Grade 5

Copyright © by Houghton Mifflin Harcourt Publishing Company

Printed in the U.S.A.

ISBN 978-0-358-29965-3

3 4 5 6 7 8 9 10 0607   29 28 27 26 25 24 23 22 21

4500823195

r2.21

© Houghton Mifflin Harcourt Publishing Company

Whose book is this?

_____

Observe the cover.

I notice _____

_____

I wonder _____

_____

What does it mean to ...

observe

infer

investigate

communicate

Design your own robot.

Science makes me feel ...

    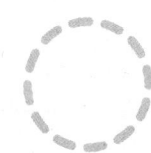

I like science because ... _____

_____

_____

_____

_____

Consulting Authors

Michael A. DiSpezio
Global Educator
North Falmouth, Massachusetts

Marjorie Frank
*Science Writer and Content-Area
  Reading Specialist*
Brooklyn, New York

Michael R. Heithaus, PhD
*Dean, College of Arts, Sciences &
  Education Professor, Department
  of Biological Sciences*
Florida International University
Miami, Florida

Peter McLaren
Executive Director of Next Gen Education, LLC
Providence, Rhode Island

Bernadine Okoro
*Social Emotional
Learning Consultant
STEM Learning Advocate & Consultant*
Washington, DC

Cary Sneider, PhD
Associate Research Professor
Portland State University
Portland, Oregon

Program Advisors

Paul D. Asimow, PhD
*Eleanor and John R. McMillan Professor of Geology and
  Geochemistry*
California Institute of Technology
Pasadena, California

Eileen Cashman, PhD
Professor of Environmental Resources Engineering
Humboldt State University
Arcata, California

Mark B. Moldwin, PhD
Professor of Climate and Space Sciences and Engineering
University of Michigan
Ann Arbor, Michigan

Kelly Y. Neiles, PhD
*Associate Professor
  of Chemistry*
St. Mary's College of Maryland
St. Mary's City, Maryland

Sten Odenwald, PhD
Astronomer
NASA Goddard Spaceflight
  Center
Greenbelt, Maryland

Bruce W. Schafer
Director of K-12 STEM Collaborations, Retired
Oregon University System
Portland, Oregon

Barry A. Van Deman
President and CEO
Museum of Life and Science
Durham, North Carolina

Kim Withers, PhD
Assistant Professor
Texas A&M
  University-Corpus Christi
Corpus Christi, Texas

Classroom Reviewers

Julie Ahern
Andrew Cooke Magnet School
Waukegan, Illinois

Amy Berke
South Park Elementary School
Rapid City, South Dakota

Pamela Bluestein
Sycamore Canyon School
Newbury Park, California

Kelly Brotz
Cooper Elementary School
Sheboygan, Wisconsin

Andrea Brown
HLPUSD Science and STEAM TOSA,
    Retired
Hacienda Heights, California

Marsha Campbell
Murray Elementary School
Hobbs, New Mexico

Leslie C. Antosy-Flores
Star View Elementary School
Midway City, California

Theresa Gailliout
James R. Ludlow Elementary School
Philadelphia, Pennsylvania

Emily Giles
Assistant Principal
White's Tower Elementary School
Independence, KY

Robert Gray
Essex Elementary School
Baltimore, Maryland

Stephanie Greene
Science Department Chair
Sun Valley Magnet School
Sun Valley, California

Roya Hosseini
Junction Avenue K–8 School
Livermore, California

Rana Mujtaba Khan
Will Rogers High School
Van Nuys, California

George Kwong
Schafer Park Elementary School
Hayward, California

Kristin Kyde
Templeton Middle School
Sussex, Wisconsin

Marie LaCross
Sulphur Springs United
    School District
Santa Clarita, California

Bonnie Lock
La Center Elementary School
La Center, Washington

Imelda Madrid
Assistant Principal
Montague Charter Academy for the
    Arts and Sciences
Pacoima, CA

Imelda Madrid
Bassett St. Elementary School
Lake Balboa, California

Susana Martinez O'Brien
Diocese of San Diego
San Diego, California

Kara Miller
Ridgeview Elementary School
Beckley, West Virginia

Mercy D. Momary
Local District Northwest
Los Angeles, California

Dena Morosin
Shasta Elementary School
Klamath Falls, Oregon

Craig Moss
Mt. Gleason Middle School
Sunland, California

Joanna O'Brien
Palmyra Elementary School
Palmyra, Missouri

Wendy Savaske
Education Consultant
Wisconsin Department of
    Public Instruction

Isabel Souto
Schafer Park Elementary School
Hayward, California

Michelle Sullivan
Balboa Elementary School
San Diego, California

April Thompson
Roll Hill School
Cincinnati, Ohio

Tina Topoleski
District Science Supervisor
Jackson School District
Jackson, New Jersey

Terri Trebilcock
Fairmount Elementary School
Golden, Colorado

Emily R.C.G. Williams
South Pasadena Middle School
South Pasadena, California

These are some smart people!

Look!

Unit 3 Energy and Matter in Organisms

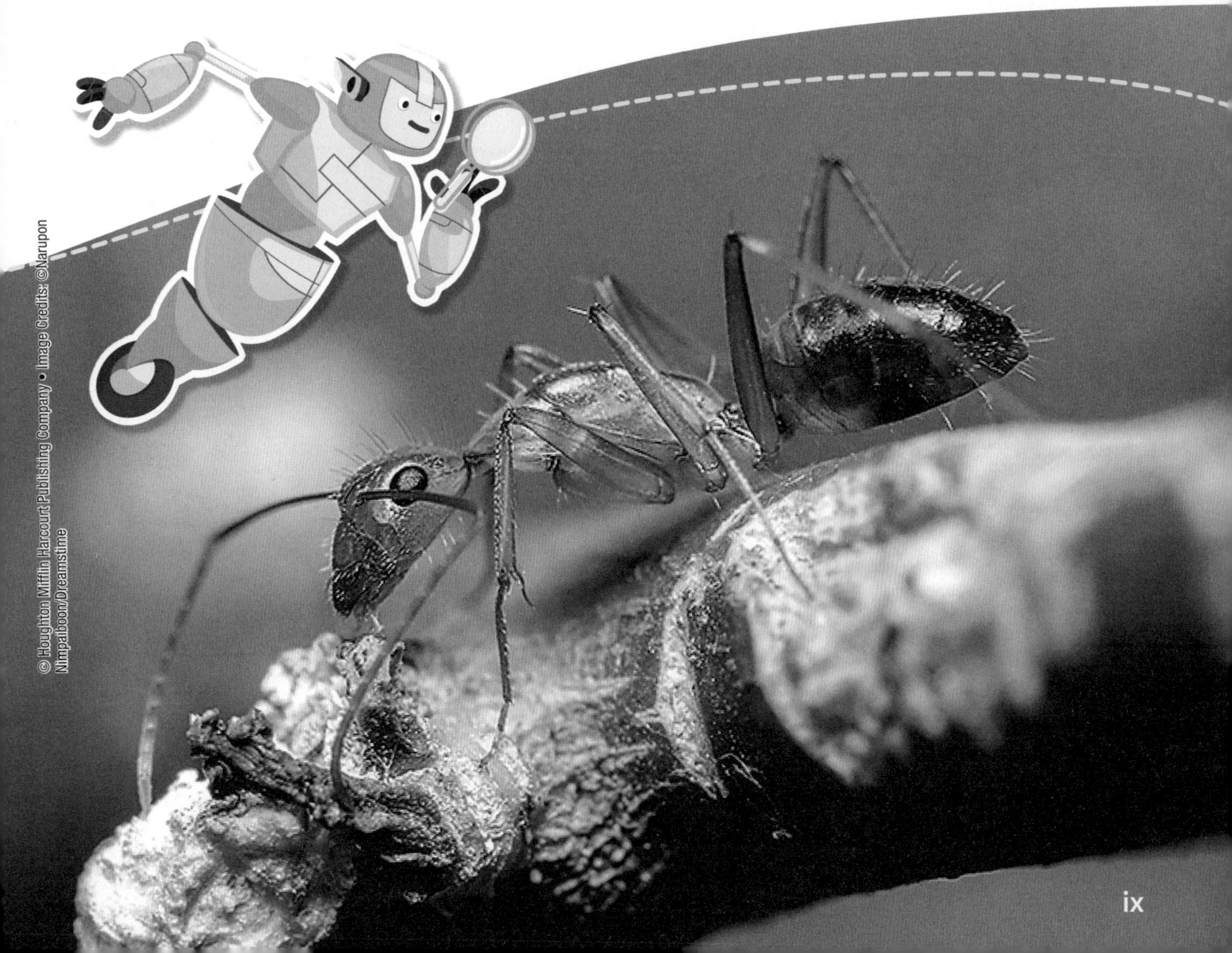

Unit 5 Earth Interactions and Resources

Engineering

Engineers develop solutions for all types of problems. Engineers use an engineering design process to help them find a good solution to a problem. They use this process to solve problems to meet people's wants and needs. One engineering design process is shown here.

This engineering design process has three main parts, or *phases*. You may use this three-phase process to solve many different types of problems.

EXPLORE

In the *Explore* phase, you learn more about the problem by asking questions and doing research. Can you think of other ways to learn more about a problem? After you have gathered information about the problem, you state the problem clearly. Then you identify what features a good solution should have. The desirable features of a solution are called **criteria**. You may also identify limits, or **constraints**, on an acceptable solution. The problem is defined when you've identified criteria and constraints and stated the problem clearly.

MAKE and TEST

In the *Make and Test* phase, you develop a good solution. This phase may include the following steps:

- Brainstorm
- Plan
- Design
- Test
- Evaluate

When you brainstorm, you think of as many ideas as you can. These ideas may or may not solve the problem you defined in the *Explore* phase. Use the criteria, constraints, and problem statement to choose which solutions you think will work best. Then you can plan and make a prototype to test. A **prototype** is a model of a solution that can be tested.

Testing a prototype helps you know how well a solution works. If a solution does not solve the problem, you may change the solution and test again. You must test a solution after each change so you know how well the changed solution works. You may also find out that you need to choose a different solution to make and test.

There may be more than one acceptable solution to a problem. Use test results to choose which solution is better. The solution that best meets the criteria and constraints is the better solution. Once you have found a good solution to solve the problem, you can move to the third phase, *Improve and Test*.

IMPROVE and TEST

In the *Improve and Test* phase, you do many of the same steps as the *Make and Test* phase. You may replan, redesign, and retest many small changes. You may even return to an earlier phase if needed. Throughout the process, you communicate with others to share information or learn more. At the end of the process, you should have as good a solution as possible, given the constraints. Your solution is ready to use or share with others.

Hana wants to attract pretty birds to her backyard. Talk with a partner about how Hana might use an engineering design process to solve this problem.

Claims, Evidence, and Reasoning

Constructing Explanations

A complete scientific explanation needs three parts—a claim, evidence, and reasoning.

A **claim** is a statement you think is true. A claim answers the question, "What do you know?" **Evidence** is data collected during an investigation. Evidence answers the question, "How do you know that?" **Reasoning** tells the connection between the evidence and the claim. Reasoning answers the question, "Why does your evidence support your claim?"

Suppose you're investigating what combination of baking soda and vinegar will produce the largest "volcanic" eruption. Specifically, you are increasing the amount of vinegar but leaving the amount of baking soda the same.

The largest amount of vinegar will react the most.

You have three containers of vinegar—50 mL, 100 mL, and 200 mL—and one tablespoon of baking soda for each container. Before you begin, you make a **claim**.

Then you add the baking soda to each container and observe. The data you gather is your **evidence**. You can use data to show if your claim is true or not. Now you're ready to construct a scientific explanation with a claim, evidence, and reasoning.

Claim	I think the largest amount of vinegar will react the most.
Evidence	The container with 200 mL of vinegar made more bubbles than the containers with 50 mL and 100mL.
Reasoning	The evidence showed that more vinegar makes a larger reaction than a little vinegar.

Evidence used to support a claim can be used to make another claim.

You decide to try a different type of investigation. Describe it below, then record your possible claim, evidence, and reasoning.

Warm vinegar will produce a larger reaction than cold vinegar.

My investigation is

_____

_____

_____

Claim	
Evidence	
Reasoning	

Safety in the Lab

Doing science is a lot of fun. But, a science lab can be a dangerous place. Falls, cuts, and burns can happen easily. **Know the safety rules and listen to your teacher.**

☐ **Think ahead.** Study the investigation steps so you know what to expect. If you have any questions, ask your teacher. Be sure you understand all caution statements and safety reminders.

☐ **Be neat and clean.** Keep your work area clean. If you have long hair, pull it back so it doesn't get in the way. Roll or push up long sleeves to keep them away from your activity.

☐ **Oops!** If you spill or break something, or get cut, tell your teacher right away.

☐ **Watch your eyes.** Wear safety goggles anytime you are directed to do so. If you get anything in your eyes, tell your teacher right away.

☐ **Yuck!** Never eat or drink anything during a science activity.

☐ **Don't get shocked.** Be careful if an electric appliance is used. Be sure that electric cords are in a safe place where you can't trip over them. Never use the cord to pull a plug from an outlet.

☐ **Keep it clean.** Always clean up when you have finished. Put everything away and wipe your work area. Wash your hands.

☐ **Play it safe.** Always know where to find safety equipment, such as fire extinguishers. Know how to use the safety equipment around you.

Safety in the Field

Lots of science research happens outdoors. It's fun to explore the wild! But, you need to be careful. The weather, the land, and the living things can surprise you.

- ☐ **Think ahead.** Study the investigation steps so you know what to expect. If you have any questions, ask your teacher. Be sure you understand all caution statements and safety reminders.

- ☐ **Dress right.** Wear appropriate clothes and shoes for the outdoors. Cover up and wear sunscreen and sunglasses for sun safety.

- ☐ **Clean up the area.** Follow your teacher's instructions for when and how to throw away waste.

- ☐ **Oops!** Tell your teacher right away if you break something or get hurt.

- ☐ **Watch your eyes.** Wear safety goggles when directed to do so. If you get anything in your eyes, tell your teacher right away.

- ☐ **Yuck!** Never taste anything outdoors.

- ☐ **Stay with your group.** Work in the area as directed by your teacher. Stay on marked trails.

- ☐ **"Wilderness" doesn't mean go wild.** Never engage in horseplay, games, or pranks.

- ☐ **Always walk.** No running!

- ☐ **Play it safe.** Know where safety equipment can be found and how to use it. Know how to get help.

- ☐ **Clean up.** Wash your hands with soap and water when you come back indoors.

Safety Symbols

To highlight important safety concerns, the following symbols are used in Hands-On Activities. Remember that no matter what safety symbols you see, all safety rules should be followed at all times.

Dress Code

- Wear safety goggles as directed.
- If anything gets into your eye, tell your teacher immediately.
- Do not wear contact lenses in the lab.
- Wear appropriate protective gloves as directed.
- Tie back long hair, secure loose clothing, and remove loose jewelry.

Glassware and Sharp Object Safety

- Do not use chipped or cracked glassware.
- Notify your teacher immediately if a piece of glass breaks.
- Use extreme care when handling all sharp and pointed instruments.
- Do not cut an object while holding the object in your hands.
- Cut objects on a suitable surface, always in a direction away from your body.

Electrical Safety

- Do not use equipment with frayed electrical cords or loose plugs.
- Do not use electrical equipment near water or when clothing or hands are wet.
- Hold the plug when you plug in or unplug equipment.

Chemical Safety

- If a chemical gets on your skin, on your clothing, or in your eyes, rinse it immediately, and tell your teacher.
- Do not clean up spilled chemicals unless your teacher directs you to do so.
- Keep your hands away from your face while you are working on any activity.

Heating and Fire Safety

- Know your school's fire-evacuation routes.
- Never leave a hot plate unattended while it is turned on or while it is cooling.
- Allow equipment to cool before storing it.

Plant and Animal Safety

- Do not eat any part of a plant.
- Do not pick any wild plant unless your teacher instructs you to do so.
- Treat animals carefully and respectfully.
- Wash your hands throughly after handling any plant or animal.

Cleanup

- Clean all work surfaces and protective equipment as directed by your teacher.
- Wash your hands throughly before you leave the lab or after any activity.

Safety Quiz

Name _____

Circle the letter of the BEST answer.

1. At the end of any activity, you should
   a. wash your hands thoroughly before leaving the lab.
   b. cover your face with your hands.
   c. put on your safety goggles.
   d. leave the materials where they are.

2. If you get hurt or injured in any way, you should
   a. tell your teacher immediately.
   b. find bandages or a first aid kit.
   c. go to your principal's office.
   d. get help after you finish the activity.

3. Before starting an activity, you should
   a. try an experiment of your own.
   b. open all containers and packages.
   c. read all directions and make sure you understand them.
   d. handle all the equipment to become familiar with it.

4. When working with materials that might fly into the air and hurt someone's eye, you should wear
   a. goggles.
   b. an apron.
   c. gloves.
   d. a hat.

5. If you get something in your eye, you should
   a. wash your hands immediately.
   b. put the lid back on the container.
   c. wait to see if your eye becomes irritated.
   d. tell your teacher right away.

In this unit, you will use the engineering design process to define problems, design solutions, and test and improve your solution. You will also find out how technology changes as user priorities change.

UNIT 1 Engineering and Technology

Engineering and Society

Building 'em better and better...

What do you notice about the two cars?

I notice _____

_____

_____

_____

What do you wonder about the differences between the car from 60 years ago and the more modern car?

I wonder _____

_____

_____

_____

Can You Explain It?

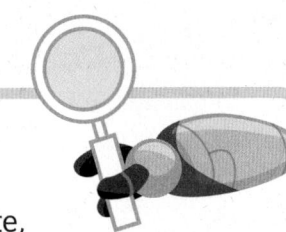

How and why have cars changed structure over time? Sketch, write, or model your answer.

Engineer It
What Makes a Good Toy Car?

Suppose that your school is hosting a Family STEM Night during which families will participate in science and engineering activities, such as building toy cars. The school provides a model of a balloon-powered toy car and the basic materials needed to construct it. You and your team are to construct a similar car, but your teacher thinks the model can be improved. Work together with your team members to improve the car using the materials provided. Your solution should be easy to build, work reliably, and roll in a straight line.

Identify a problem   What problem are you trying to solve?

_____

_____

_____

Did you know?

People can actually go to college to study toy design and learn about engineering, art, child development, materials, and modeling.

POSSIBLE MATERIALS

- ☐ balloon
- ☐ bendable straws
- ☐ cardboard rectangle
- ☐ paper cups
- ☐ ruler
- ☐ scissors
- ☐ stir straws
- ☐ tape
- ☐ additional materials as provided by your teacher

Explore

STEP 1 **Explore the problem** Begin by exploring the balloon-powered car solution the school provided. Build the toy car, and investigate how well it works.

a. Cut two large straws to be the same width as your cardboard.

b. Tape the cut straws to the cardboard, parallel to the short ends. This is the bottom of your car.

c. Cut the bottom off four cups to make wheels. Poke a hole in the center of each wheel with a pencil.

d. Insert the stir straws through the larger straws to make axles.

e. Push each end of the axles through the holes in the wheels.

f. Cut the last large straw to 15 cm, including the bendable portion. Insert the straight portion into the balloon. Fit the balloon opening over one end of the straw and wrap it with tape to make a tight seal.

g. Tape the straw with the balloon to the top of your toy car so that the balloon opening is in the center of your car.

h. Blow air through the straw to inflate the balloon. Hold your finger over the end of the straw while you place the car on the table. Let go, and notice how the car rolls forward as air flows out of the balloon.

Research how the toy car solution works. Investigate how it moves, and make notes. In particular, look for ways it works well and ways it could be made to work better.

I did...	I observed...

Make a **claim** identifying one way the car could be improved. Support your claim with **evidence** from your investigation, and explain your **reasoning**.

Now that you have conducted research to understand the problem better, revise your problem statement.

STEP 2
Define the problem Fill in the chart with desired features of good solutions and factors that limit possible solutions.

Desired features	Limitations

STEP 3
Brainstorm solutions Look over the materials your teacher gives you. As a group, brainstorm at least three solutions. Solutions should include ways to modify and improve the existing toy car.

STEP 4 **Evaluate solutions** Evaluate three of the possible solutions that your group identified. Decide how well they will provide the desired features within the limitations.

Possible solutions	How well solutions will work

STEP 5 **Develop a model** Sketch a model of the possible solution your group thinks is best. Label all parts of your model with the materials you plan to use.

Making Sense

Why do you need to conduct research, define the problem, and brainstorm before making changes to the toy car? Connect your ideas to the ways and reasons real cars have changed in structure over time.

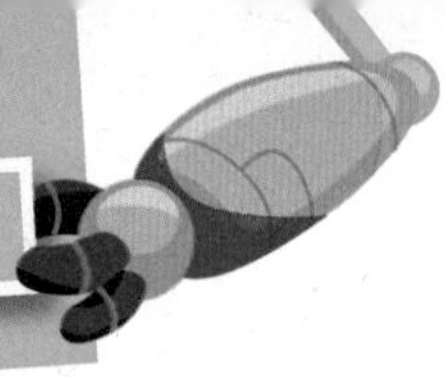

Engineer It
Improving Toy Cars

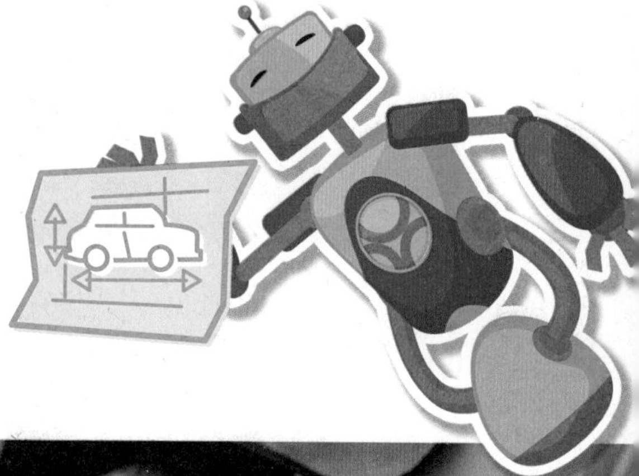

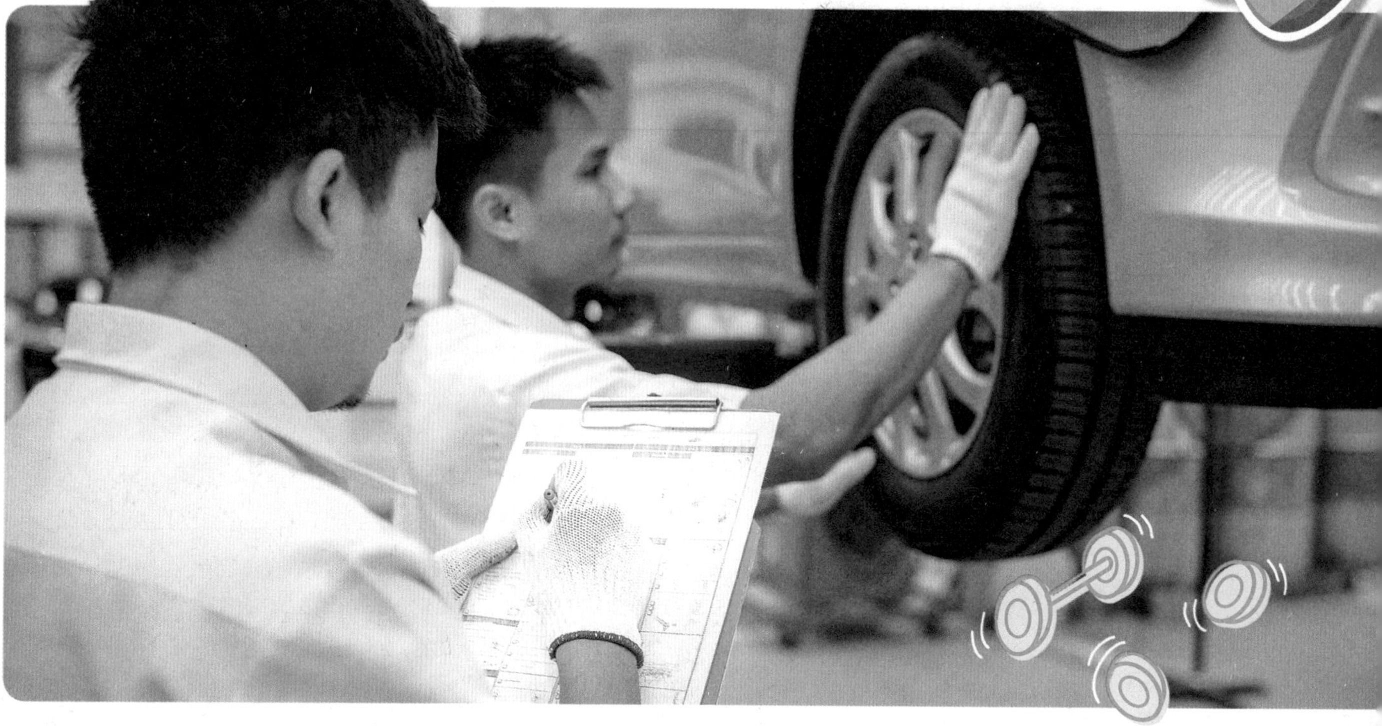

The school leaders who hosted the Family STEM Night are pleased to hear about your improvements to the balloon-powered toy car they provided. However, they are worried that you have no evidence to show that your solution is an improvement on the original car. This need for evidence also applies to engineers who build real cars that are sold to consumers and driven on public highways. The cars the public buys are never the first version an engineer came up with. Instead, automotive engineers work on every aspect of a car, from its engine to its tires to its seat belts, before releasing it for public use. They gather evidence at each step to ensure that the car will operate safely and reliably.

Form a question   Form a question that summarizes the worries of the school leaders. In this activity, you will develop an answer to this question.

> **Did you know?**
>
> The world record for most tires made per year is held by a toy company, not a car tire company.

Make and Test

STEP 1   **Make a solution**   Review the model you drew in the previous activity. Modify the basic toy car you built and tested using the materials provided by your teacher and the information from the model.

STEP 2   **Plan an investigation**   Review the problem definition, desired features, and limitations from the previous activity. Plan a fair test of your possible solution. Describe your test plan, and then have your teacher review your plan.

Identify the important variables in your test plan.

What is different for each set of trials	What is the same for each trial	What you will measure

STEP 3   **Test your solution**   Test your possible solution. Record your observations in the space below. You may want to use a table or other method to organize your data.

Air, like all matter, is made of particles too small to see. Describe how the balloon functions in the toy car system, and explain how the inflating and deflating balloon provides evidence that air is made of very small particles.

Improve and Test

STEP 4 **Improve your solution** Did your possible solution provide the desired features within the limitations? Why or why not? How could you improve your possible solution?

_____

_____

_____

Sketch a model of your plan for improving your solution. Add labels to your model to explain how you will make changes.

STEP 5 **Test your solution** Test your improved model, and evaluate the results. If you have time, make another change. Then test and evaluate again.

How well did your final solution provide the desired features within the limitations?

_____

_____

_____

STEP 6 **Communicate** Compare each group's results. Record your observations about each group's possible solution and how well it solved the problem.

_____

_____

Drawing conclusions Why did some solutions fail to provide the desired features within the limitations? How could you improve them?

_____

_____

_____

Based on your investigation, make a **claim** to answer the question you formed. Support your claim with **evidence,** and explain your **reasoning**.

_____

_____

_____

 Think back on your work as a group, and discuss one good contribution each team member made to help develop the solution.

Making Sense

What would you need to do if the desired features and limitations changed? Connect your ideas to the ways and reasons cars have changed in structure over time.

_____

_____

_____

Technology, Engineering, and Science

What Is Technology, and What Is Not?

Look over each of the items below. Decide which ones are examples of technology and which are not examples of technology. Draw lines to match each item to the proper category.

calculator
wooden chair
truck
tree
computer
insect

Technology

Not technology

What reasoning did you use to decide how to sort the items? Discuss your answers in a small group.

Look around you. What are some of the things that you see? Chairs? Windows? Books? All of these things are products of engineering, which is the practical use of science and math to solve problems to meet society's needs and wants. Engineered objects can be simple, such as a shovel. Engineered objects also can be complex, such as a communication satellite that orbits Earth. Now, revise your answers above as needed.

 **Turn and Talk** With a partner, take turns describing what today's trip to school would have been like if there were no technology. While one partner shares their ideas, the other will listen carefully. Then, the second partner will summarize what they heard before sharing their own ideas. Together, come up with one true statement about technology that your descriptions show. Be prepared to share it.

Classroom Technology

Match Read the descriptions of classroom technology in the image. Write the name of the technology on the line. Then write its letter on the picture.

a. _____

An engineer helped to design the case and keys, and a computer engineer helped program it to help solve complex math problems.

b. _____

A chemical engineer improved the quality of the glass, while a mechanical engineer designed the frame so that it is easy to open and close.

c. _____

A mechanical engineer helped make it by designing machines to print, cut the paper, and bind it together.

d. _____

A mechanical engineer helped build the machines that are used to cut and stitch the cloth together.

Compare What two things do all the objects have in common as examples of technology?

_____

_____

Looking at What They Do

The similar ways that scientists and engineers do their jobs might seem confusing. Use the question below to compare and contrast their work.

Classify For each activity, draw a box around who does it. Some activities may be done by both scientists and engineers.

Activity	Who does it?
analyzing test data to find the best boat design	scientist or engineer
asking questions to find out if Earth's surface is changing	scientist or engineer
planning and carrying out a fair test	scientist or engineer
using evidence to argue for the best solution	scientist or engineer

Both scientists and engineers see a problem and ask questions about it. They follow many of the same methods to find answers. However, their goals differ. Scientists conduct research and investigations to add to our scientific knowledge. Engineers, on the other hand, focus on designing and testing solutions to problems.

Although science and engineering have different goals, they complement each other. For example, before engineers design solutions to problems, they conduct research to explore and define the problem. This research relies on the work of scientists. Advances in science often lead to advances in engineering, and advances in engineering often lead to advances in science.

Making Sense

How do engineering problems, such as improving car technology, connect to science?

_____

_____

_____

© Houghton Mifflin Harcourt Publishing Company

How Do Engineers Solve Problems?

Explore

Once you have identified a problem, you need to learn more about it before you can develop a solution. Consider the school STEM night. This time, the problem is that you need to design a game to play at the event.

Plan What would you want to know before you started to design a game? After writing down your thoughts, discuss your ideas with a small group.

_____

_____

Learning more about the problem is the best way to make good decisions about what you want to do. This additional knowledge helps you to define the criteria you will use and also determine any constraints. **Criteria** tell the desirable features of a solution. A **constraint** is an absolute limit on acceptable solutions.

Classify Identify each item as _criteria_ or _constraint_ by drawing a line to the correct word.

budget to make the game

availability of materials

(Criteria)   works with a big group   (Constraints)

fun for students and adults

15 minutes to play, at most

rules are easy to learn

Discuss with a partner the reasoning you used to determine which items are criteria and which are constraints.

In the Background

Predict What is the advantage of doing research before you begin planning your solution? Discuss your answer with a partner.

_____

_____

To solve a problem, it is often helpful to do some background research to see what is already known about it. If another solution worked somewhere else, then you may want to try to follow it. If a past solution failed, then that failure might help you identify what not to try next.

Make and Test

Once you have decided on a problem to solve, it is important to gather as many ideas as possible before deciding how to go about solving the problem. This is a process called *brainstorming*. When you brainstorm, you collect as many different ideas as you can, no matter how good you think they are. This technique is especially useful when working with a group of people.

a. First, generate as many ideas for the STEM night game as you can in 5–10 minutes. Listen to everyone's ideas without judging. Select one person to serve as the recorder. It can be helpful to use a whiteboard so everyone can see the ideas that have been identified.

b. Next, discuss the ideas as a group. Give each person a chance to explain what they meant.

c. After all the ideas are discussed, eliminate any ideas that do not meet the constraints of the problem. Narrow the list down to two or three ideas. Then label the ideas *A*, *B*, and *C*. Continue to the next section to see how to use a decision matrix to choose the best idea.

Make a Decision

A decision matrix can help people look at specific criteria and evaluate each solution to help make the best decision. When you evaluate something, you determine its value. A decision matrix can be used for personal decisions as well as engineering decisions. Read the text below and help Shania decide which bike best fits her criteria.

Shania saves up money for a new bike that she hopes will last her three or more years. Her plan is to purchase it this weekend. Her grandmother insists she ride with a helmet for safety. Shania would like a red-and-white striped bike, but it's not at the top of her priorities.

Bike A	Bike B	Bike C
$180	$135	$150
3 years free repairs	1 year free repairs	1 year free repairs
comes with a helmet	no additional items	comes with a helmet
red with white stripes	purple with stars	yellow and green

a. In the chart below, list the criteria in the left column. This has been done for you.

b. Prioritize the criteria using a number scale. The higher the number, the more important the criterion is. In this decision matrix, safety is more important than the warranty. Discuss why you think this is. Work with a partner to decide what number, 1 or 4, to assign to price and to design.

c. After prioritizing, the next step is to look at each bike and decide if it meets the criteria. If it does, write the priority number in the column; if it doesn't, write a zero. Complete the rows for price and color/design.

d. Finally, add up the numbers in each column for each of bikes to get a total of the points. The choice with the highest total number is the best one because it meets the criteria the best. Discuss the outcome with a small group.

Criteria	Priority of Importance	Solutions/Choices		
		Bike A	Bike B	Bike C
free repairs	2	2	0	0
saftey	3	3	0	3
price				
design				
total points	—			

Engineers use tools like decision matrices to evaluate solutions against criteria. Engineers also evaluate solutions against constraints. If a solution does not meet a constraint, it is not acceptable. If Shania can only spend $160, the price would be a constraint. Bike A does not meet the price constraint, so it would not be an option.

What Is Fair?

After engineers evaluate solutions, they make a **prototype**, or a model for testing. Imagine you chose two promising school STEM night game ideas. Once you build your prototypes, you need to test them to get data about how well each game satisfies the criteria and constraints.

If you tested one game with ten first-grade students and another game with four adults, would it be a fair test? It would be very difficult to judge which game took less time under these conditions. A fair test should have one factor that changes—an independent variable—while all other factors stay the same—controlled variables. In your game test, each game may vary, but all the other factors must remain the same. This should include the location of the test, the way it is measured, and the number of test trials.

Archers do tests and make decisions in similar ways to engineers. When archers practice, they make adjustments over multiple trials. After shooting each arrow, the archer evaluates where it hit the target. Then, archers adjusts their stance, grip, or aim, and shoot again. Archers improve and try again until they consistently hit the center of the target.

© Houghton Mifflin Harcourt Publishing Company • Image Credits: ©Wavebreak Media ltd/Getty Images Plus/Getty Images

Improve and Test

 **Turn and Talk** How often do you get things perfect on the first try? With a partner, list some things that you had to do many times before you got it right. Then, discuss your process and what would have happened if you had given up.

Every success comes from a history of failures. It often takes many trials before a working solution is found. Keeping detailed notes about what worked and what did not allows you to learn from your mistakes and make improvements to your solution.

Engineering design solutions improve as you test different ideas and evaluate the results. Each trial gives you more information. Over time, you will develop a prototype that meets the criteria and constraints. Repeating tests several times helps you see how well the prototype solves the problem. If something happens once during a test, it might just be a random error. If it happens many times, you can rely on it more.

Infer How does repeating tests and building on your successes lead to better solutions?

_____

_____

_____

_____

_____

a. The first shot lands too low and to the left of the bull's-eye. How would you adjust the next shot?

b. The second arrow is too high and to the right. How would you adjust now?

c. Bull's-eye! You hit the center of the target. Repeating tests and improving solutions is important.

It's a Process

Engineers follow steps in the engineering design process to develop solutions. Depending on the problem, engineers may combine, repeat, or skip steps. The steps occur in three phases: defining the problem, making and testing a solution, and improving and testing the solution.

Review what you did to design the toy car. Then, sort the engineering activities into the three phases of the process. You may use each activity more than once.

Analyze test results	Make a prototype	Define the problem
Brainstorm possible solutions	Modify the prototype	Model a solution
Evaluate possible solutions	Research the problem	
Identify criteria and constraints	Test the prototype	

Explore	Make and Test	Improve and Test

Making Sense

How would you describe the process engineers use when solving problems like designing cars or improving existing technology?

_____

_____

Improving Over Time

So Many Changes!

Discuss the following questions with a small group as you review these pages: Why have some things remained generally unchanged in cars? Why have other features been added over time?

In the 1950s, people wanted cars that resembled fast flying machines. Today, cars have a much more streamlined, rounded shape. The streamlined shape reduces drag between the car and the air. This increases the car's fuel efficiency, or how far it can go using a certain amount of fuel.

early lap seat belt

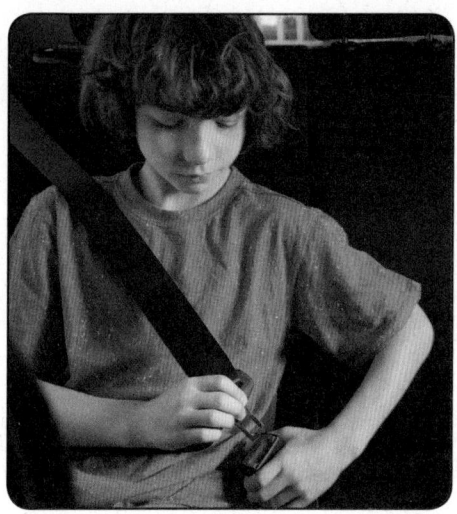

added shoulder belt for better safety

Safety in automobile engineering is influenced by society in two ways: choices people make and regulations put in place by the government. In the 1950s, seat belts were not required. In the 1960s, the U.S. government required all cars to have seat belts to reduce injuries and deaths from accidents. Like all engineering solutions, car makers have to test that safety features such as seat belts solve the problems they were designed to address.

Making Sense

Why have engineers made changes to car technology?

_____

_____

You Can't Have Everything

In the activity, you designed a car that had certain design features. It might have been fast, or maybe it had a good safety rating. A **tradeoff** involves giving up a quality or feature of a solution to gain a different quality or feature.

Take a look at Shania's bike choices again. Bike B has the best price, but it doesn't include a helmet. Work with a partner to discuss the tradeoffs for each bike choice.

Bike A	Bike B	Bike C
$180	$135	$150
3 years free repairs	1 year free repairs	1 year free repairs
comes with a helmet	no additional items	comes with a helmet
red with white stripes	purple with stars	yellow and green

Recall that technology is developed based on people's needs and wants. Automotive engineers need to think about these criteria as they design cars. They also need to think about regulations, such as safety standards and mileage requirements, as they design cars.

← better power   better mileage →

For cars that run on gasoline, more power often means fewer miles per gallon of gas. Automotive engineers must think about the tradeoff between engine power and fuel efficiency as they design vehicles.

← better appearance   lower cost →

The appearance of cars varies widely. Some features that improve a car's appearance also increase the cost of the car. Engineers must decide which features to include as they design a particular model of automobile.

Mark an X on each arrow above to show how important each feature is to you. Discuss your choices, and compare the vehicles you each would prefer.

Name _____

Lesson
Check

Can You Explain It?

Review your ideas from the beginning of this lesson about how and why cars have changed over time. How have your ideas changed? Be sure to do the following:

- Explain how science and engineering relate to car technology.
- Explain the process engineers use to make improvements to car technology.
- Explain how society plays a role in changes in car technology.

Now I know or think that _____

_____

_____

_____

_____

Making Connections

These two vision technologies were made several hundred years apart. Both serve the same function, but they have very different structures. Based on your exploration of how car technology changed, how and why do you think vision technology has changed over time?

_____

_____

_____

Checkpoints

1. It is the job of engineers to _____. Select all that apply.

   a. discover how natural things work.

   b. apply technology.

   c. develop solutions.

   d. eliminate technology.

   e. improve solutions.

2. The student needs to reach a book on a high shelf. How could he evaluate a few possible solutions to determine which one best solves his problem?

_____

_____

_____

_____

_____

3. Which of the following are true about the engineering design process? Select all that apply.

   a. The steps are always the same, no matter what the problem.

   b. Each step needs to be followed in an exact order.

   c. Sometimes steps are repeated or blend together.

   d. Some solutions work better than others.

4. Why is communication important in the engineering design process? Choose all that apply.

   a. Engineers want to know what mistakes others have made.

   b. Engineers need to brainstorm after the experiment is designed.

   c. Engineers want to share information about solutions.

   d. Engineers need it to keep track of where others are living.

5. Formulate a list of questions a student could ask to determine if a design test is fair. Recall any patterns you observed in tests discussed in the lesson.

_____

_____

_____

6. Why do engineers test solutions before implementing them? Select all that apply.

a. to determine if a solution solves the problem

b. to determine ways the solution could be improved

c. to determine how others have solved similar problems in the past

d. to determine how well the solution meets the criteria and constraints

7. Choose the correct words for each sentence.

problem solutions	conclusion criteria	background research constraints	more brainstorming brainstorming

After a _____ has been identified, it is important to

do _____ to learn as much as possible about the

issue. This will lead to a more complete set of _____

and _____. Once all these factors are in place, the

solution can be designed.

8. Give an example of how people's changing needs and wants have led to changes in technology. Support your claim with evidence and reasoning.

_____

_____

_____

_____

Unit Review

1. Examine the photo. Define the problem the student is facing in terms of the bicycle system and its function.

_____

_____

_____

_____

2. Describe two topics you would need to research in order to understand the problem with the bicycle system. Explain why each of these topics is important.

_____

_____

_____

_____

3. Underline the text that correctly completes each sentence. Reflect on patterns in examples of engineering work and scientific work from the lesson.

Engineers _____.

a. discover things about the world and universe.

b. use scientific discoveries to develop technology.

Scientists _____.

c. discover things about the world and universe.

d. use scientific discoveries to develop technology.

4. What factors can cause car technology to change over time? Choose all that apply.

a. new legal requirements

b. new scientific knowledge

c. new understanding of risks

d. new needs and wants

5. Choose the correct words for each sentence. You may use the words more than once.

criterion	constraint

Birdhouse designers make decisions when evaluating possible solutions. One desired feature, or _____, of a good birdhouse is that it shelters the birds from rain. One limitation, or _____, on a birdhouse solution is that the opening must be large enough for a bird to enter and exit safely. A birdhouse that does not meet the _____ is not considered as an option.

6. Explain what a fair test of a solution is and why it is important.

_____

_____

_____

_____

_____

7. Reflect on patterns of problem solving in the lesson. Using the numbers 1–5, label these steps of a possible engineering design process to show their most likely order.

_____ Choose and test the best solution.

_____ Modify and retest the solution.

_____ Identify a purpose/problem/goal.

_____ Brainstorm possible solutions.

_____ Evaluate the test results.

© Houghton Mifflin Harcourt Publishing Company • Image Credits: ©Nancy R. Cohen/ Photodisc/Getty Images

8. Which of these would an engineer do? Select all that apply.

    a. investigate to explain how the sun moves across the sky

    b. investigate how a computer battery might fail

    c. model how long a pen will work if used daily

    d. model to explain how a drought affects animal populations

9. Write an argument, supported by evidence from this unit, that testing systems is a necessary part of the engineering design process.

_____

_____

_____

10. Engineers design technology to meet wants and needs. Use your knowledge from this unit to explain how features and components of the car system meet wants and needs of car users.

_____

_____

_____

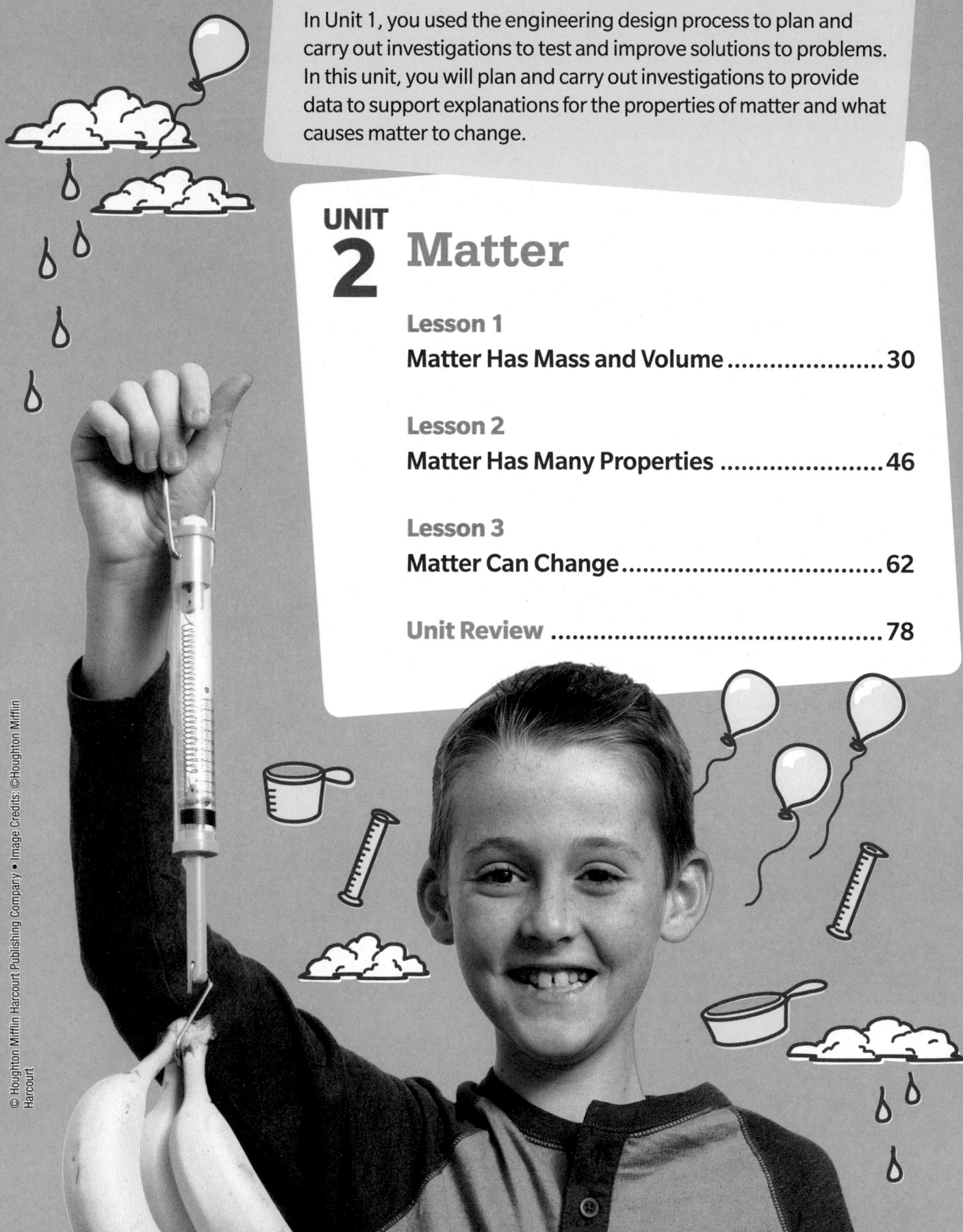

In Unit 1, you used the engineering design process to plan and carry out investigations to test and improve solutions to problems. In this unit, you will plan and carry out investigations to provide data to support explanations for the properties of matter and what causes matter to change.

UNIT 2 Matter

Matter Has Mass and Volume

Rockets are exhausting!

What do you notice about this toy rocket?

I notice _____

_____

_____

_____

What do you wonder about how the rocket works?

I wonder _____

_____

_____

_____

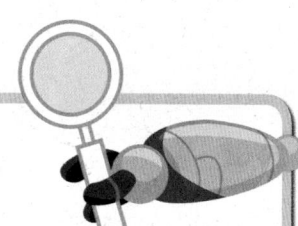

Can You Explain It?

How do properties of matter enable the rocket to launch? Sketch, write, or model your answer.

HANDS-ON ACTIVITY

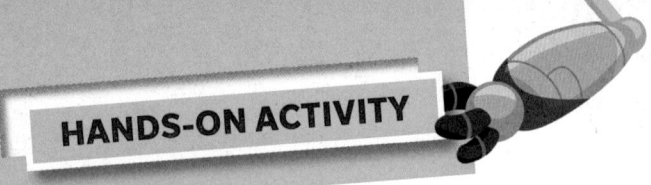

Measuring Mass and Volume

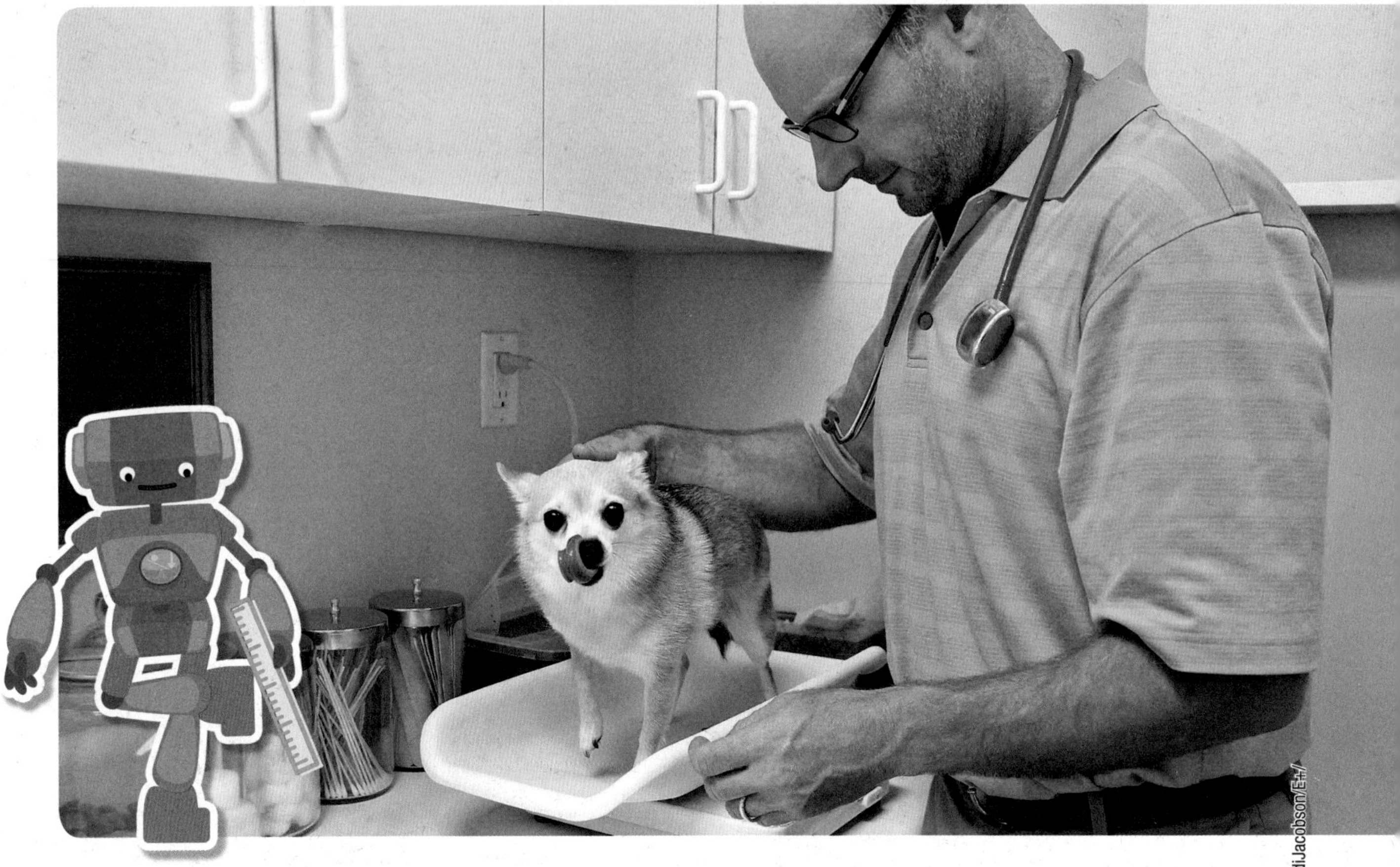

Anything that takes up space, such as a dog or a chair, is **matter.** Matter can be measured in different ways. For example, weight and height are two ways a veterinarian might describe a dog. Using the same measurements and the same units of measurement makes it easy to share data and observations with other pet health workers.

Did you know?

An inch was once defined as the length of three grains of barley, or barleycorns.

Form a question Ask a question about measuring matter.

POSSIBLE MATERIALS

☐ objects to measure   ☐ metric ruler or tape

☐ balance   ☐ unit cubes

☐ beaker   ☐ other objects you need to complete your plan

☐ graduated cylinder

STEP 1 With your class, determine which are the most important questions students had about measuring matter. Record the questions your class chose as most important.

_____

_____

_____

_____

STEP 2 How can you investigate the questions your class selected as most important? Think about the materials your teacher shows you and what else you might need. Write out your plan and show it to your teacher to see if you can request the other objects you require. If you use other materials than those shown by your teacher, be sure to include them in your plan.

_____

_____

_____

_____

STEP 3 Carry out your plan, and record your results. Present your data in a way that conveys what you did and what happened as a result. You might choose a table or a graph as a presentation tool, or you might choose to make a poster with photographs and other visuals.

_____

_____

_____

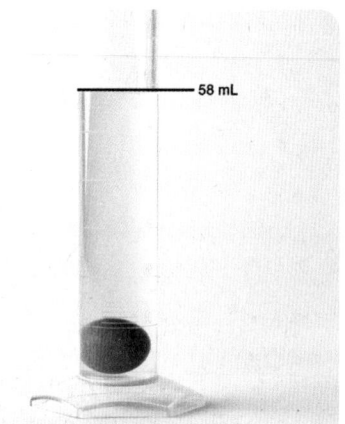

Make a **claim** that answers the question or questions your class decided to explore. You may need to have a claim for each question. Support your claim with **evidence** from your investigation and **reasoning** to explain how the evidence supports your claim. Use a separate piece of paper to record your findings.

_____

_____

_____

Making Sense

How could measuring mass and volume help you explain how to operate the rocket?

_____

_____

_____

Evidence of Matter

What a blowup!

When a bike tire goes flat, you first need to patch the leak or replace the tire's inner tube. Then, you must pump the tire full of air. However, what exactly does it mean to be "full of air"?

Form a question Ask a question about particles of matter.

Did you know?

A typical scuba tank holds enough air for an hour of swimming at a depth of 15 m (49 ft).

MATERIALS

Group A:
- ☐ dosing tube
- ☐ cup of water

Group B:
- ☐ paper towel
- ☐ clear plastic cup
- ☐ bowl of water

Group C:
- ☐ sugar cube
- ☐ clear plastic cup
- ☐ water
- ☐ spoon or stir stick

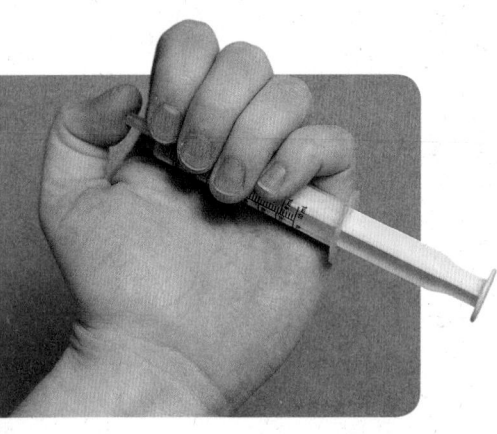

For this activity, your teacher will assign you to one of three groups.

Group A

1. Fill a dosing tube with air. Place your finger firmly over the opening, and then push the plunger.

2. How does the air inside the tube change?

3. Sketch the air particles before and after you pushed the plunger.

4. Discuss your sketches with a partner. How are "before" and "after" different?

5. Repeat Steps 1–4, this time filling the dosing tube with water instead of air.

6. What was different? Why?

Group B

1. Pack the paper towel into the bottom of the plastic cup. Holding the cup upside down, push it straight down into the bowl.

2. Hold it there for a minute, and then pull the cup straight up and out of the water.

3. What happened to the paper towel? Why?

_____

_____

_____

4. Draw and label a simple model that shows how matter is interacting to cause what you observed.

Group C

1. Drop a sugar cube into a cup of water, and then stir until the sugar disappears.

2. Draw a model to explain what happened to the sugar cube.

After groups A, B, and C share their results, make a **claim** about the matter that makes up air, sugar, and water. Support it with **evidence** from the explorations, and explain your **reasoning**.

Making Sense

How did the ideas you explored here add to your explanation of the backyard water rocket?

How did respectful cooperation among the three activity groups help build your understanding?

© Houghton Mifflin Harcourt Publishing Company • Image Credits: ©Turtle Rock Scientific/Science Source

A Matter of Particles

What Makes Up Matter?

Matter takes up space. But what is it made of? You can break down an object into smaller parts. At first, you can see the broken pieces. Eventually, you would need to use a tool such as a microscope to see the smaller parts. At that stage, the parts can still get smaller, all the way down to their basic particles—the smallest parts of matter that exist.

You cannot see these basic particles, but they make up all matter. The sun, a whale, air, and an apple are all forms of matter made of particles.

Where do you find things made of matter? If you can taste, smell, or touch something, it's matter. Anything that takes up space is matter. Matter can take different forms and can behave in different ways. However, some things you see are not made of matter.

Think of a local or state fair. People at a fair are able see the sights and play the games because there is light. Light is not matter. It doesn't take up space or have mass. Mass is the amount of matter in object. Read on to learn about another example of matter.

If your family has cooked outdoors, you may have used a grill that burns charcoal. Let's explore the particles of the charcoal. A bag of charcoal holds dozens of large chunks, or briquettes.

A briquette is made up of particles that are stuck together. But you'll get black grit on your hands from touching it.

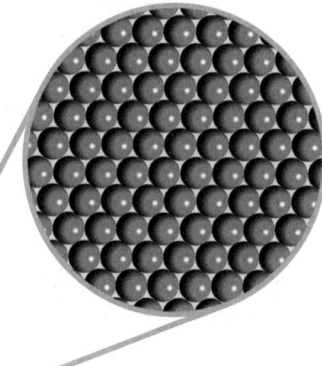

Even the tiniest speck of a charcoal briquette is made of hundreds of millions of carbon particles.

Break up a briquette and you can see both large and small parts that make up the whole. Notice how even the smallest particles, such as the grit on your hands, all look the same. This is because they are made from the same type of matter, called carbon.

The piece of charcoal is a form of matter. By zooming in, you can see that the makeup of the whole is the same as the makeup of the charcoal's smaller pieces.

Fill in the blank with either *the same* or *different*: A large piece of matter

has _____ traits as the smaller pieces and the individual

particles of the same matter.

 Turn to a partner. Discuss ideas about how you could test and compare one or two properties of large and small samples of the same matter. Agree on a plan. Write it below.

_____

_____

_____

States of Matter

Look at the images and models of matter, and then write down your observations. Focus on shapes and sizes. Do they change easily?

The shoe is made up of different solid materials.

At 22 °C (72 °F) honey is a liquid. The glass bear is a solid.

The gas-filled bouncy house can be inflated and deflated by fans.

Matter has particular properties. One property is the state in which matter exists. The term *state* refers to how the particles of the matter are behaving. Another word for state of matter is *phase*.

In a **solid**, matter has a definite shape and volume. A solid's particles are tightly-packed together. In a **liquid**, matter has no definite shape but does have a definite volume. A liquid's particles are not as tightly packed and can move around each other. In a **gas**, matter has neither definite shape nor definite volume. The particles of a gas are far apart and move freely.

Gases

Air is clear, colorless, and all around us. Wave your hand back and forth. Can you feel it? Air is made of particles of different gases, including water vapor.

Why can't we see most gases, such as air? After rainfall, liquid water in a puddle turns into a gas and becomes part of air. Gases such as water vapor are invisible because their tiny particles are very far apart. The white smoke produced by a blown-out candle has gas-like properties. How can you tell that the parts you see are probably not a gas?

_____

_____

When the trigger is pressed, the gas squeezed inside this fire extinguisher rushes out. It carries a dry powder with it.
....

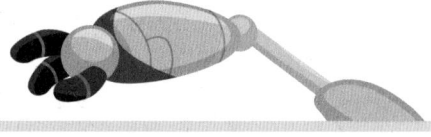

Making Sense

How do the properties of solids and liquids and the particle nature of gases such as air add to your explanation of the rocket?

_____

_____

_____

Name _____

Lesson Check

Can You Explain It?

Review your ideas from the beginning of the lesson about how the types of matter shown in the image enable the rocket to function. How have your ideas changed? Be sure to do the following:

- Describe three states of matter.
- Explain how you know matter is made of particles.
- Identify ways to measure different forms of matter.

Now I know or think that _____

_____

_____

Making Connections

How do the properties of solids, liquids, and gases enable this sprayer to work?

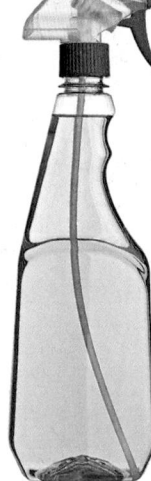

_____

_____

_____

_____

_____

Checkpoints

1. In the space below, draw and label a model that shows how the matter inside a tire changes as the tire is inflated.

2. Label each model with the term that describes the state of matter.

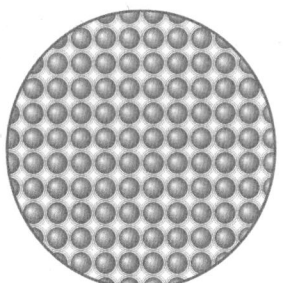 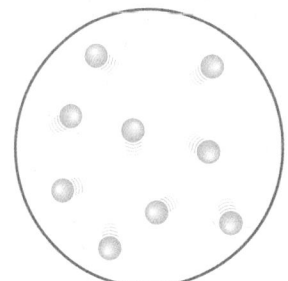 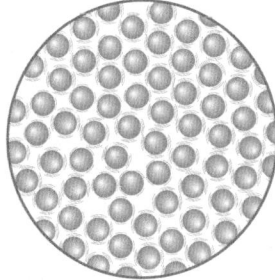

3. Why is important to include units in measurements of length and mass? What happens if you change units during an investigation?

_____

_____

_____

_____

4. Draw lines to match the tools in the right-hand column with the things they measure.

volume   balance

length   graduated cylinder

mass   metric ruler

5. Which of these are considered matter?

  a. a feeling of happiness

  b. a thought

  c. a chicken laying an egg

  d. a container filled with milk

  e. five minutes passing by

  f. bowling pins set up on an alley

6. Which property of matter did you use to answer Question 5?

_____

_____

_____

7. Compare and describe the arrangement of particles before and after squeezing for water and for air.

_____

_____

_____

8. What could you measure to test your model in Question 1? Why?

_____

_____

_____

Matter Has Many Properties

ZZZZZZZZ

What do you notice about this chair?

I notice _____

_____

_____

_____

What do you wonder about how this chair should work and feel compared
to a regular chair?

I wonder _____

_____

_____

Can You Explain It?

Why is sitting on a beanbag different from sitting on a typical
classroom chair? Sketch, write, or model your answer.

So Many Properties

What would a mini me be made of?

The materials used to make everyday products are chosen based on their properties. For example, a baseball cap is made of soft, durable fabric, with a bill that sticks out and shades your eyes. A bicycle helmet is padded on the inside, with a lightweight outer shell that can absorb impacts. Chairs are padded and support your body.

Form a question Ask a question about choosing materials for repairing or making a beanbag chair.

Did you know?

All bicycle helmet designs in the United States must pass a series of tests before they can be sold—including being dropped on a metal plate.

STEP 1 Your teacher will give your group some materials that can be used to make a beanbag chair. Describe the properties of each sample.

_____

_____

STEP 2 Make a **claim** about the best sample to use. Use **evidence** from your observations and **reasoning** to support your claim.

_____

_____

_____

STEP 3 How might you use math to get more numeric data to support your claim? Be ready to share your answer.

_____

_____

_____

Making Sense

How does focusing on the properties of materials help you tell what makes a beanbag chair different from a typical chair?

_____

_____

Engineer It
Beat the Heat

A company that makes chocolate bars wants to start selling their product in outdoor marketplaces. The problem is that chocolate melts in warm weather! The company has hired your team to help design new packaging, and they give you these goals:

- Minimize wasteful packaging. The package can be no more than three times as big as the chocolate.
- Keep chocolate from melting for a minimum of 15 minutes. Minimize use of materials.
- Make the prototype easy to open and close in order to demonstrate its effectiveness to the company.

Form a question Ask a question about this design challenge.

Did you know?

The U.S. military gave out special chocolate bars during World War II. The chocolate didn't melt easily. It was tough to chew and bitter.

POSSIBLE MATERIALS

- [ ] a small piece of unwrapped chocolate (place inside container)
- [ ] small container with lid
- [ ] foam cup
- [ ] tape
- [ ] glue
- [ ] aluminum foil
- [ ] cardboard
- [ ] wax paper
- [ ] paper cup
- [ ] cotton balls
- [ ] felt
- [ ] brown bag
- [ ] zip-top bag
- [ ] clock or timer

Explore

STEP 1 **Research** Begin by conducting research about how to keep items from melting. Write your findings below.

STEP 2 **Define the problem** Review the problem on the previous page, and then fill in the criteria and constraints below.

Criteria	Constraints

STEP 3 **Brainstorm** Brainstorm at least three solutions for your problem. Recall the criteria and constraints, including available materials. Evaluate each solution below. Are all constraints met? How well are criteria met (1–4 points each)?

Make and Test

STEP 4 **Develop and test a model** Choose the best-rated solution and sketch it. Label all parts. Think about your test procedure.

Build and test your design. Record your data and observations below.

Improve and Test

STEP 5 **Improve** If time allows, build and test an improved model. Did you meet the criteria and constraints better this time? Why or why not?

_____

_____

Make a **claim** based on your investigation. Support your claim with **evidence,** and explain your **reasoning**.

_____

_____

Why did some designs fail? How could you improve the designs that failed?

_____

_____

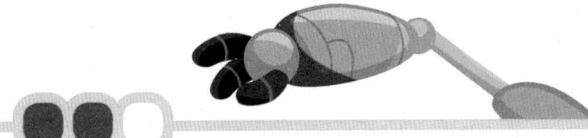

Making Sense

How might understanding the properties of packaging materials and constraints help you choose materials for a beanbag chair?

_____

_____

_____

Turn to a team member. Discuss a time during the activity when you disagreed with a team member, and share how you positively resolved the disagreement.

What Matter Can Do

A change in state is also called a phase change. Work with a partner and use the phrases *more energy* and *less energy* to describe the phase changes that occur to water in a teakettle before and after it is taken off a stove.

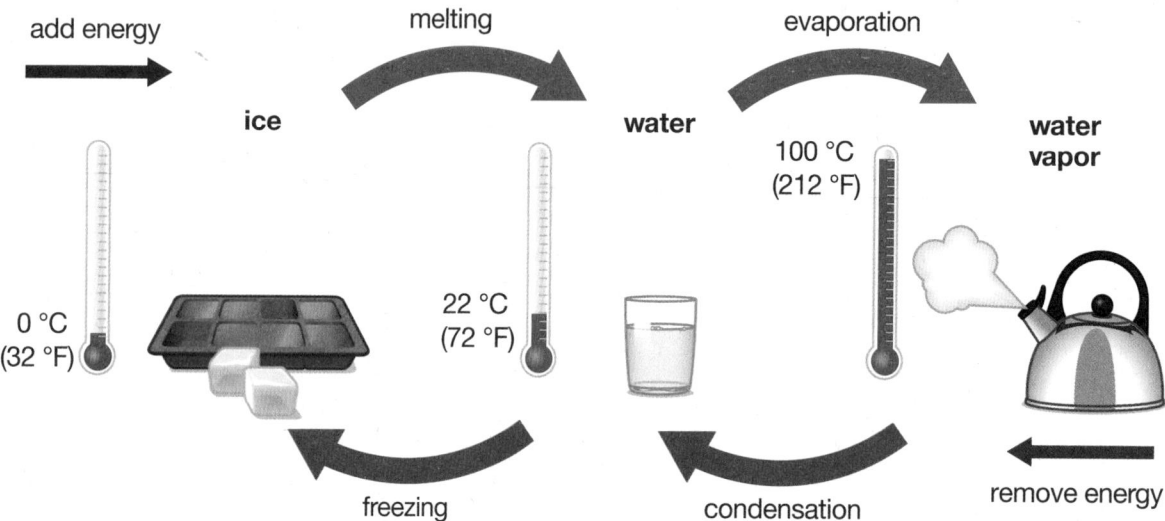

Changes from solid to liquid to gas and back do not ever change the matter. For example, a teakettle gains energy as it warms up. As the water inside reaches its boiling point, it turns rapidly into a gas. As the kettle cools, it loses energy. Any water vapor still in the kettle turns back into a liquid. If the kettle is put into a freezer, the water loses more energy. At its freezing point, the water becomes solid ice. During these changes nothing new has been made. It is still water, just in different states. A boiling point of 100 °C and a freezing point of 0 °C are properties of water.

This sculptor is using high heat to polish the sculpture. The torch melts and then boils away, or *evaporates*, a thin layer of ice.

Conductivity

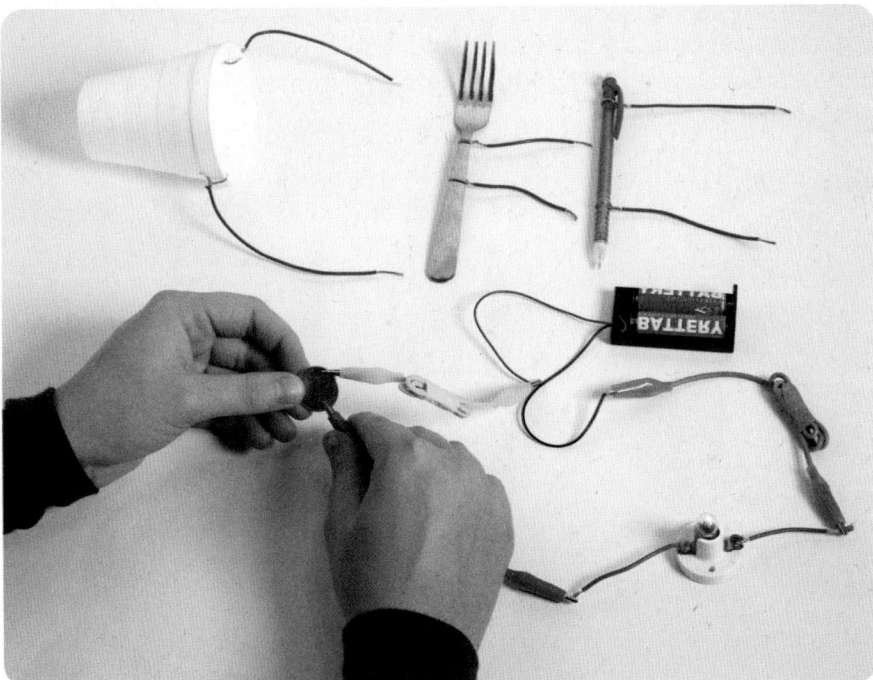

Many things conduct electricity and heat, while others do not. Which samples do you think will make the light turn on?

....

Test Conductivity Another property of matter is conductivity, the ability to transfer heat or electricity. To test conductivity, you can use a light bulb in a bulb holder, two pieces of wire, an AA battery, and a samples of materials to test. Put on safety goggles before starting.

Build a complete circuit that lights the bulb. To begin, disconnect one wire from the battery. Test samples by using them to complete the circuit between the wire and the end of the battery. Write a **claim** about a pattern of test results, support it with **evidence**, and explain your **reasoning.**

_____

_____

Just looking at something isn't a good way to determine its conductivity. For example, plastic objects may be very polished so that they look like metal. A fairly good predictor for electrical conductivity is to see if the object heats up, just like the spoons in the photos on the next page.

Would holding up a metal umbrella during a lightning storm be a bad idea? What evidence allows you to argue your point to a friend?

_____

_____

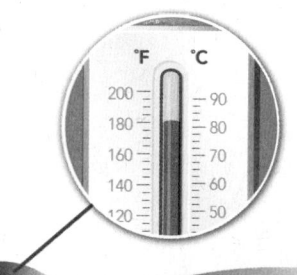

Use math to calculate the temperature difference between the spoons. ___ °C _____

Using a metal spoon to stir the pot could result in a burn to your hands because metal conducts heat well from the boiling water.

Using a spoon with a nylon (plastic) handle is a much better idea. Nylon does not conduct heat well.

Conductors and Insulators

Materials that let heat or electricity travel through them easily are conductors. Most conductors are made of metal, although other materials can also be conductors. A conductor may transfer only heat energy or only electrical energy.

Materials that conduct heat or electricity poorly are called insulators. Cloth, plastic, and rubber are insulators. Have you ever noticed the material that covers the electric cords of devices? The plastic insulation around the wires prevents short circuits, fires, and shocks (electrocution).

You probably used an insulator to keep the chocolate bar from melting. Insulation, such as layers of cotton or cardboard, reduced the heat reaching the bar.

Tell a partner how your team used insulation in the packaging you designed. Give an example of how you collaborated well to develop the insulation part of the design. What evidence supports your argument?

INGREDIENT LIST

- [ ] sugar
- [ ] oranges
- [ ] tomatoes
- [ ] carrots
- [ ] cucumbers
- [ ] lettuce
- [ ] water

What Is a Mixture?

A **mixture** is a combination of two or more substances, or materials, that keep their identities. This means the materials do not change when mixed together.

Use the images and ingredient list to answer the questions and fill in the chart below. In a small group, take turns listening and speaking to check your answers.

A mixture that has the same composition throughout is called a **solution.** This means that the parts are mixed together evenly.

Think of lemonade, ocean water, or orange juice. Can you see the different parts that make up these liquids? Probably not. That is because the solids, such as the sugar in lemonade, have dissolved into the water. The particles are too small to be seen.

	Salad	Orange juice
What are the ingredients?		
Would you be able to taste each ingredient?		
Can you see each ingredient easily?		
If you can't see it, why not?		
Do you think this is a mixture?		
Why or why not?		

Dissolving

Another property of matter can be seen when sugar mixes with water.

Look at the image. Consider what you know about matter and sugar. Then, draw a model below to show what is happening to the sugar and water before and after the sugar dissolves.

When something dissolves to form a solution, it may look like as if it has disappeared, but those particles are still there! They are just too small to be seen. **Solubility** describes how much of a substance will dissolve in a given amount. For example, table salt's solubility in room-temperature water is 357 mg/mL. Ask your teacher about testing this number, then leaving the solution on a window sill for a few weeks to observe.

Making Sense

How does knowing more about other properties of materials affect your choice of materials for the beanbag chair?

_____

_____

© Houghton Mifflin Harcourt Publishing Company • Image Credits: ©Houghton Mifflin Harcourt

Lesson Check

Can You Explain It?

Review your ideas from the beginning of the lesson about properties of matter to describe why sitting on a beanbag chair is different from a typical classroom chair:

- Which properties must be considered for the chair to work right? Why?
- Which optional properties could also be considered?

Now I know or think that _____

_____

_____

_____

Making Sense

How do the properties of a pencil eraser relate to how well or poorly it works?

_____

_____

_____

_____

_____

Checkpoints

1. Suppose you were asked to identify the desirable properties of the glass used in fire trucks. Select all of the terms that describe the desirable properties.

   a. breaks easily

   b. withstands high temperatures

   c. expensive

   d. easy to replace

   e. melts easily

   f. difficult to see through

   g. flexible

   h. transparent

2. For one of the fire truck glass properties that you selected, tell how it helps the fire truck function.

   _____

   _____

   _____

3. Water boils at 100°C. In the space below, tell how you might find the temperature at which another common liquid starts to boil. What pattern of data would be the most convincing evidence?

   _____

   _____

   _____

4. Suppose you wanted to learn more about the properties of a new substance. Which of the following investigations would help you determine its properties? Choose all that apply.

   a. placing the substance in warm water

   b. testing it in a circuit

   c. trying to bend it

5. Suppose you were asked to design a machine that would be made of materials that best conduct electricity. Select those that would be useful to you.

    a. plastic

    b. wood

    c. aluminum

    d. gold

    e. rubber

    f. silk

    g. flannel

6. Why is a vegetable salad considered a mixture?

    a. The particles are very small.

    b. The vegetables can be put together easily.

    c. Each part keeps its own identity.

    d. All of the colors and flavors fit well together.

7. A scientist has a small container of ocean water. She wants to keep it from changing so that she can study it further. Her lab gets a lot of sunlight every day. What can she do to keep the ocean water from changing?

    a. Cover the container.

    b. Increase the temperature of the container.

    c. Separate the water into different containers.

    d. Add more plain water to the container.

8. Give an argument to support your answer for Question 7.

_____

_____

_____

_____

Matter Can Change

What do you notice about this sculpture?

I notice _____

_____

_____

_____

What do you wonder about the sculpture?

I wonder _____

_____

_____

_____

Can You Explain It?

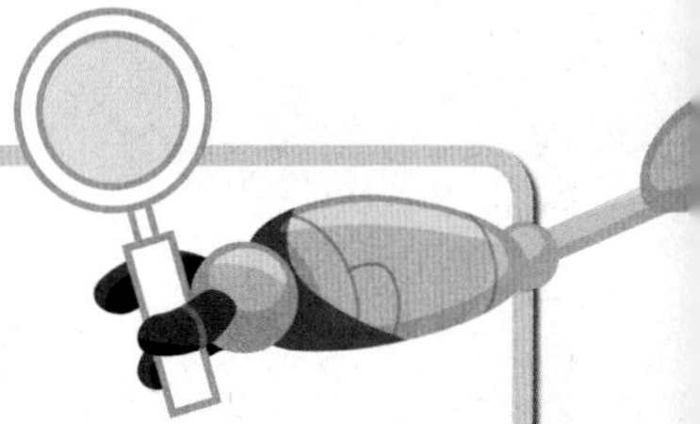

Why does part of the sculpture stay dark and dull even though it's rained on? Sketch, write, or model your answer.

_____

_____

_____

Changes in Matter

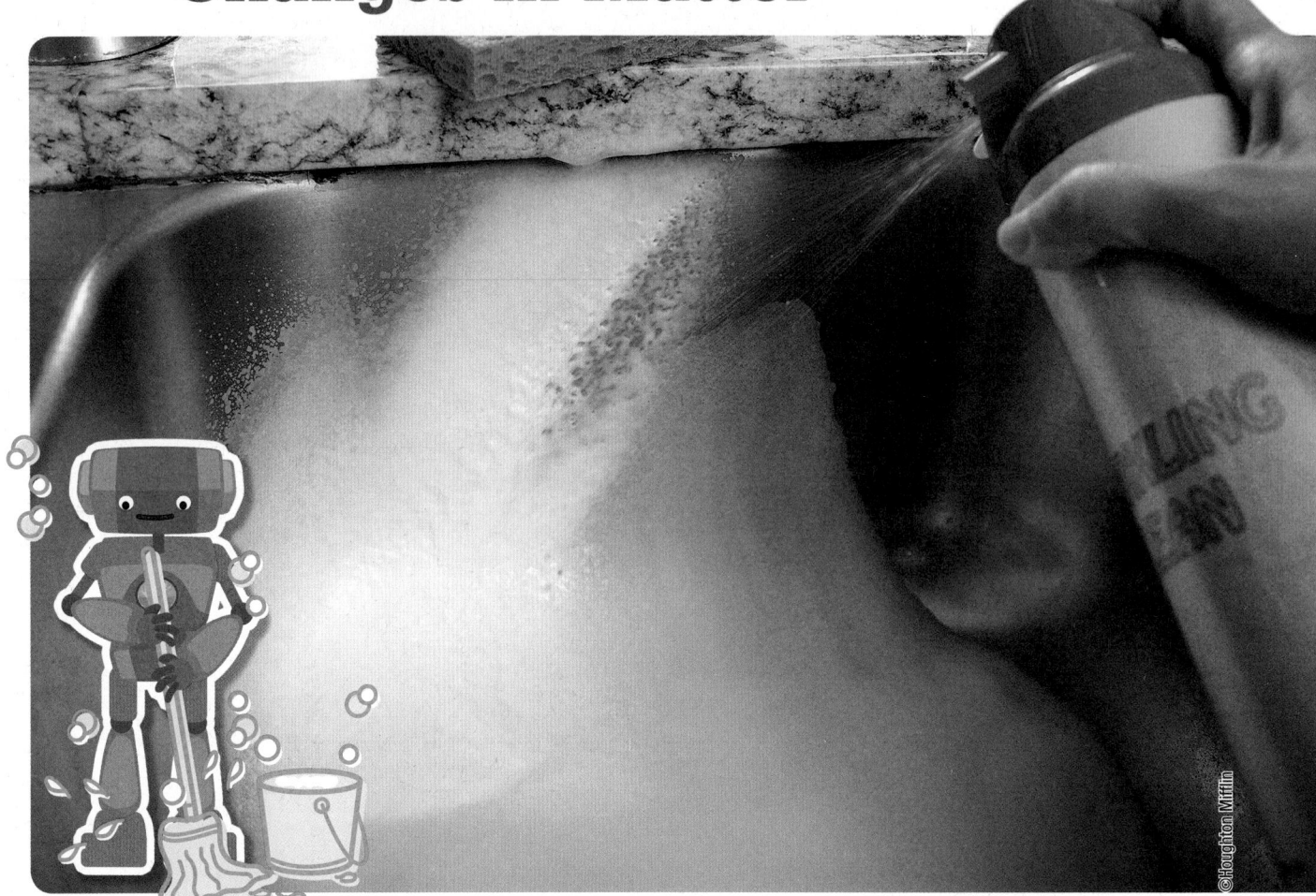

Water can dissolve many things, but people also use soap and other materials to clean objects. These cleaners interact with dirt, stains, and grime in ways that water alone can't.

Form a question What question do you have about how substances can change when they are mixed?

_____

_____

_____

_____

Did you know?

Water is called the _universal solvent_ because it dissolves many kinds of substances.

POSSIBLE MATERIALS

- ☐ used toothbrush
- ☐ 6 tarnished pennies
- ☐ small paper plate
- ☐ goggles
- ☐ gloves
- ☐ paper towel
- ☐ water dropper
- ☐ baking soda, pinch
- ☐ vinegar dropper
- ☐ table salt, pinch

Try to shine a penny with each cleaning method below, using no more than 6 drops of each liquid. Be sure to wipe the penny clean after each trial.

Cleaning method (with toothbrush)	Penny observations	Other observations
No liquid		
Water		
Water and baking soda		
Baking soda and vinegar		
Vinegar and table salt		

Make a **claim** about which cleaning method works the best. Use **evidence** from your tests, and give **reasoning** to support the evidence.

●○○○

Making Sense

How do the changes you observed here help you explain the shiny and dark areas on the sculpture?

Which Will React?

Some containers of ingredients in a kitchen have lost their labels. Can you tell the cornstarch, cream of tartar, and baking soda apart just by looking at them? You can't, but by observing how a substance changes when it reacts with other substances, you can often determine the identity of a mystery substance.

Form a question What question do you have about solving this problem?

_____

_____

_____

> **Did you know?**
>
> Cream of tartar isn't tartar sauce. It's a powder often used to make whipped egg whites fluffier.

POSSIBLE MATERIALS

- ☐ safety goggles
- ☐ apron
- ☐ 3 droppers
- ☐ 3 plastic spoons
- ☐ 9 test tubes

- ☐ test tube holder
- ☐ powder 1
- ☐ powder 2
- ☐ powder 3
- ☐ iodine solution

- ☐ vinegar
- ☐ water
- ☐ labels and pen
- ☐ test tube brush
- ☐ soap

STEP 1 Label three water test tubes *A*, *B*, and *C*. Prepare similar test tubes for the vinegar and iodine, and then carefully place each test tube in the test tube holder.

STEP 2 Add a tiny spoonful of powder 1 to all the tubes labeled *A*.

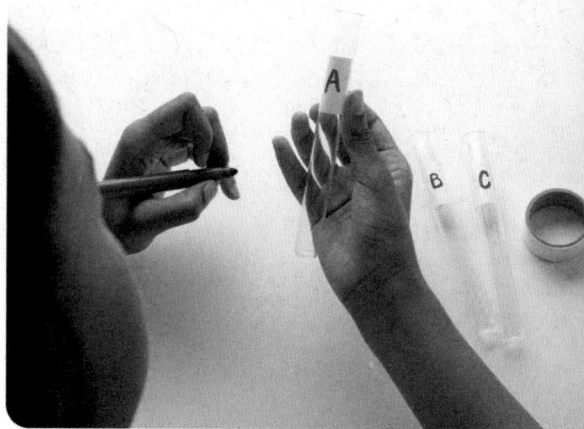

STEP 3 Repeat Step 2 with powder 2 and powder 3, using a clean spoon for each. Add powder 2 only to *B* test tubes, and add powder 3 only to *C* test tubes.

STEP 4 Use a dropper to add three drops of water to all three water test tubes. Record your results in the table on the next page, and then repeat for the vinegar and iodine test tubes, using a new dropper for each liquid.

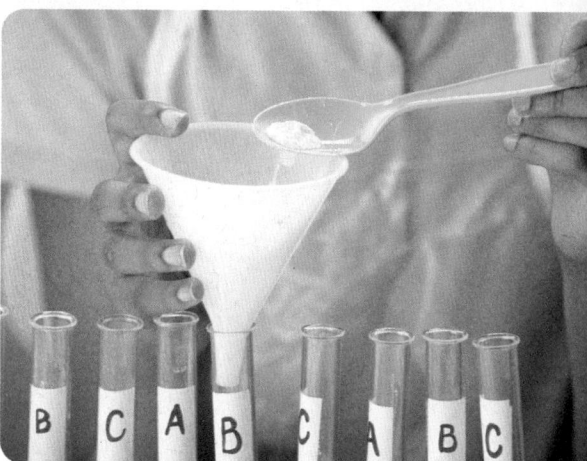

Powder Identification Key

Baking soda: reacts with vinegar to produce a gas

Cornstarch: changes color when mixed with iodine.

Cream of tartar: doesn't react to water, iodine, or vinegar

Each test tube is a unique system with parts that interact. What are the two parts of each system? What is different between the test tubes?

Reactions			
Liquid	**A (powder 1)**	**B (powder 2)**	**C (powder 3)**
Water			
Vinegar			
Iodine			

STEP 5 Analyze your results in the table. Using your observations and the identification key, name the powder containers based on the liquids that reacted with each one.

Make a **claim** about which types of changes took place in this investigation. Support your answer with **evidence** and **reasoning**.

_____

_____

_____

_____

_____

 How did your group show responsible, safe behavior during this activity?

_____

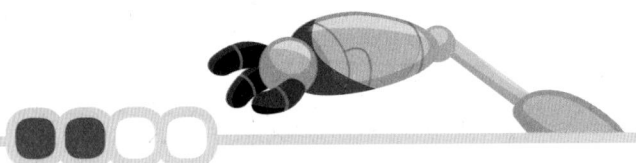

Making Sense

How does this activity add to your explanation of the sculpture's dark areas and shiny areas?

_____

_____

When Matter Changes

One of the ways that matter can be changed is in how it looks. For example, white paper can be cut into many pieces. Paper can also be folded into different shapes. The matter itself is still the same. This type of change is called a **physical change.** The key to a physical change is that nothing new is made. It is still paper.

Another example of a physical change happens when you mix things together. Imagine you have a bag of blue beads and a bag of red beads. Then you put them together into the same bag and shake it up. What happens? The beads mix with one another. Can you still see the different colors? Yes! This is because nothing new has formed. The physical change is just the mixing of the beads.

This can is made of steel. It is used to hold soup or vegetables. What happens to the can after it gets crushed? Is the can still made of steel? Sure! All you have done by crushing it is change its shape. It is still the same kind of matter.

....

Choose the correct words for each sentence.

color	number	makeup	shape	cutting
burning	matter	temperature	flammability	size

Physical changes happen when matter changes in _____,

_____, or _____.

An example of this type of change would be _____ a piece of

wood.

In this type of change, no new _____ is formed.

Before and After Are Different

Another type of change that can occur is a chemical change. During a **chemical change,** a new substance forms as two or more substances combine. During a chemical change, a gas or a precipitate—a solid material—may form. There can also be a change in temperature. A new substance with new properties shows that the original matter has changed. All these new parts come from the original system, but they can never have their original properties again. Burning is an example of a chemical change. When things burn, heat is released and new substances with different properties form.

What happens when you leave food out on the counter or in the refrigerator for a long time? It "goes bad," or rots. The chemical makeup of the food changes.

When chemicals inside glow sticks mix, they start to glow. Can you ever separate those chemicals? No, because a chemical change has happened. Once the reaction is over, the light will fade out.

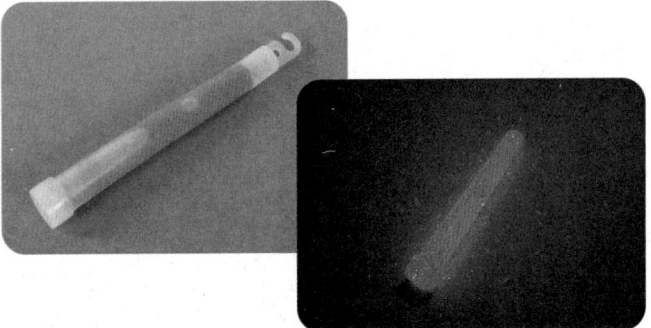

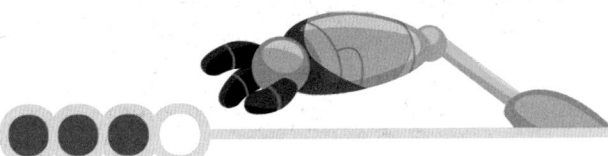

Making Sense

How does your understanding of physical and chemical changes add to your explanation of the shiny and dark parts of the sculpture?

_____

_____

Conservation of Matter

Where Does the Matter Go?

You found the mass of the orange below with the skin on. Then you decided to peel the skin off and place all of the pieces back on the scale. Predict the mass of the peeled orange on the scale. Write it down. Discuss your ideas with a classmate.

a. The mass of the orange is shown on the digital scale.

b. The same orange has been peeled. How does its weigh compare with that of the unpeeled orange?

c. These materials will be added together. What is their combined mass here?

d. What is the mass now? Did it change from before they were added together? This is how the conservation of matter works.

Physical Changes

During a physical change, the amount of matter in the object stays the same. This happens because no new matter is being formed. When you cut a piece of paper in half, you still have the same amount of paper, just in two pieces. The fact that the amount of matter stays the same is called the **conservation of matter.**

Imagine you have a pile of building blocks. You build a tower using all of the blocks. Then you are asked to take apart the tower and build another shape using the same number of blocks. The new shape looks totally different than the tower but still has the exact same number of blocks in it. This is the conservation of matter during a physical change.

Identify Choose the correct words. Words can be used more than once. When you're finished, draw and label a model to support your answers.

chemical	physical	increase	decrease	stay the same

Phase changes are considered _____ changes. This means that no

new matter is formed. When changing from solid to liquid form, the mass of

the matter will _____. When changing from liquid to gas form, the

mass will _____. This supports the conservation of matter.

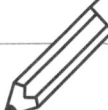

Conservation in a Phase Change

Remember that changing from a solid to a liquid, and a liquid to a gas are both physical changes. The amount of matter does not change, only its energy. If you were to melt solid gold metal, the liquid would have the same mass as the solid block you started with.

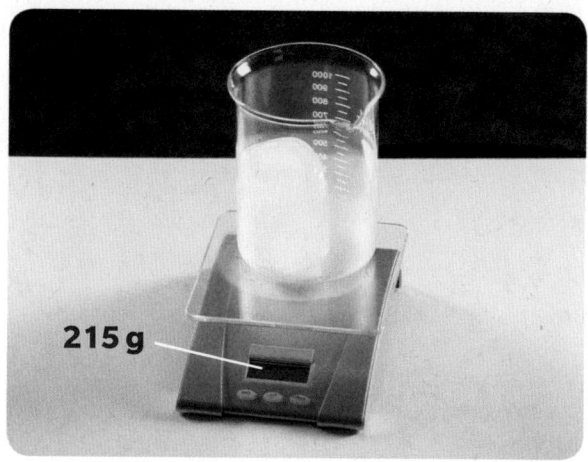

Here is a block of ice sitting in a beaker. Notice what the scale says. The room is 22 °C (72 °F).

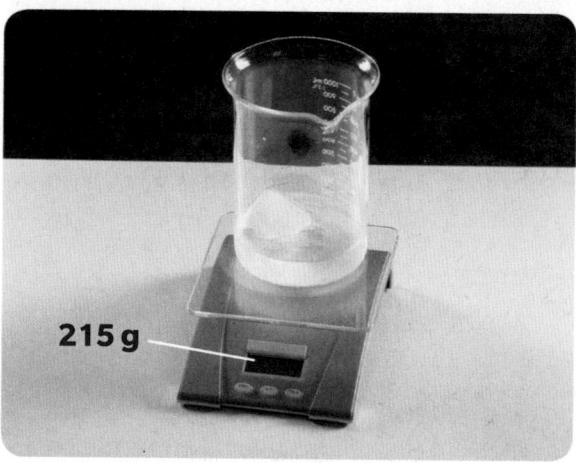

What does the ice look like now? What does the scale say the mass is?

All the ice has melted and the liquid water is near its boiling point. What does the scale say the mass is now?

The water is boiling. What does the scale say the mass is now?

The boiling water released water vapor. If you could capture and return the vapor as liquid, the total mass would still read 215 g.

Conservation of Matter: Chemical Change

Chemical changes also demonstrate the conservation of matter. In a chemical change, new substances form. But the mass of the new substances is equal what you started with.

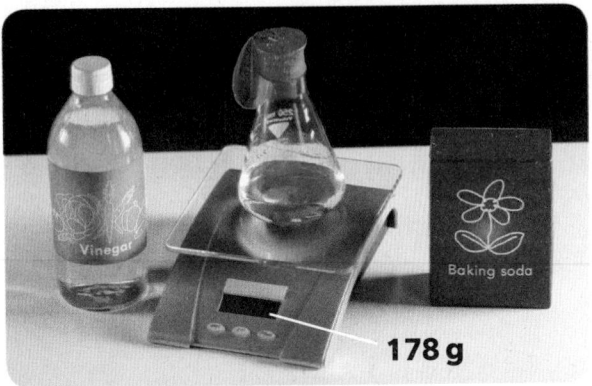

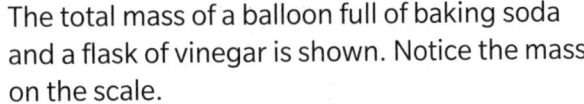

The total mass of a balloon full of baking soda and a flask of vinegar is shown. Notice the mass on the scale.

Vinegar and baking soda produce a liquid and a gas when they react. The flask is sealed with a balloon, which traps any gas. The total mass of inputs equals the mass of the outputs.

Predict What would happen if the reaction between baking soda and vinegar occurred in an open container with no balloon? Would it be easy to show conservation of matter?

_____

_____

 Turn to a partner. Share another way you could demonstrate conservation of matter.

Making Sense

How does your understanding of physical and chemical changes and conservation of matter add to your explanation of the dark and shiny parts of the sculpture?

_____

_____

_____

Name _____

Lesson Check

Can You Explain It?

Review your ideas from the beginning of this lesson about the shiny and dark parts of the outdoor sculpture. How have your ideas changed? Be sure to do the following:

- Explain the differences between chemical and physical changes.
- Explain what type of change likely happened in the photo.
- Explain how the conservation of matter relates to both kinds of changes.

Now I know or think that _____

_____

_____

_____

_____

Making Connections

The lighter colored crust on this faucet built up over time. It won't dissolve easily in water. How could you find the best way to clean it?

_____

_____

_____

Checkpoints

Answer the following questions to test your knowledge.

1. What property could you use to help identify baking powder?

   a. odor

   b. conductivity

   c. fizzes with vinegar

   d. temperature

2. When Sefa got home from school, he knew something inside the garbage can had a undergone a chemical change. What evidence did he most likely use to come to this conclusion?

   Choose all that apply.

   a. The can had three-day-old food in it.

   b. There was an odor.

   c. The can contained smashed containers.

   d. He threw ice cubes in there last night.

   e. An old, rusty spoon was thrown out.

3. Decide which terms relate to chemical changes of matter and which to physical changes of matter.

Chemical change	Physical change

energy release
odor
boiling
gas release
burning
shape change
phase change
energy release

4. You leave a glass of ice outside on a sunny day. The ice melts. What does the conservation of matter predict? How could you test that prediction?

_____

_____

_____

_____

5. Which of the following would be physical changes? Choose all that apply.

   a. folding paper

   b. breaking a window

   c. baking bread

   d. rotting food

   e. building a tower of blocks

   f. boiling water

For one of your choices, tell how you know it is a physical change.

_____

_____

6. Which of the following would be chemical changes? Choose all that apply.

   a. bending a metal bar

   b. breaking a glass

   c. baking brownies

   d. molding fruit

   e. building a wall out of bricks

   f. burning wood in a fireplace

For one of your choices, tell how you know it's a chemical change.

_____

_____

7. What would happen to the amount of matter of a piece of wood if it were cut it into pieces and then burned?

   a. It would go up.

   b. It would go down after cutting.

   c. It would go up, then down.

   d. There would be no change.

8. What evidence and reasoning would you use to convince a friend of your answer to Question 7?

_____

_____

Unit Review

1. Describe a simple test you can perform to show there is matter inside all three sealed bottles.

_____

_____

_____

2. Draw and label a model comparing matter in an inflated balloon and an empty balloon.

3. Fill in the second column. Then, draw a line from each word in the first column to its correct description in the second column.

air   _____ : definite shape and volume

bus

tea   _____ : definite volume, varying shape

milk

sidewalk _____ : no definite volume or shape

Use this image to answer questions 4 and 5.

4. A user needs to temporarily attach several pieces of paper. What criteria would matter for a good solution? How do the properties of the material used to make paper clips meet these criteria?

_____

_____

_____

5. Suppose each block is a different substance. What would you do with the blocks to determine which substances to use when designing and building a wall? Explain how your conclusions based on the blocks can be applied to a full-size wall.

_____

_____

_____

6. The art teacher has a mixture of crayons, colored pencils, and markers. He made a system to separate them. The first filter separates out objects that weigh as much as a marker. The second filter separates out objects longer than a crayon. What failure points will he identify when testing the system? Select all that apply.

  a. A used colored pencil may be shorter than a new crayon.

  b. A colored pencil could pass through the second filter at an angle.

  c. A crayon could leave marks on the filters.

  d. A sideways crayon could get caught in the second filter.

7. Which are examples of physical changes? Circle all that apply.

   a. paper burning   **d.** wood burning

   b. paper being torn   **e.** cake being cut

   c. wood being chopped down   **f.** cake baking

For an answer you didn't circle, what could you measure and observe to show it isn't a physical change?

_____

_____

_____

8. Choose the correct answer. What type of change is happening in the picture to the right?

   a. metal rusting; a chemical change

   b. metal rusting; a physical change

   c. metal rotting; a chemical change

   d. metal rotting; a physical change

9. A classmate claims that the reddish color on the nails was caused by melting the nails. What data would you collect to evaluate the claim?

_____

_____

_____

10. When a chemical change occurs between substances in a system, what do you know about the amount of matter in the system? What is this known as? Draw a diagram or write a math sentence that models this.

_____

_____

In Unit 2, you planned and carried out investigations to explain what causes matter to change. In this unit, you'll use a model to explain how plants use energy to change one form of matter into another and how the energy stored in the new matter is transferred throughout an ecosystem.

UNIT 3 Energy and Matter in Organisms

© Houghton Mifflin Harcourt Publishing Company • Image Credits: (bl) ©weyo/Adobe Stock

LESSON 1
Plants Transform and Use Energy and Matter

nutrient return

nutrient pump

Lettuce look closely at this garden.

© Houghton Mifflin Harcourt Publishing Company • Image Credits: (c) ©nuwatphoto/istock / getty Images Plus/Getty Images

What do you notice about these plants?

I notice ______________________________

____

____

____

What do you wonder about the conditions in which the plants are growing?

I wonder ______________________________

____

____

____

Can You Explain It?

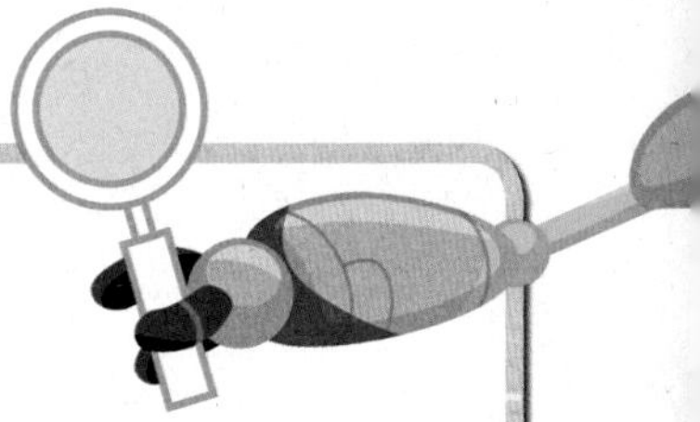

How do these plants get the energy and matter they need to grow without soil? Sketch, write, or model your answer.

© Houghton Mifflin Harcourt Publishing Company

A Tree in a Forest

In a rain forest, mature trees make up the canopy layer. In this layer, the limbs of various trees are so close that they nearly touch. On the forest floor, there is more space, but there are very few young trees. It is difficult for young trees to grow in a rain forest.

Form a Question Ask a question about the growth of young trees in the shade formed by the canopy layer.

> **Did you know?**
>
> The tallest tropical tree is the yellow meranti. It is 100 m tall, the height of a 33-story building!

POSSIBLE MATERIALS

- ☐ 2 small potted plants
- ☐ shoebox and lid
- ☐ masking tape
- ☐ marker
- ☐ metric ruler
- ☐ measuring cup
- ☐ water
- ☐ colored pencils

STEP 1   **Investigate your question**   In the space below, plan a fair test to gather evidence to help you explain why few young trees grow on the rainforest floor. List the materials you will use. You may choose to write or sketch the steps.

STEP 2   **Organize your data** Use this space to organize your data.

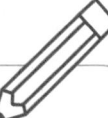

STEP 3   **Analyze your data** Describe any changes that happen to the plants.

_____

_____

_____

STEP 4   **Draw conclusions** Share your data with other groups.

Explain any differences or similarities among the groups' data.

_____

_____

_____

_____

Make a **claim** about the pattern of young tree growth on the rainforest floor. Support your claim with **evidence** from your investigation, and explain your **reasoning**.

_____

_____

_____

_____

Making Sense

How does your claim or the evidence you gathered in this investigation help you begin to explain why plants can grow without soil? Describe or draw your evidence.

_____

_____

_____

_____

_____

In the space below, list two examples of good communication and teamwork that you followed during this investigation.

_____

_____

_____

Needs for Growth

Even the largest plants usually start out as small seeds. Inside a seed is a tiny plant. On the outside, the seed has a coating that protects the seed and its contents. When conditions are just right for a seed to sprout and grow, the tiny plant pushes open the coating and grows toward the sun. As it grows, it gains more mass, or matter.

Form a question What question do you have about how the mass of a plant changes over time?

Did you know?

One type of palm tree has the world's largest seed. It is 30 cm (1 ft) long and can weigh up to 18 kg (40 lb).

Use the table below to show the mass of a seed or seedling and its system. Then, carefully measure a plant that is six weeks old.

	Starting mass (g)	Mass after 6 weeks (g)
Seed/plant		
Soil		
Pot		

POSSIBLE MATERIALS
☐ one-week-old seedling in pot
☐ six-week-old plant in pot
☐ pan balance or scale

Analyze your data Make a **claim** about the plant's mass. Tell how the **evidence** supports your claim, and explain your **reasoning**.

_____

_____

_____

Briefly tell how you might gather more data to support a deeper explanation of added plant mass.

_____

_____

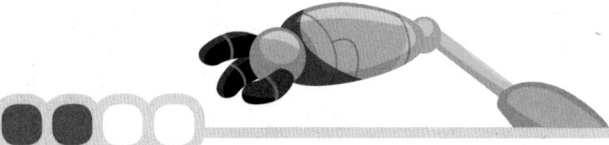

Making Sense

How does understanding how plants add mass as they grow help you explain how plants can grow without soil?

_____

_____

Plant Needs

Drink It In

All organisms need water to live. Plants contain more water than most other living things. In fact, water makes up 90% of most plants. If a plant does not get enough water, it will wilt, as the plant on the left shows.

Water enters a plant through the roots, travels up through the stem, and spreads out into the leaves. Without enough water, the leaves and stem of a plant become weak and start to droop. Unlike a healthy plant, a wilted plant is not able to make food for itself and survive.

Nutrients

Water is not the only thing plants take in through their roots. Nutrients in the soil are dissolved in the water in the soil, and these nutrients are delivered to a plant via its roots. Nutrients are materials from the environment that plants need to be healthy. In a hydroponic system, where plants are grown in water instead of soil, nutrients are added to the water.

Name three things plants need to grow and thrive.

In and Out

Plants need to take in fresh air and release waste gases. How do they do this? The underside of a leaf has tiny holes that can open and close. Air moves into and out of a plant through these holes.

There are structures on the sides of the holes. The structures control whether the holes are closed or not. When these structures are swollen, the holes are open. When they are shrunken, the holes are closed.

A magnified view of the underside of leaves.

Making Sense

Describe the evidence you have found to support your claim about how plants can grow without soil.

_____

_____

 Discuss your answer with your group. Provide constructive feedback for each answer and make sure everyone has a chance to speak.

Making Food

How do plants use the light, water, air, and nutrients they need? Plants use energy and matter to make food. Study the model and the captions for each step, then match each caption to what it describes in the model by writing the correct letter in each circle.

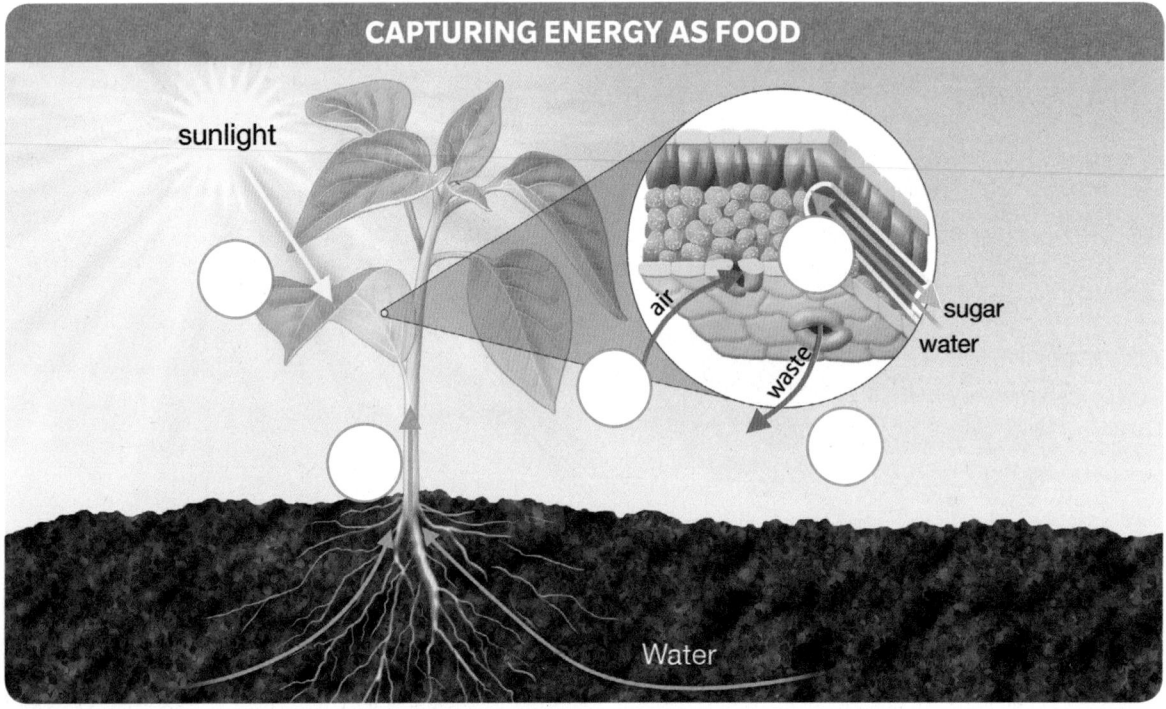

CAPTURING ENERGY AS FOOD

sunlight

air

sugar
water

waste

Water

a. Plant roots take in water. It moves up the stem and into the leaves.

b. Plant structures capture light energy.

c. Plant leaves take in air.

d. Plants use light energy, air, and water to produce food (sugar). Plants use this food to survive and grow.

e. Waste is released as a gas.

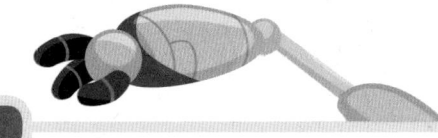

Making Sense

Analyze images in this lesson to make a word model of how plants meet their needs. How does a model help you explain how plants can grow without soil?

_____

_____

Lesson Check

Can You Explain It?

Review your ideas from the beginning of this lesson about what plants need to survive and grow. How have your ideas changed?

Be sure to do the following:

- Explain how these plants are growing even though they aren't being grown in soil.
- Describe what plants need to survive and grow.
- Use data from investigations and explorations to explain how plants make their own food.

Now I know or think that _____

_____

_____

Making Connections

Potatoes can start growing in water. How is this like the plants growing without soil at the beginning of the lesson? How is it different?

_____

_____

_____

_____

Checkpoints

1. Complete the model of a plant process of making food by labeling the matter and energy inputs and outputs.

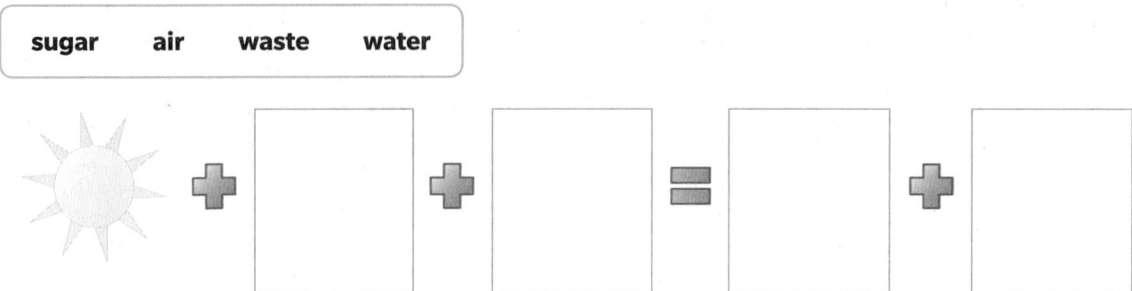

| sugar | air | waste | water |

2. Suppose that the two plants in the photograph are each getting the same amount of sunlight, air, and nutrients. What could cause the one on the left to look the way it does? Choose all that apply.

   a. It is the effect of getting too much sun.

   b. It is the effect of not getting enough air.

   c. It is the effect of getting too much water.

   d. It is the effect of not getting enough water.

3. Suppose a plant gets only 2 hours of sunlight every 24 hours. Construct an explanation about how the lack of energy affects how a plant is able to use matter.

_____

_____

_____

_____

4. Match each statement to the process part in the illustration. Write the letter in the correct circle on the model.

   a. It is the energy source used to change matter that isn't food into matter that is food.

   b. These structures help the plant absorb nutrients and water.

   c. Air, water, and waste pass through these structures.

© Houghton Mifflin Harcourt Publishing Company

5. You are investigating plant needs with a computer simulation. You develop a model to test what happens when one plant gets no air for a week and another gets no water. How will a plant be affected if it does not get enough water or air? Explain your answer.

_____

_____

_____

6. Draw a line to each term to identify whether it is needed for a plant to make food or is made by the plant. Put a box around the energy input.

air

Needed to make food	sugar	Made by the plant
	sunlight	
	water	

waste

7. Which of the following is not a necessary part of a system for growing plants? Choose all that apply, then explain your answer.

a. air

b. soil

c. water

d. sunlight

e. bacteria

f. nutrients

_____

_____

_____

8. Which plant part would likely be larger in a dry environment and why?

_____

_____

Organisms Use Matter and Energy

Here's the rest of lunch!

What do you notice about how this giant panda eats?

I notice _____

_____

_____

_____

What do you wonder about how this giant panda uses its food energy?

I wonder _____

_____

_____

_____

Can You Explain It?

How do you think this giant panda obtains enough food to survive?
Sketch, write, or model your answer.

A Filling Morsel

Giant pandas eat bamboo for 16 hours a day! You might have heard about people who require special foods or diets. For example, athletes closely monitor what they eat to get energy to perform their sport. The unit of measurement for energy available in food is called a *Calorie*. The energy stored in food originally came from sunlight.

Form a question What questions come to mind when you think about the amount of energy in foods for athletes compared with the amount of energy in foods for pandas?

> **Did you know?**
>
> Wild animals often seek out fatty food because it provides a lot of energy.

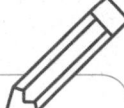

STEP 1

Investigate your question How can you investigate the questions your class chose as most important? Think about the materials your teacher shows you, what else you might need to research, and where you will find it. Write your plan and show it to your teacher to see if you can get the other things you need. Use extra paper if needed.

Organize your data Carry out your plan, and record your results. Communicate your data in a way that everyone can see what you did and what the outcome was. You might choose a table or a graph as a presentation tool, or you might choose to make a poster with photographs. Summarize your findings below.

Draw conclusions Make a **claim** that answers the question your class decided to explore. Support your claim with **evidence** from your investigation and **reasoning** to explain how the evidence supports your claim.

Explain how the matter from air, matter from water, and energy from the sun transfer to food and then from food to you.

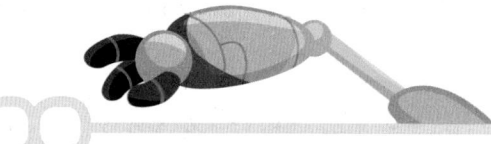

Making Sense

How does your new understanding of energy needs help explain the giant panda's eating habits?

© Houghton Mifflin Harcourt Publishing Company • Image Credits: (tl) ©Houghton Mifflin Harcourt

Where's the Heat?

This deer is searching for food on a very cold day. Animals' energy needs can change depending on the weather or how active they are, and that is also true for humans. Think about a day you needed a lot of energy. Maybe you had soccer practice, did chores around your home, and helped to prepare a meal.

Form a question What questions come to mind when you think about your energy needs for soccer, chores, and preparing dinner?

_____

_____

_____

_____

Did you know?

A dog's average body temperature is 39.2 °C (102.5 °F). So, your pet may feel a little warm normally.

POSSIBLE MATERIALS

- [ ] thermometer
- [ ] thermometer strips

STEP 1 **Investigate your question** Measure the room temperature with a thermometer, and then measure your skin temperature with a forehead strip.

STEP 2 **Organize your data** Record your data.

STEP 3 Compare your classmates' skin temperatures. What do you notice? How do they compare with the room's temperature?

STEP 4   **Research**   Find out the daily Calorie needs for an active fifth-grader, a typical adult, and an adult backpacker in warm weather and in cold, snowy weather. Use books, the Internet, or other reliable media sources.

_____

_____

Analyze your data   Make a **claim** to answer your question about energy needs. Show how the **evidence** supports your claim, and explain your **reasoning**.

_____

_____

Draw conclusions   Where does the energy to keep your body temperature consistent come from? What would happen if you had a lower-energy diet?

_____

_____

To support your answer, draw and label a model of energy inputs to your body system on a separate piece of paper.

Making Sense

Bamboo isn't a great source of energy. How does what you've just learned add to your explanation of how a giant panda survives?

_____

_____

 Turn and talk with a classmate about your answers.

Growth, Change, and Regrowth

Body Building

In the past, horses did a lot of the work that cars, trucks, tractors, and bulldozers do today. In some places, they still do. A baby horse, or foal, cannot do the same work that an adult horse does. Discuss in your group how a foal is different from an adult horse.

What do you think a foal needs to grow into an adult horse? Select all that apply.

a. air   **d.** nutrients   **g.** grooming

b. water   **e.** hay for bedding   **h.** a saddle

c. a barn   **f.** food

Growth and repair of body parts require matter, which, for animals, are materials found in the environment. When food is eaten, matter is broken down into simpler forms. These can be used to build or repair an animal's body.

Growth, repair, and other life processes also require energy. When food matter is broken down, energy is released. The animal's body can then use the energy.

A bird may obtain matter and energy by eating fruits, seeds, insects, or other small animals.

Producers to Consumers

Animals drink and eat food to obtain the matter and energy they need for their life processes. Some organisms, such as plants, can make their own food. An organism that makes its own food is called a **producer**. Plants are producers because they are able to use the energy from sunlight to produce sugars, which are a source of energy and matter.

On the other hand, an animal cannot make its own food. An animal is a **consumer**, an organism that obtains energy and matter by feeding on other organisms. Animals are consumers and get what they need from the environment. All the food energy consumers take in can be traced back to sunlight captured by plants.

 Class pets need healthy foods in order to grow and repair body parts. How do you think it feels to make responsible choices for class pet meal times and foods? Share your thoughts with a partner.

Snails use the matter they obtain from food in many ways. Unused matter is released from the body as waste.

While animals take in matter from the environment, they also release wastes into the environment. Wastes are produced when matter is converted into materials that are not used by the body. Some wastes are from the breakdown of food. Others may be byproducts from life processes. Wastes are then released into the environment.

For example, used-up air is a waste product released when an animal breathes out. Animals also eliminate the remains of digested food out of their bodies as waste.

Making Sense

How does your understanding of energy and matter needs of organisms help you explain the giant panda's food needs?

© Houghton Mifflin Harcourt Publishing Company • Image Credits: (tc) ©mypokcik/ istock/Getty Images

Animal Energy

Brrr! It's Cold Outside!

Think about running fast with and without a heavy backpack. How does the energy you need to run change?

Keeping a home warm in winter takes energy, too. How do you think a home's size affects the amount of energy needed?

Now, think about a large animal such as the bison below. Does it need more or less energy than a squirrel? Use reasoning to explain your answer.

It's bitterly cold in the Antarctic. Here, temperatures may be "high" at –20 °C in the summer and dip below –60 °C in the winter! So how do these penguins stay warm? By eating! In addition to providing matter and energy for growth and body repair, food provides energy to keep their bodies warm.

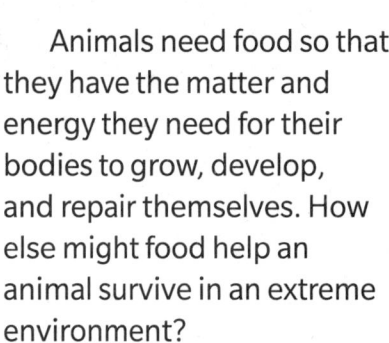

Animals need food so that they have the matter and energy they need for their bodies to grow, develop, and repair themselves. How else might food help an animal survive in an extreme environment?

Energy and Body Temperature

Energy stored in matter can be released through chemical reactions. Some animals have internal body parts that use chemical reactions to break down food and produce heat. Think about how heat flows in or out of these animals. Share your ideas with other students.

Animal	Daytime temperature (°C)	Nighttime temperature (°C)
Human	37	37
Mouse	37	37
Green iguana	35	26
Chicken	42	42

Animals such as iguanas, snakes, and other reptiles use the energy in food to grow and move. They use sunlight to keep their bodies warm. Evaluate the information in the table. In a small group, share ideas about how heat flows in and out of reptiles and birds. Then look at the images on this page. How do you think the animals shown are affected by conditions in the environment, such as climate?

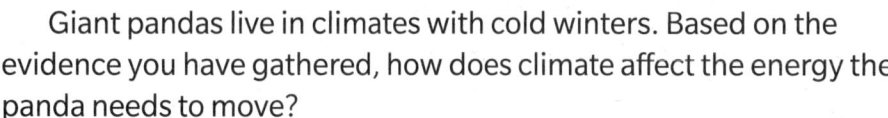

Making Sense

Giant pandas live in climates with cold winters. Based on the evidence you have gathered, how does climate affect the energy the panda needs to move?

_____

_____

_____

Name _____

Lesson Check

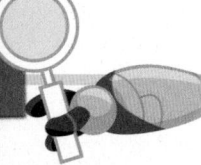

Can You Explain It?

Review your ideas from the beginning of this lesson about how pandas get the energy and matter they need for life. How have your ideas changed?

Be sure to do the following:

- Describe the roles of energy and matter in body processes.
- Explain why pandas need food.
- Identify the source of the energy in panda food.

Now I know or think that _____

_____

_____

_____

_____

Making Connections

This snake only needs to eat every few weeks. Explain why the snake does not need to eat daily by making a claim about how the snake's energy and matter needs compare to what is available in its food.

_____

_____

Checkpoints

1. Study the photo to answer the question. What is the original source of the energy that the horse uses to grow and survive? How do you know?

_____

_____

2. Develop a model to show how these organisms might interact in an ecosystem.

lettuce	grasshopper	hawk
grass	lizard	chicken

3. Use the words below to complete the statements.

chemical process	physical process	some	most	all

A _____ releases the energy stored

in food. _____ organisms use

this energy to keep warm. _____

organisms use the energy from food to carry out

life functions.

4. Which of the following show(s) that animals use energy?

   a. sunlight   **c.** motion

   b. plants   **d.** body temperature

5. Use the concepts of energy and matter to explain why each boldface word or phrase is wrong.

Animals are **producers** that get the materials necessary for body growth and repair by **taking in sunlight.** Animals obtain gases and water from the environment and release **consumers** back into the environment.

6. Draw a model to explain a panda's food needs. Use the words below as labels. Add more labels if you need them.

consumer	matter	energy	grow	animal	warm

Plenty of plants here!

© Houghton Mifflin Harcourt Publishing Company • Image Credits: (c) ©Jeff McGraw/Shutterstock

What do you notice about this tundra ecosystem?

I notice _____

_____

_____

_____

What do you wonder about the availability of plants and its effect on caribou and other organisms in the tundra?

I wonder _____

_____

_____

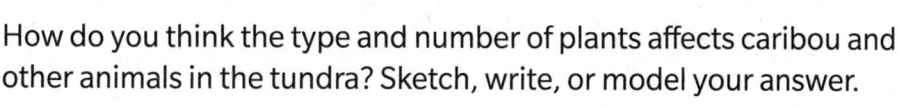

Can You Explain It?

How do you think the type and number of plants affects caribou and other animals in the tundra? Sketch, write, or model your answer.

Modeling Matter Moving Within an Ecosystem

Organisms in an ecosystem have complex relationships. For example, sometimes they compete for space, water, and other resources. Sometimes they interact when one catches and eats another, like the heron and the fish, and sometimes animals compete to catch and eat the same food.

Form a question Ask a question about how energy and matter move between organisms in a food chain.

© Houghton Mifflin Harcourt Publishing Company • Image Credits: (c) ©Ondrej Prosický/Dreamstime

Did you know?

Where there are lots of mosquitoes for prey, some bats can eat 1000 an hour.

POSSIBLE MATERIALS

- ☐ scissors
- ☐ index cards
- ☐ markers
- ☐ paste
- ☐ string or yarn
- ☐ stapler

STEP 1   **Investigate your question**   With your partner, choose an ecosystem to model. Research the organisms that you will include in your model ecosystem.

Which ecosystem are you researching?

_____

_____

_____

Use your research to complete the table below.

Ecosystem	
Energy Source	
Producers	**Consumers**
Organisms that Break Down Matter	

STEP 2   Discuss with your partner how you want to model your ecosystem. For example, you could choose to make a diorama, draw a poster, or design a digital model.

Describe how you will model your ecosystem.

_____

_____

_____

STEP 3   Develop your model by making the pieces of your system. Label organisms that are producers or consumers. Some organisms may not be either one, such as organisms that break down remains and waste.

STEP 4   Arrange the organisms into chains that show what eats what.

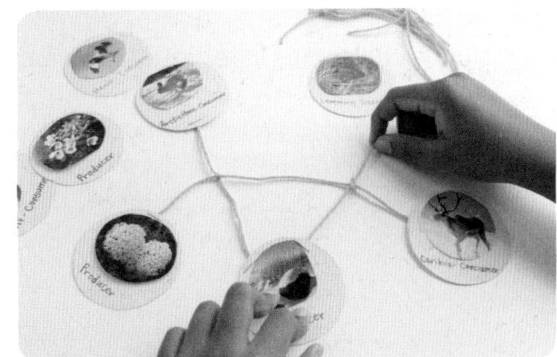

STEP 5   Find the chains that overlap. Connect the chains together. Your end result should look like a web.

Describe how this models your ecosystem.

_____

_____

_____

Predict what might happen if one of the organisms in your web disappeared. Remove one of the organisms from your web, and describe the results.

_____

_____

Is your web a system? If so, what are the components in the web?

_____

_____

Draw conclusions Make a **claim** based on your model of how energy and matter move through an ecosystem. Cite **evidence** from your web to support your claim, and explain your **reasoning.**

_____

_____

_____

How does listening to ideas from all team members about how to make the model help you find the best solution? Discuss with your team.

Making Sense

How does an understanding of what eats what help you explain how plants on the tundra relate to other parts of the ecosystem?

_____

_____

_____

Break It Down

These mushrooms are getting food from this dead tree. All plant and animal matter decays. Ever notice a brown and stinky tomato that someone dropped outside? After it sat on the ground for a while, it began to change.

Form a question Ask questions about what happens to a piece of fruit that is left outside for a long time.

Did you know?

Botanically speaking, tomatoes are a fruit because they contain seeds and grow from ripened flowers.

© Houghton Mifflin Harcourt Publishing Company • Image Credits: (c) ©yakonstant/ Shutterstock

POSSIBLE MATERIALS

- ☐ gloves
- ☐ flower pots, labeled A–F
- ☐ plastic spoon
- ☐ small brush
- ☐ pan balance
- ☐ hand lens

STEP 1   **Investigate your question**   Put on gloves. Use a spoon to uncover the apple slice buried in the pot that your teacher gives you. Gently brush the dirt off the slice.

STEP 2   **Organize your data**   Closely observe the slice. Weigh it to the nearest gram, and record your observations in the graphic organizer on the next page.

STEP 3   Dispose of materials as your teacher directs. Wash your hands when you're done.

Plant Data	
Pot label:	
Starting weight from label:	
Weight now:	
Observations:	

Analyze your data Compare the buried apple slice with a fresh apple slice. How has the buried slice changed?

_____

_____

_____

_____

© Houghton Mifflin Harcourt Publishing Company

Draw conclusions What do you think caused the changes?

_____

_____

_____

With your group, decide how you could test the cause you identified. What **evidence** supports your **claim**? Explain your **reasoning**.

_____

_____

_____

_____

Think of one thing that might slow down or speed up the apple's changes. Tell how you could test your idea.

_____

_____

_____

_____

Making Sense

The recycled matter from rotting things often goes into the soil. What part of a tundra ecosystem is most likely to benefit and why?

_____

_____

Moving Energy and Matter

Energy and Matter Flow

You know that organisms need energy and matter to live and grow. You also know that all the energy in living systems can be traced back to the sun. But how does that energy move through organisms in the environment? Share your ideas with others in your class.

CAPTURING ENERGY AS FOOD

Using the evidence below, draw or write the names of the organisms in the circles to model how matter and energy move through organisms in this environment.

 **Rabbits** are herbivores, or organisms that eat only producers, such as grass. This means that they are first-level consumers.

 The **sun** is the initial source of energy for most living things on Earth.

 **Grass** uses energy from the sun to change matter that is not food into matter that is food.

 **Owls** are carnivores. This owl only eats other animals, such as rabbits. This owl is a second-level consumer.

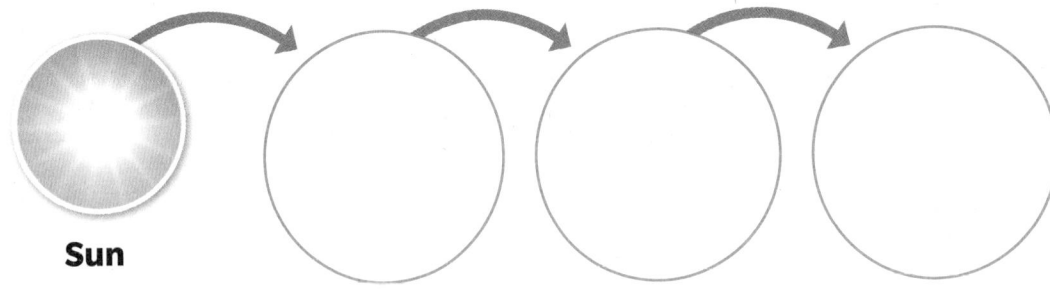

Sun

Explore the Tundra

A tundra is one of the coldest and driest places on Earth. Yet many organisms thrive here. These organisms interact and exchange matter and energy with each other and the environment to form an ecosystem.

Work with a partner to identify the resources in this ecosystem that are used by all organisms.

TUNDRA ECOSYSTEM

 The **sun** supplies energy to producers so that they can change matter that is not food into matter that is food.

 **Caribou** eat reindeer moss and other producers. They are prey to wolves. **Prey** are animals that are caught and eaten by predators.

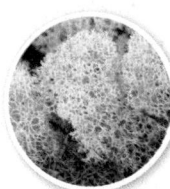 **Reindeer moss** uses energy from the sun to make matter in the form of sugars from air and water.

 A **wolf** is a **predator**—an animal that hunts, catches, and eats other animals. Animals such as caribou are their prey.

 Scavengers such as this **Arctic gull** feed on the dead bodies of other plants and animals.

 **Fungi and bacteria** do the cleanup work as they decompose the remains of tundra organisms.

Modeling Matter and Energy Movement

Each time an organism eats another organism, energy and matter are transferred from one organism to another. This transfer of energy and matter from one organism to the next in an ecosystem is called a **food chain**. So, how do you model the way energy and food matter move through a tundra ecosystem?

TUNDRA FOOD CHAIN

In the circles, draw or write the names of the organisms from the tundra ecosystem in the order that you think energy and matter move through the food chain. You can use the evidence provided on the previous page.

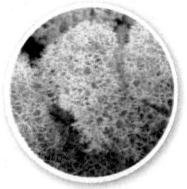  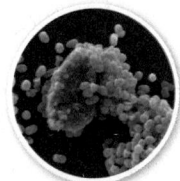   

Reindeer moss   **Arctic gull**   **Bacteria**   **Caribou**   **Fungi**   **Wolves**

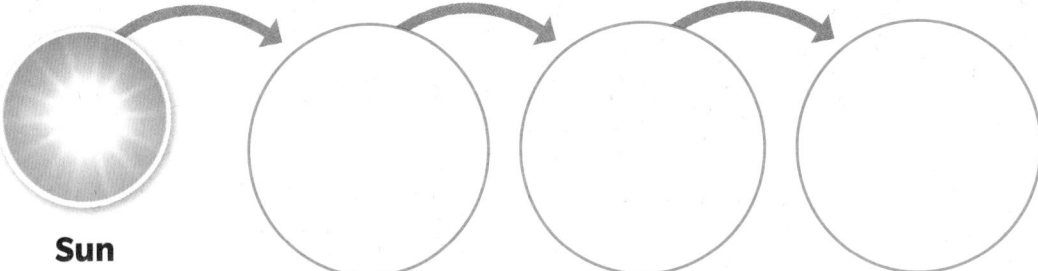

Sun

Explain Which organisms were not included in your food chain? Explain your reasoning.

_____

_____

_____

 Turn to a partner and discuss your reasoning for the tundra food chain. Provide constructive feedback and make sure that each partner has a chance to speak.

Scavengers and Decomposers Are Important

Have you ever wondered what happens to the bodies of plants and animals after they die? When plants and animals die, some organisms in the environment consume them for matter and energy.

Arctic raven

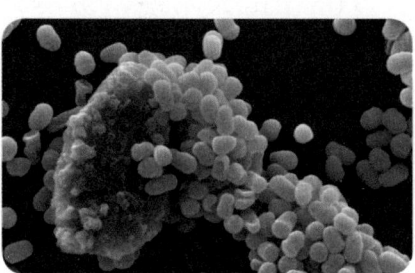

Bacteria close-up

Club fungi

Scavengers

Arctic ravens are **scavengers**. **Scavengers** are consumers that eat dead organisms. Some scavengers mainly feed on the remains of dead animals. Others mainly feed on dead plants.

Decomposers

Bacteria are tiny **decomposers**. **Decomposers** use chemicals called enzymes to break down the remains of organisms and animal wastes. They use the energy they obtain to carry out life processes. The breaking down of wastes restores materials to the soil.

Fungi are also decomposers that release enzymes. These enzymes break down dead matter, releasing nutrients that enrich the soil. Mushrooms and club fungi are two examples of this kind of decomposer.

Making Sense

How does the leftover matter and energy in dead organisms get recycled back to the soil? Which organism in the tundra food chain would use this recycled matter? Use evidence from the tundra food chain to support your inference.

_____

_____

Following Matter and Energy

TUNDRA ECOSYSTEM

Using the description of each organism in the tundra, write the role of each (producer, consumer, scavenger, decomposer) in the corresponding space in the diagram.

a. Caribou eat reindeer moss and other producers to get the energy and matter they need.

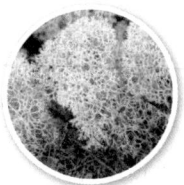

b. Reindeer moss uses energy from the sun to make matter in the form of sugars from air and water.

c. Fungi and bacteria do the cleanup work as they decompose the remains of tundra organisms.

d. The **Arctic hare** mainly gets matter and energy from grasses and wildflowers.

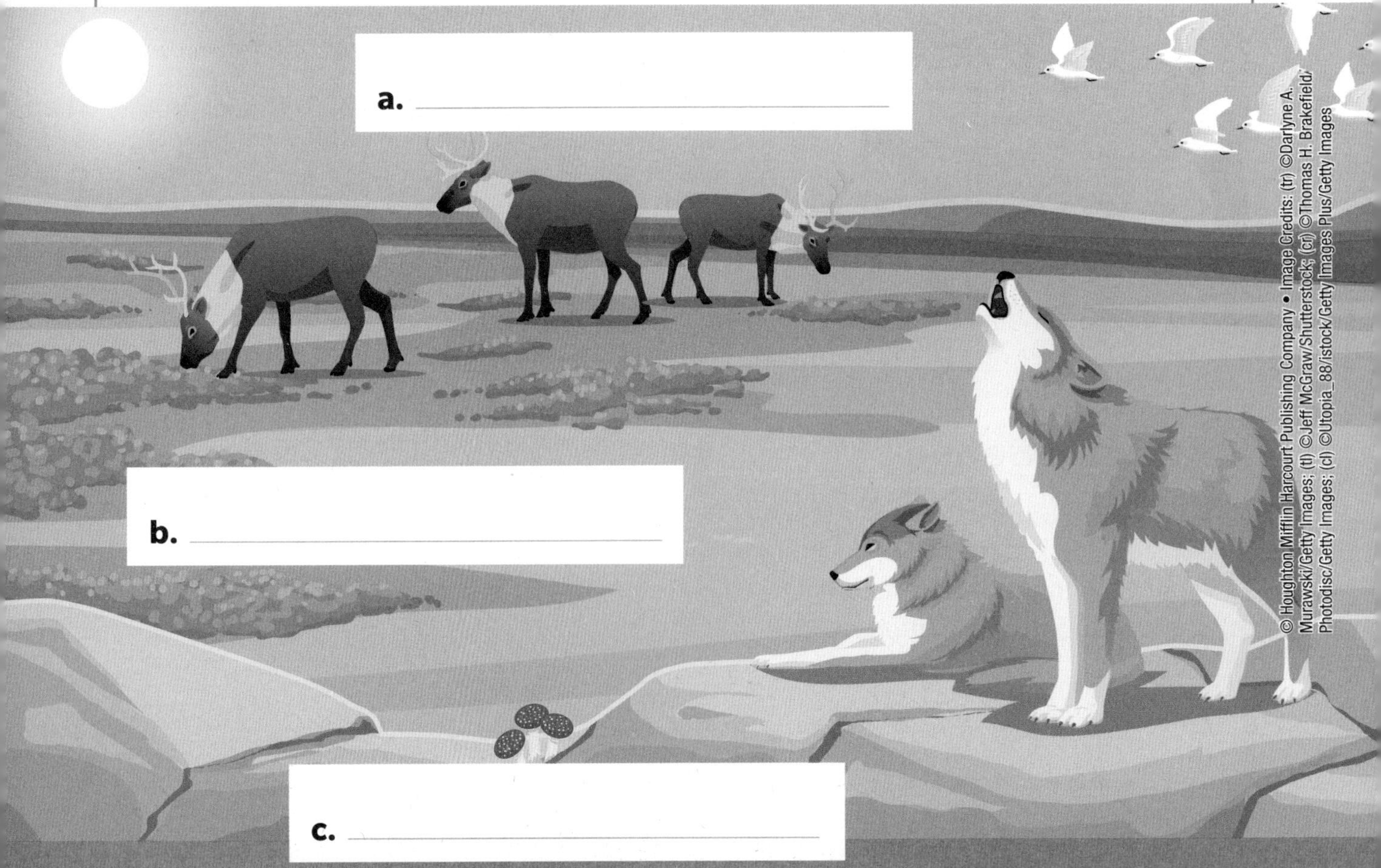

a. _____

b. _____

c. _____

e. Animals such as this **Arctic gull** feed on the dead bodies of other animals.

f. Lemmings are rodents that often live in Arctic ecosystems. They will eat any producer they can get their paws on!

g. Hawks catch and eat prey that are smaller than they are, such as lemmings.

h. Arctic wildflowers are plants. They are a favorite of first-level consumers in Arctic ecosystems.

Connecting Food Chains

In the last section, you explored matter and energy interactions among a few tundra organisms using a single food chain model. But an ecosystem is made of many organisms. These organisms form many food chains, and these food chains often overlap, creating **food webs**.

What do you think it means if an organism has many lines leading away from it showing energy flow (as food)?

_____

_____

e. _____

g. _____

d. _____

f. _____

h. _____

Adding Connections to the Tundra

Food, space, water, and predators limit the number of organisms that can live in an ecosystem. For example, if wolves were removed from a tundra ecosystem, the caribou population would increase. More caribou would eat more plants. Other first-level consumers might run out of food and die. Losing one component can greatly change an ecosystem.

Write the name of the missing organisms to complete the model.

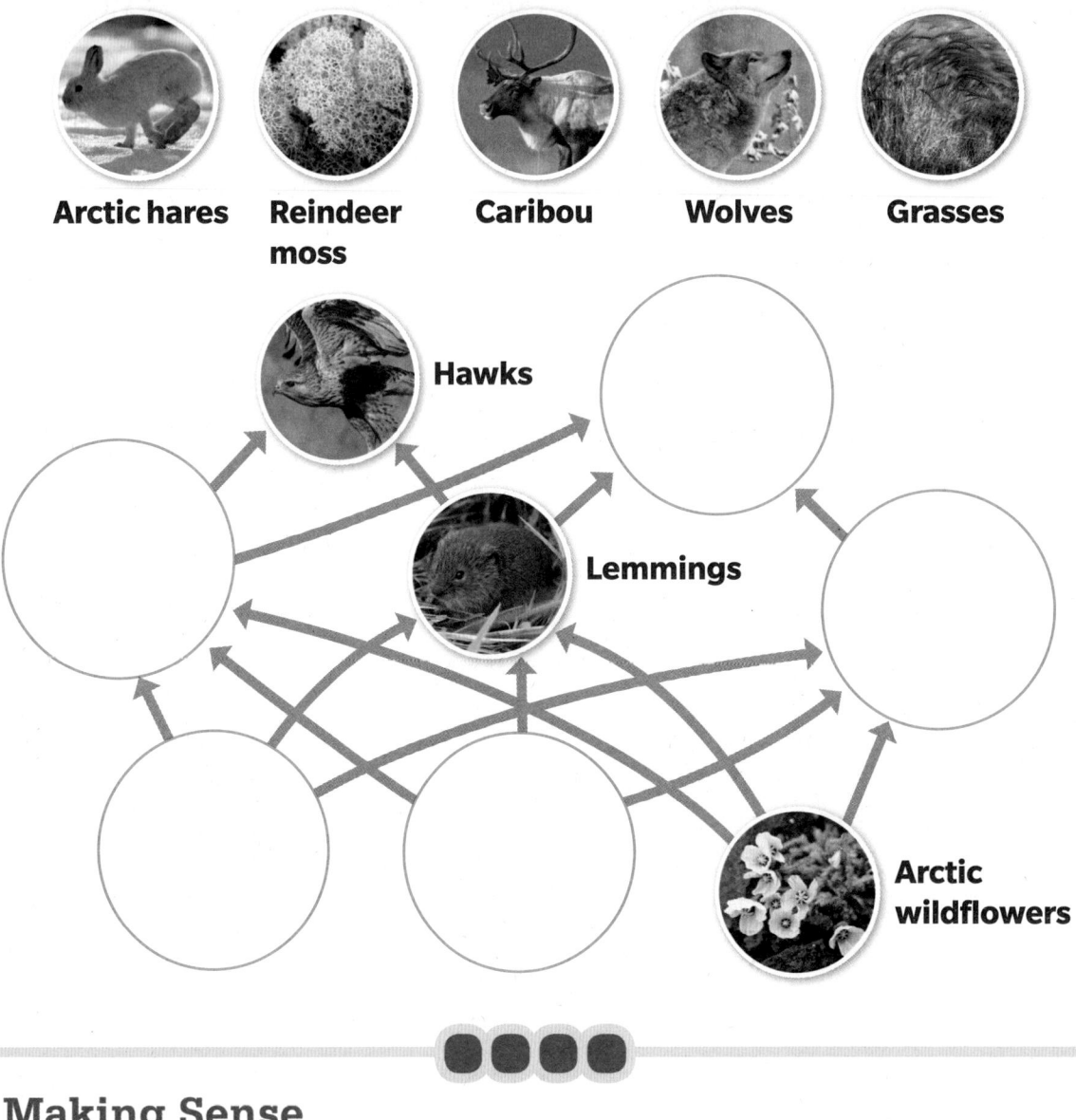

Arctic hares   **Reindeer moss**   **Caribou**   **Wolves**   **Grasses**

Hawks

Lemmings

Arctic wildflowers

●●●●

Making Sense

What happens to the tundra ecosystem if bad weather caused the plants to die?

_____

_____

Name _____

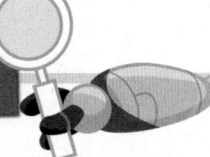

Can You Explain It?

Review your ideas from the beginning of this lesson about how the number and types of plants affect a tundra ecosystem. How have your ideas changed? Be sure to do the following:

- Identify how plants affect energy flow in the ecosystem.
- Describe how plant changes could cause other changes.
- Identify other interactions in the ecosystem.

Now I know or think that _____

_____

_____

_____

Making Connections

Describe a possible food chain made up of common organisms in the city park ecosystem shown. Tell what might happen if all of one type of organism moved away.

_____

_____

_____

_____

Checkpoints

1. Put these items in a food chain model. Add arrows to show energy and matter movement. Label the producer(s) and consumer(s).

Hawk

Sun

Corn

Mouse

2. A disease has killed many trees in an ecosystem. How will the loss of trees affect organisms in the area? Choose all that apply.

   a. Animals that use the trees for food or shelter might die off.

   b. Animals that use the trees for food or shelter will be fine and will eat other organisms.

   c. Animals that use the trees for food or shelter may have to move to a new location.

   d. Animals that use the trees for food or shelter will not be affected.

3. Use the terms in the box to make three food chains.

> tomato   grass   sun   you   cow   lettuce

_____ **sun** → _____ → _____

_____ → _____ → _____

_____ → _____ → _____ → _____ **you**

Explain why you chose the order you did for the food chains.

_____

_____

_____

_____

© Houghton Mifflin Harcourt Publishing Company • Image Credits: (tcl) ©E+/Getty Images; (tl) ©Ed Schneider/Shutterstock; (tcr) ©Shotshop GmbH/Alamy; (tr) ©Rui Miguel da Costa Neves Saraiva/iStockPhoto.com

4. Draw a model to show how energy and matter flow in an ecosystem. Show how organisms interact. Show the inputs and outputs of matter and energy.

5. This organism is a decomposer. Think about the role of decomposers. Predict the effects on an ecosystem of all decomposers dying at once.

Unit Review

1. Plants change matter that is not food into matter that is food. In the space provided, draw a model that shows how this happens. Include components of the plant system, and identify the inputs and outputs involved in the process. Then use information you learned from the text of the lessons to explain the process.

_____

_____

_____

2. How would you expect the weight of soil in a pot to change as the plant inside it grows larger? Why?

_____

_____

3. Which of the following are necessary for plants to change matter that is not food to matter that is food? Select all that apply.

   a. water   **c.** soil   **e.** air

   b. sugar   **d.** light   **f.** decomposed matter

4. If an injured animal is hungry and doesn't get the _____ it needs from food, it will likely take a _____ time to heal completely.

5. Write an explanation for how the body uses matter and energy from food in the situation pointed to in this image.

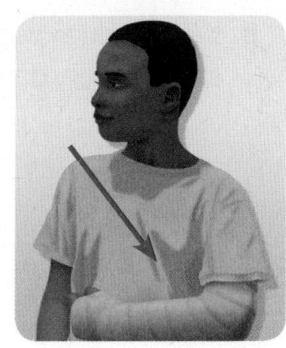

_____

_____

_____

Use this image to answer questions 6 and 7.

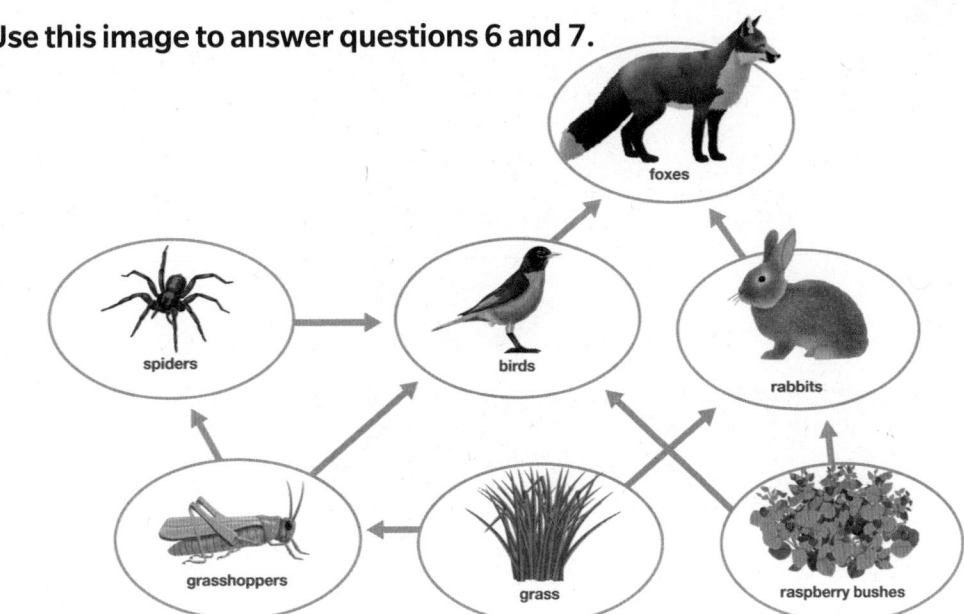

6. How does the energy and food matter move from the raspberry bushes to the fox in this food web model?

   a. The rabbit eats the raspberry bushes, the bird eats the rabbit, and the fox eats the bird.

   b. The grasshopper eats the raspberry bushes, the rabbit eats the grasshopper, and the fox eats the rabbit.

   c. The bird eats the raspberry bushes, and the fox eats the bird.

   d. The spider eats the grasses, the grasshopper eats the spider, the bird eats the grasshopper, and the fox eats the bird.

7. In the food web shown, the raspberry bushes and grasses are producers. What is true of the raspberry bushes and grasses? Select all answers that apply.

   a. They can make their own food.

   b. They use energy from the sun to make food.

   c. They get energy from other plants and animals.

   d. They decompose the remains of plants and animals for food.

8. Would you expect an Olympic swimmer to need more or less food energy every day than you do? Explain why.

_____

_____

9. Indicate whether each function is performed by a plant's green structures (G), its leaf openings (L), or its roots (R).

Releasing waste

Making food

Taking in water

Taking in nutrients

Taking in air

10. Think about why people store food in a refrigerator. How do you think the activity level of decomposers is affected by the changing seasons? Construct an explanation using evidence from the lessons to support your claim, and explain your reasoning.

_____

_____

_____

_____

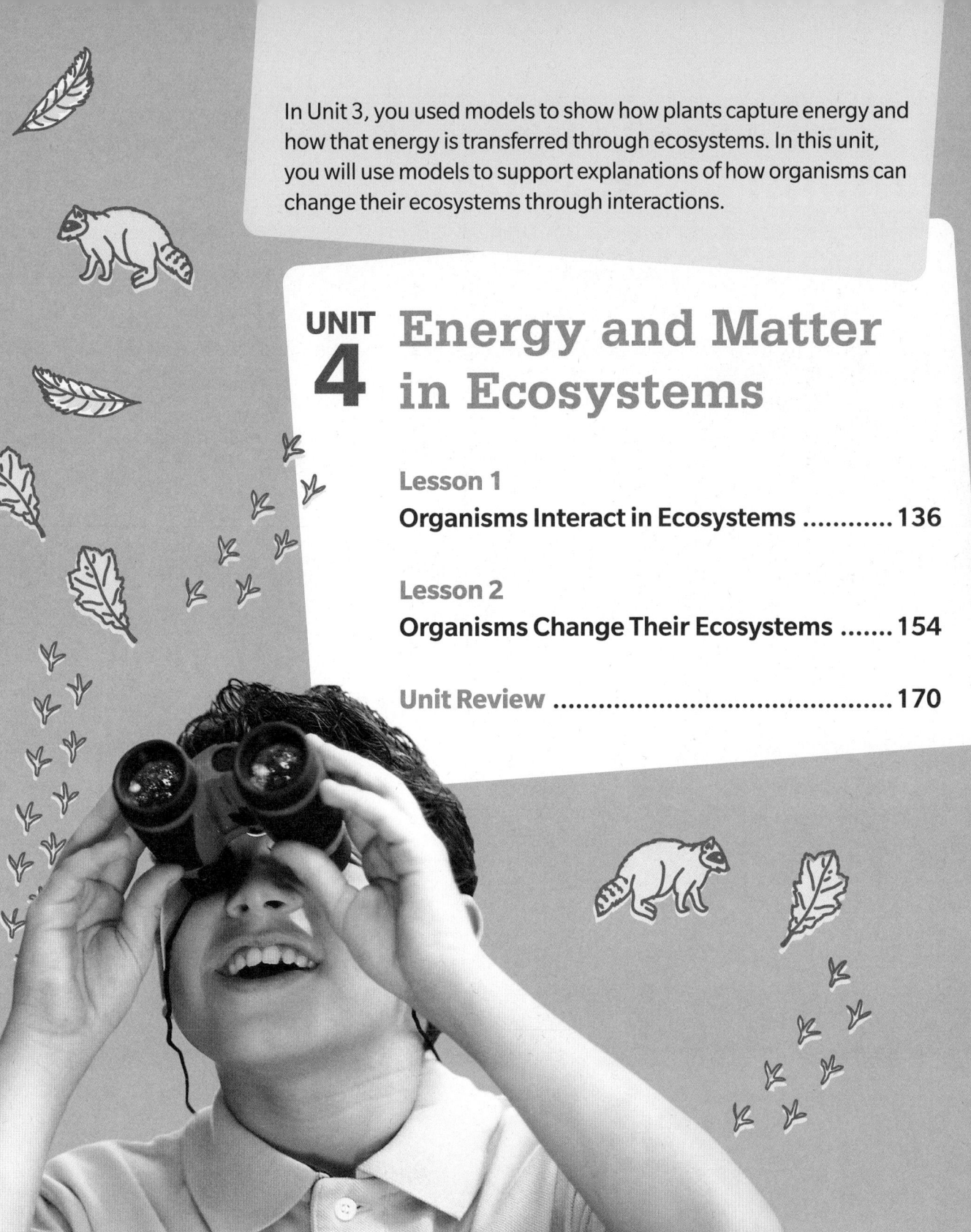

In Unit 3, you used models to show how plants capture energy and how that energy is transferred through ecosystems. In this unit, you will use models to support explanations of how organisms can change their ecosystems through interactions.

UNIT 4 Energy and Matter in Ecosystems

© Houghton Mifflin Harcourt Publishing Company • Image Credits: ©Randy Faris/Corbis

What do you notice about these organisms?

I notice _____

_____

_____

_____

What do you wonder about the ways in which these organisms interact?

I wonder _____

_____

_____

_____

Can You Explain It?

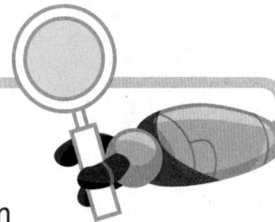

How do you think organisms live together and interact in the African savanna? Sketch, write, or model your answer.

What's Out There?

Many types of organisms live in the world around you. Some of these living things are large and easy to notice, while others are tiny or live in places where someone might not think to look, such as in holes in the ground. An **ecosystem** is a system in which organisms interact and exchange matter and energy. In a healthy ecosystem, a variety of living things can get what they need.

Form a question Ask a question about living things that can be found around your school.

_____

_____

_____

_____

Did you know?

Some earthworms can grow to be as long as 35 cm (14 in.).

| STEP 1 | **Investigate your question** With your class, select the most important questions about local ecosystems. Record the questions here. |

_____

_____

_____

| STEP 2 | **Develop a plan** How can you investigate the questions you and your classmates chose as most important? Think about the materials your teacher shows you and what else you might need. Below, write your plan and show it to your teacher to see if you can get the other things you need. Add your additional materials to the materials list. |

_____

_____

_____

_____

How might the organisms you observe be affected by your plan?
What will you do to make sure you do not harm the organisms?

_____

_____

_____

_____

STEP 3 **Organize your data** Carry out your plan, and record your results. Present your data in a way that helps everyone understand what you did and what happened. You might choose a table or a graph as a presentation tool, or you might choose to make a poster. Use the space below to record your results.

What do the organisms you observed need to live and grow, and where do they find those things?

_____

_____

Make a model of how the living things you observed interact with the environment to meet their needs. Focus on how matter moves through the whole system.

Draw conclusions Recall that a variety of living things get what they need in a healthy ecosystem. Make a **claim** about how healthy the area around your school is. Support your claim with **evidence** from your investigation, and use **reasoning** to explain how the evidence supports your claim.

_____

_____

Making Sense

The living things you observed rely on other living things and nonliving things to get what they need to live and grow. How do you think living and nonliving things interact in the African savanna ecosystem?

_____

_____

_____

Environment Matters

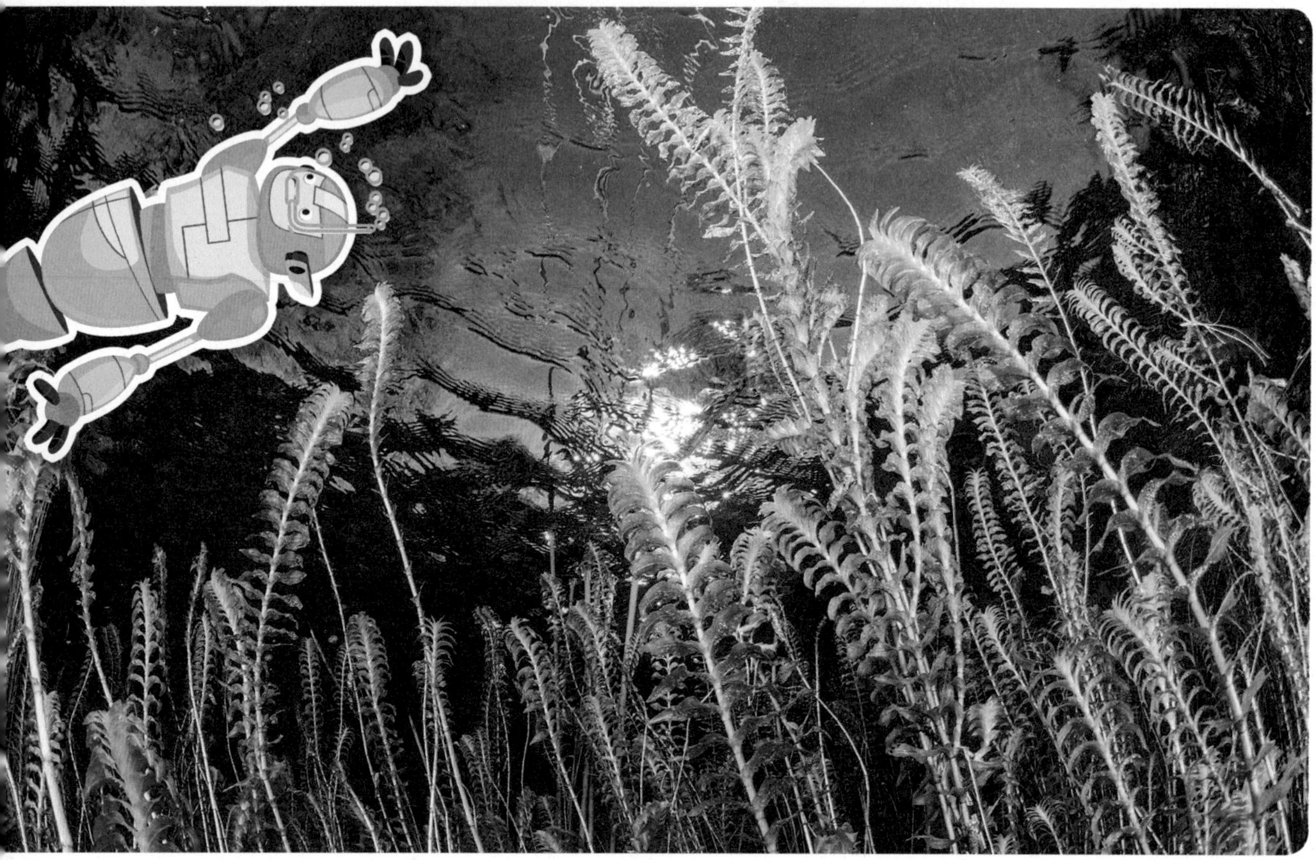

Most plants live in environments where they are in contact with air, but *Elodea* plants are different. These plants live with their roots, stems, and leaves all underwater.

Form a question Ask a question about the different environments where plants can live.

Did you know?

There are at least five different species of *Elodea*.

_____

_____

_____

_____

_____

□ container, clear, large   □ water

□ 2 plants, herbaceous,   □ weights, rocks
  live

STEP 1 Water both plants. Record how the plants look.

STEP 2 Place one plant in the container of water, including the pot. Make sure the water covers the plant's leaves and stem. Place weights on the soil to keep the plant underwater. Place the other plant on the counter next to the large container.

STEP 3 **Collect data** Observe both plants each day for several days. Use the space below to record your data.

Draw conclusions Make a **claim** about which environment was better for the plant. Support your claim with **evidence** from your investigation, and explain your **reasoning**.

● ● ○ ○

Making Sense

Elodea plants live and grow underwater, but not all plants can survive underwater. Think about how the different environments in which plants can live connect to the African savanna. What do the organisms that live on the African savanna have in common?

Living Things and Their Environment

It's Alive!

A forest is a type of ecosystem. It is very different from the African savanna ecosystem where elephants and zebras live. In both ecosystems, living things, or organisms, interact with each other and with the nonliving parts of the environment.

LIVING TOGETHER

Study the picture. Circle the living things in this ecosystem. Place an *X* through all the nonliving things.

An **environment** is made up of all the living and nonliving systems that surround and affect an organism. Nonliving systems include air, water, and rocks or soil. All living things make up one system. An ecosystem is a system in which organisms interact and exchange matter and energy with each other and the nonliving things in their environment.

Explain Explain how the black bear interacts with living and nonliving things.

Living Partnerships

Healthy ecosystems are ones in which many different types of living things meet their needs for survival. Animals get their food from plants or from a source that can be traced back to plants. But animals get more than just food from plants. Plants provide animals with tools, shelter, and a place to lay eggs or rest.

This animal is using a stick as a tool.

Some birds rely on trees for a place to rest.

Model In the space below, make a model to show how the living things in the African savanna interact with their environment and each other.

Animal Groups

A group of organisms of the same kind in an ecosystem, such as these elephants, is called a *population*. The members of a population interact with one another. They eat the same kind of food and need the same kind of shelter. They all need water and space to grow and find food.

The different populations that share an ecosystem make up a community. A community consists of all the populations of living things that live and can interact in an area. The living things in a community might not have all of the same needs. Even if they have different needs, the populations in a community interact.

System Connections

To understand interactions between living and nonliving things, scientists have classified, or sorted, everything found on and around Earth into systems. The system that includes all living things is called the **biosphere**. One system includes all the water on Earth. Another includes all the rocks and soil. Yet another includes gases on and around Earth. All living things in an ecosystem depend on all the other nonliving systems for survival.

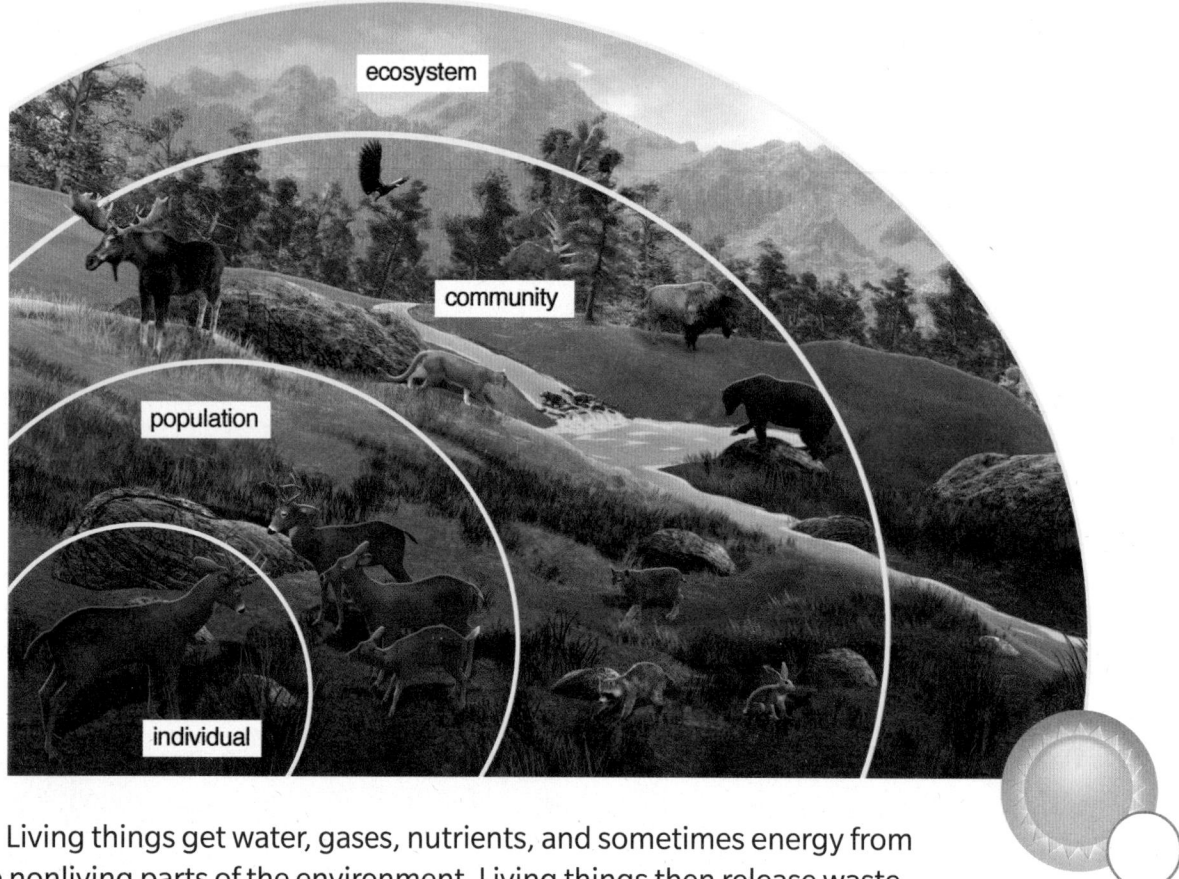

Living things get water, gases, nutrients, and sometimes energy from the nonliving parts of the environment. Living things then release waste matter back into the environment.

Explain In the bubble under each picture, write the letter of the phrase or phrases that describe how the nonliving things in the picture interact with living things in the environment.

a. gases that both plants and animals need for life
b. provides energy for plants to make food
c. anchors plant roots; stores nutrients; habitat for decomposers
d. drink for animals; plants need it to make food; some animals and plants live in it

sun

air

water

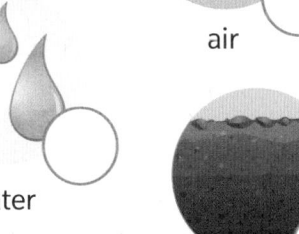

soil

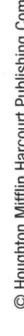

Waste Matter

The diagram below shows how matter and energy flow among three types of organisms in the biosphere. The tree is a *producer*, an organism that makes its own food. The animals are *consumers*, organisms that obtain energy and matter by feeding on other organisms. The fungi are *decomposers*, organisms that break down the remains of organisms and animal waste to obtain energy.

 **Turn and Talk** In a small group, analyze the model. Then, work together to answer questions a–d. Take turns for each question, and have a different person go first to share their ideas each time.

a. What is the relationship between nutrients and decomposers?

b. Why do producers need nutrients?

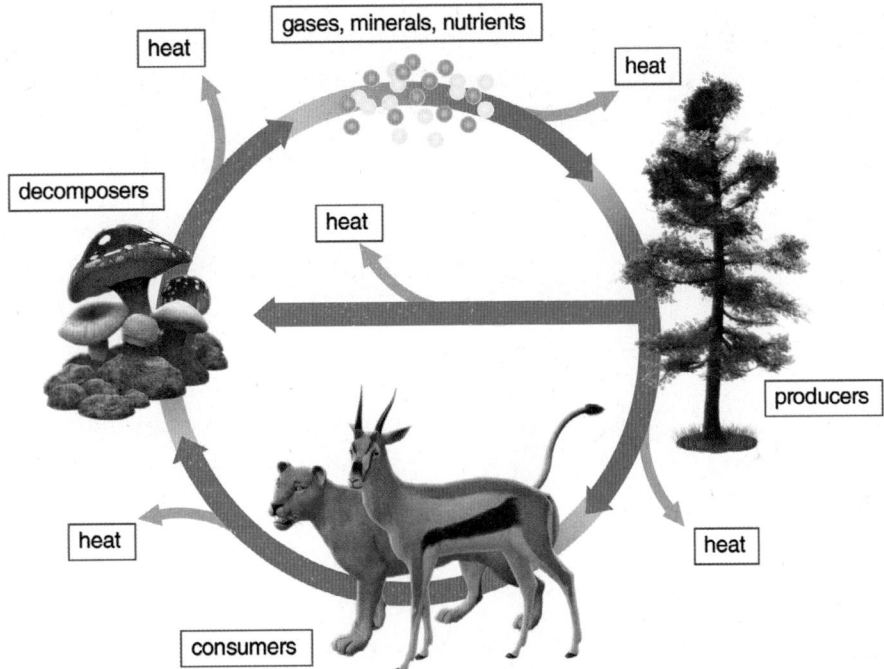

c. How do decomposers interact with producers and consumers?

d. What do consumers depend on producers for? Do consumers need nutrients?

Making Sense

How do the organisms on the African savanna interact with each other and the nonliving parts of their ecosystem?

Competition in Ecosystems

Battling for Survival

A healthy ecosystem has many different types of plants and animals that meet their needs in different ways. Organisms' needs must be met for survival.

Infer What will happen in an ecosystem if there are not enough resources to support all of the populations of living things found there? Circle the letters for all answers that apply.

a. Some living things might move to a new ecosystem.
b. Many more living things will move into the ecosystem.
c. Some living things might die.
d. More resources will be produced to meet the demands of the living things.
e. Some living things will struggle to get what they need.

Limited Supply

Resources in any ecosystem are limited. There is only so much space available in an ecosystem. Water and food may also be in short supply. Space, water, food and even sunlight are limiting factors. *Limiting factors* affect the number of individuals of a given population that an ecosystem can support.

Individuals and populations that compete successfully will get the resources they need. They will survive. Individuals and populations that do not compete successfully cannot get what they need and will not survive.

Habitat Factors

How would you describe an animal? You might talk about how it looks or moves. Another way to describe an animal is to tell where it lives, what it eats, and other ways it interacts with its environment. Some animals can live in a variety of places, eat many foods, and be part of many different ecosystems. Other animals can only live in specific places and eat one or two kinds of food. A *habitat* is the place where an animal lives and can find everything it needs to survive. Read about each animal in the next section.

Infer Circle the animal that would more easily adapt to a change in its habitat or move to a new habitat if its current habitat were destroyed.

Raccoons live in a great variety of habitats, including prairies, forests, marshes, and large cities. They eat all kinds of food, ranging from frogs to fruit. Raccoons will even eat garbage! They are nocturnal animals, which means that they are active at night. Wolves, coyotes, and bobcats prey on raccoons. By carrying seeds in their fur, raccoons help plants reproduce.

Giant pandas are found in the bamboo forests of Central China. They survive mainly on bamboo. They have special bacteria in their stomach that helps them break down the nutrients in the bamboo. They eat a lot and are active both day and night. These pandas have almost no predators.

The Difference Is Night and Day

Animals that live in the same habitat usually play different roles in their habitat. This enables them to get what they need from the environment. In a group, discuss what would happen if the animals had the same role.

Red-shouldered hawks are hunters. They live in forest habitats and catch prey such as snakes, frogs, and mice. Red-shouldered hawks mostly hunt and catch their prey during the day.

The barred owl also lives in forest habitats. It hunts and eats the same types of prey that the red-shouldered hawk eats. Barred owls hunt at night and at dawn and dusk.

Compare the red-shouldered hawk and the barred owl. Identify the resource or resources for which these animals compete.

CASE STUDY

Black bears are powerful animals found in many ecosystems across the United States. They can be a threat if they lose their natural fear of people. This can happen if they get used to eating food from garbage cans left outside people's homes and businesses.

In order to avoid dangerous encounters, some communities have laws in place that require people to use bear-proof garbage cans. People have mixed reactions to these laws.

Some people argue that they have lived in "bear country" all their lives and have never had a problem with bears. They claim that if people just waited to put their garbage out in the mornings, then there would be no problem. They also argue that the bear-proof cans are very expensive.

Other residents argue that having bears in their neighborhoods makes them worry about the safety of their children and pets. They would like everyone to buy and use the bear-proof trash cans to solve the problem.

Put the causes and effects of the bear issue in order. Begin by writing a 1 by the original cause.

Laws may be passed to require bear-proof garbage cans.

Bears could harm people when they go on people's property for the garbage.

Food in garbage cans attracts bears.

Making Sense

How do the amounts and types of resources on the African savanna affect how organisms live together and interact there?

Lesson
Check

Can You Explain It?

Review your response about the animals at the start of this lesson. Now that you have explored how living things interact with living and nonliving elements of the environment, think about this again. Be sure to do the following:

- Describe how the animals interact with nonliving parts of their environment.
- Describe how the animals interact with living parts of their environment.
- Explain what happens if the organisms' needs are not met.

Now I know or think that _____

_____

_____

_____

_____

Making Connections

Bears and fish are some of the organisms that make up communities in forest ecosystems. Based on what you learned about the African savanna, how do you think these organisms live together and interact?

_____

_____

Checkpoints

1. Look at the ecosystem in the picture. Identify one living and one nonliving thing. Tell how they interact.

_____

_____

_____

2. What other systems does the biosphere interact with?

   a. air   **c.** soil

   b. water   **d.** all of the above

3. Use the model to order the steps below the image to describe the flow of nutrients between organisms.

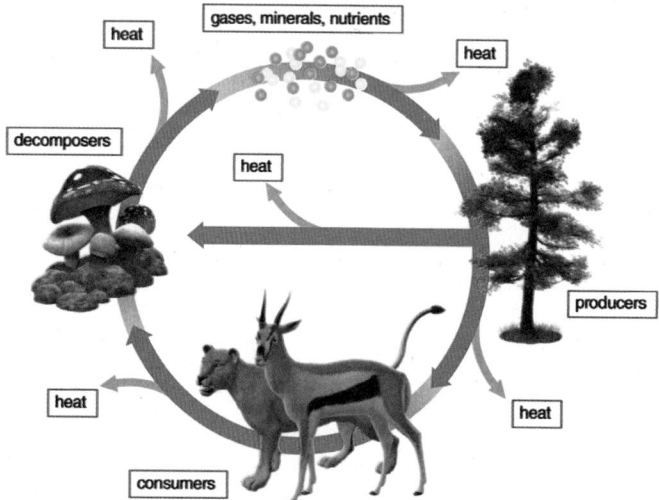

Decomposers leave nutrients in the soil.

Consumers get nutrients from eating producers.

Producers take in nutrients from the soil.

4. How can a food web or other diagram of community interactions model how living things may compete for the same food source?

_____

_____

_____

5. Use some or all of terms below to make a model that shows competition for resources in an ecosystem. Add more terms if you need them.

predators	prey	unlimited
limited	cooperate	compete

6. Add phrases to this sequence to model possible interactions among nonliving and living parts of an ecosystem. Include a producer and a consumer.

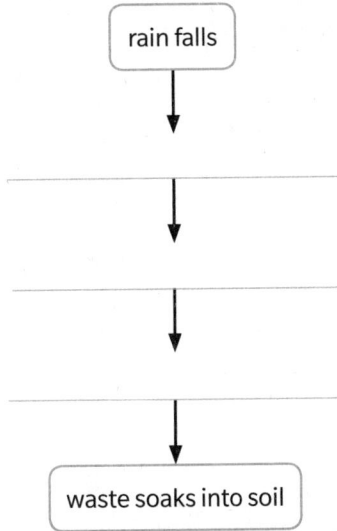

rain falls

↓

_____

↓

_____

↓

_____

↓

waste soaks into soil

Organisms Change Their Ecosystems

This is getting out of hand...

What do you notice about these kudzu vines?

I notice _____

_____

_____

_____

What do you wonder about the relationship between these kudzu vines and the other plants in the area?

I wonder _____

_____

_____

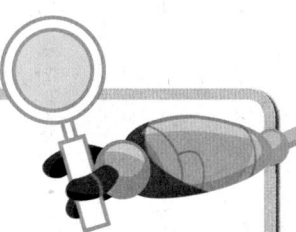

Can You Explain It?

How can kudzu vines affect an entire ecosystem? Sketch, write, or model your answer.

Invasion!

Invasive species are nonnative species that compete for resources better than existing species in the ecosystem. Invasive species damage the balance in ecosystems by using resources and harming native species. The northern snakehead fish is native to Korea, China, and Russia. It was first found in the United States in 1997. Adult northern snakeheads eat other fish and insects. Scientists use models to understand how invasive species such as the northern snakehead fish can affect the food supply of an area.

Form a question Ask a question about how northern snakehead fish affect the food supply for native species.

_____

_____

_____

_____

Did you know?

In addition to using gills to get oxygen underwater, northern snakehead fish can breathe air directly.

POSSIBLE MATERIALS

☐ 4 index cards

☐ small squares of construction paper
(10 squares each of red, blue, and yellow paper)

☐ paper clips

In what ways could a northern snakehead damage the balance in an ecosystem?

STEP 1 **Investigate your question**

With your group, research three fish species found in U.S. ecosystems affected by northern snakeheads. Write the name of these species or draw each of them on their own index card. On the fourth card, draw a northern snakehead. Place a paper clip on each card.

How do you think the northern snakehead could affect the other fish species? Make a model to show your thinking.

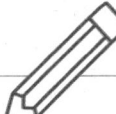

STEP 2   **Model** Set out the ecosystem's food supply—the colored construction paper squares—on the table in front of your group. Fill out the chart with the species you have selected. For this part of the activity, you can place any of the native species in any of the rows.

Native species	Food requirement (one round)
	3 blue squares, 2 red squares
	3 yellow squares
	3 red squares, 1 blue square

STEP 3   **Analyze data** Allow the native fish in the ecosystem to feed by placing the required amount of food squares—based on the information in the chart—into the paper clips on the index cards.

Is the ecosystem in balance? Why or why not?

_____

_____

_____

_____

STEP 4 After the first round of feeding, the northern snakehead is introduced into the ecosystem. The snakehead can outcompete the native species for food. To model this, the snakehead gets to eat first. The snakehead eats the following: 2 yellow squares, 4 red squares, and 3 blue squares.

Model three rounds of feeding in total, first with the snakehead eating what it needs, then all of the other species trying to meet their own needs. Use the space below to make a table to record your data, including how much food is left after each round and whether each species has survived, or died or moved away.

Did the northern snakehead change the ecosystem? How?

_____

_____

Which fish species did not have enough to eat in the second round? Would those species have had enough to eat without the snakehead?

_____

_____

Turn and Talk Compare your results with other groups. Paraphrase what you hear them say, and then share your own results. Discuss any similarities or differences you notice.

Draw conclusions How do you think your results would be similar or different if you modeled a different way in which northern snakeheads affect ecosystems?

_____

_____

Make a **claim** based on your investigation about how invasive northern snakeheads affect other species in ecosystems. Support your claim with **evidence**, and explain your **reasoning**.

_____

_____

Draw a graphic organizer to show the cause and effect of introducing northern snakeheads to the ecosystem.

Making Sense

What does the relationship between the native fish and the northern snakeheads tell you about the relationship between the native plants and the kudzu vines?

_____

_____

_____

Engineer It
Balance Restored

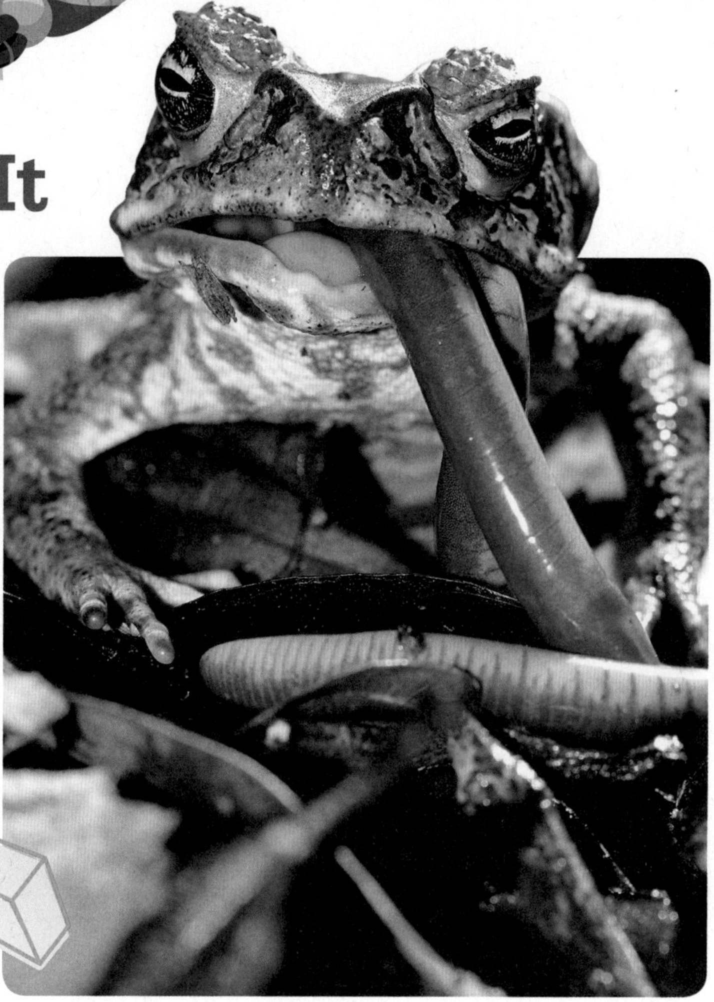

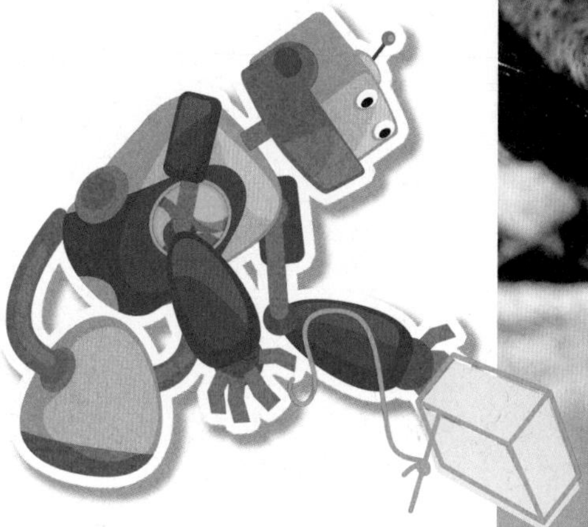

The cane toad is an invasive species that can damage the balance of ecosystems. Scientists have worked to remove or lower the cane toad population. The toads are active at night and can be found near light sources, which attract the insects they eat. Toads enjoy the rain. They grow to be 13–15 cm (5–6 in.) long. Engineers are trying to trap the cane toads. Because there are so many cane toads, engineers want to create a trap that is easy to set and retrieve. The trap should be durable enough to be reused many times. A local wildlife protection organization requires that traps do not harm the cane toads.

Did you know?

A single female cane toad can lay 30,000 eggs at one time.

Define the problem Based on the background information, what problem are you trying to solve? What are the criteria and constraints for the cane toad traps?

_____

_____

_____

Explore

STEP 1 **Design a solution** Draw a solution to the problem. Based on the criteria and constraints, how well do you think your solution will work?

_____

_____

Make and Test

STEP 2 **Develop a model** Make a poster to model your solution. Use labels to explain how it will work.

STEP 3 **Share information** Examine other groups' posters. Compare and contrast solutions.

Turn and Talk Engineering solutions can have unintended effects. Discuss how traps might affect other species. How would knowing these effects help engineers make responsible design decisions?

Draw conclusions What factors should engineers consider for the cane toad problem? Support your **claim** with **evidence**, and explain your **reasoning**.

_____

_____

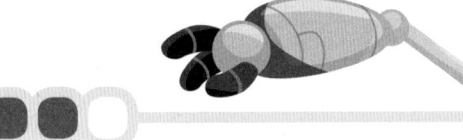

Making Sense

How can humans help restore balance to entire ecosystems when organisms like the kudzu disrupt native species?

_____

_____

Introduced and Invasive Species

New in Town

Sometimes species are introduced into an ecosystem they have never been a part of before, causing big changes to the ecosystem. For example, consier how these beetles eat the ash trees in this ecosystem. With a small group, discuss the possible effects this could have on the other things found in this ecosystem.

The emerald ash borer is a green jewel beetle native to northeastern Asia. It feeds on ash trees. In the 1990s, the beetle was accidentally introduced to the United States and Canada. The trees in this area are not adapted to be resistant to the beetles. Soon after the beetle's arrival, people in Michigan and Ohio noticed ash trees dying.

Newly introduced species, also known as nonnative species, can cause changes in ecosystems. In many cases, newly introduced species do not survive well in their new ecosystem. They might not find the right food, or the physical conditions of the ecosystem might not allow them to survive.

Sometimes, though, introduced species thrive and take over an ecosystem. An invasive species is a nonnative species that is better able to compete for resources than the existing species in the ecosystem. As a result, the existing, or native, species might not be able to get what they need to survive. When few species are able to meet their needs, the entire ecosystem is less healthy. Invasive species can spread rapidly, causing native species to die out or move away. Newly introduced species like cane toads and ash borer beetles can damage the balance of an ecosystem forever.

Losing Balance

The images below show several kinds of plants that have invaded new ecosystems and caused damage.

The water chestnut is an aquatic plant introduced to ecosystems in the United States more than 100 years ago. Its leaves spread on the surface of water, blocking sunlight needed by other species in the ecosystem.

Brazilian *Elodea* is an invasive aquatic plant that was introduced in the United States more than 100 years ago. It is for sale for use in aquariums. *Elodea* grows into dense, mat-like structures and outcompetes native plants for space.

Garlic mustard, native to Europe, was brought to the United States in the late 1800s for use as medicine and food. It uses up resources needed by native forest species. Because few animal species eat this plant, it is hard to control.

Japanese honeysuckle is native to East Asia. It was brought to the United States in the late 1800s for use as a garden plant. This invasive vine grows in field and forests. Like kudzu, it climbs, covers, and crowds out other plants.

How do invasive plants change the balance in an ecosystem? Describe two ways that invasive plant species can prevent native species from meeting their needs.

Animal Invasion

Animals can also be invasive species. Unlike plants, they do not usually smother other species, but they can cause a lot of damage.

European starlings were introduced to the United States in the 1890s. They destroy crops and compete for nest sites with native species.

Tegu lizards were probably released as pets. These lizards are invasive in Florida, where they eat the eggs of native species.

Nutria were introduced to the United States from South America for fur production. They damage the wetlands and marshes by destroying vegetation.

Zebra mussels were probably brought to the United States on ships from Europe. They compete with native species for space and nutrients. Unlike most invasive animals, they can smother similar native species.

Compare and contrast how invasive plant and animal species affect native species in ecosystems.

_____

_____

_____

_____

Pig Populations

Wild pigs are an invasive species causing big problems in parts of the southern U.S. from Texas to North Carolina, and in California. They eat almost anything and destroy vegetation as they trample over it. Few animals, such as bears, panthers, and wolf packs, prey on grown wild pig. The pig population is growing quickly.

Model Suppose a pair of wild pigs get to a location where there are no other wild pigs. The female can reproduce about ten times in her lifespan. Each time she reproduces, she has an average of six offspring. How many offspring can a female wild pig produce in her lifetime?

_____

_____

_____

Turn and Talk What factors should people think about to make a responsible decision on whether or not to introduce a non-native species into an environment? Discuss with a partner.

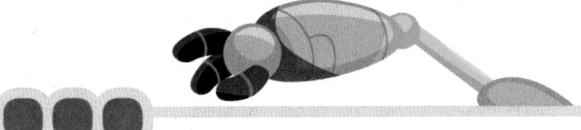

Making Sense

How can the kudzu vines affect more of the ecosystem than just the parts they interact with?

_____

_____

_____

Lesson Check

Can You Explain It?

Review your response to the kudzu vine question at the start of this lesson. How have your ideas changed now that you have learned how organisms affect their environment? Be sure to do the following:

- Describe how kudzu vines could affect native plant species they interact with directly.
- Explain how kudzu vines could damage the balance in the entire ecosystem.

Now I know or think that _____

_____

_____

_____

_____

Making Connections

Crazy ants are an invasive species in the southeastern United States. Based on what you learned about the kudzu vines, how do you think crazy ants might impact the native species and the ecosystem as a whole?

_____

_____

_____

Checkpoints

1. Kudzu interacts with many nonliving systems. Which of the following is not a way kudzu interacts with Earth's systems?

   a. using too much air

   b. root growth moving soil

   c. releasing gases into the atmosphere

   d. absorbing water from the soil

2. Which of these describe(s) an invasive species? Choose all that apply.

   a. better able to compete for resources than native species

   b. any species that is added to a new ecosystem

   c. usually dies out rapidly in its new ecosystem

   d. can damage the balance of an ecosystem

   e. usually lacks predators in the new ecosystem

3. What evidence could you use to argue that the Brazilian *Elodea* in the picture affects other plants in the ecosystem it enters? Choose all that apply.

   a. It crowds out other plants.

   b. It produces resources needed by other plants.

   c. It increases the number of native plants in the ecosystem.

   d. It blocks sunlight from plants that live deeper in the water.

4. Use one of your answers from Question 3 to construct an argument for a law requiring safe disposal of *Elodea*.

   _____

   _____

   _____

   _____

   _____

5. Model one negative way in which organisms can affect their ecosystems. Use labels to tell why the effect is negative.

6. Suppose that you have designed a trap for capturing an invasive animal species, such as a cane toad. Tell how you might test the trap to demonstrate that it works.

7. Assume your trap tests are successful. Make a claim about how traps for other invasive species such as the northern snakehead fish might affect native organisms and human communities. Use evidence and reasoning to convince people to use the trap.

Unit Review

1. List three nonliving things found in nature that you use. Cite evidence why each thing is important to you.

_____

_____

_____

2. Think of two animals in your area. Compare them, and state which one is most likely to adapt well to a change in the ecosystem based on whether their needs are very specific or can be met by a range of habitats and diets. Cite evidence to support your claim.

_____

_____

_____

3. What is true of how invasive species interact as part of an ecosystem? Select all that apply.

   a. They are typically harmful to the new environment.

   b. They can limit resources available to other species.

   c. They are eaten by native animal species.

   d. They typically spread slowly.

   e. They are native to an area.

4. Which of the following things are involved in the flow of energy and matter in ecosystems? Circle all that apply.

   a. producers

   b. rocks

   c. consumers

   d. decomposers

5. Model a population interacting with a community. Show an effect this has on the ecosystem.

6. Select all the ways living things in the biosphere interact with other living things.

   a. Fish live in a pond.

   b. Plants use air to make food.

   c. A cow uses a tree for shade.

   d. A ladybug lays eggs on a leaf.

7. Living things in the biosphere interact with nonliving things in Earth's other systems to get the matter or energy they need to live and grow. Which are examples of this? Choose all that apply.

   a. Hawks eat mice.

   b. Koalas live in trees.

   c. Plants use nutrients from the soil to make food.

   d. Deer drink water from a pond.

8. A beaver dam affects an ecosystem. Write *P* for positive or *N* for negative next to each of the effects listed below.

Dams make water cleaner.

Trees are chopped down.

Dams can store water during long dry times.

Dams can cause flooding.

Fish can't migrate past dams.

Use evidence to justify one of your choices.

_____

_____

_____

9. An invasive plant species in this ecosystem is harming native organisms. Which professionals would an engineer need to work with when developing a method for removing the invasive plants? Select all that apply.

  a. an advertising manager for the local news network

  b. another engineer who does computer modeling

  c. a legal expert on environmental protection rules

  d. a scientific expert on ecosystems and invasive species

10. Zebra mussels are small shell animals native to Asia. They're now found in freshwater lakes and streams in the U.S., such as the Great Lakes. A female zebra mussel can make up to 500,000 eggs at a time. The many zebra mussel offspring can cause problems.

- They smother native mussels by attaching to them.
- They absorb pollution, which can kill organisms that feed on them.
- They compete for space and nutrients with native species.

Model a possible long-term effect of zebra mussels on the Great Lakes ecosystem.

In Unit 4, you used models to support explanations of how organisms interact and change their ecosystems. In this unit, you will use models and computational thinking to describe how Earth's systems interact and how people can also interact with Earth's systems to find solutions to problems.

UNIT 5 Earth Interactions and Resources

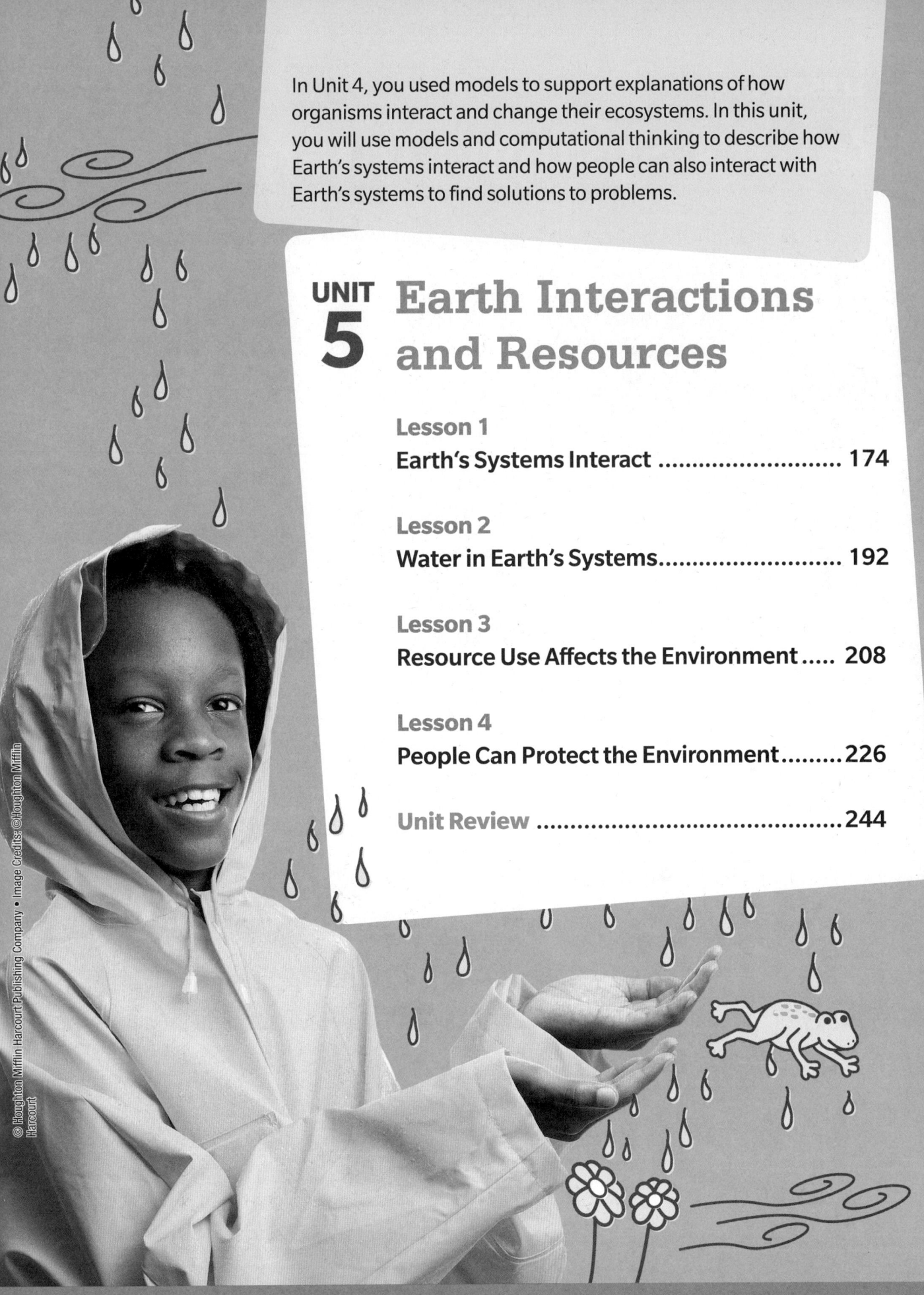

Earth's Systems Interact

Boy, that's hot!

Hawai'i is a collection of volcanic islands. What do you notice about the way the materials from the volcanic eruption interact with air, water, land, and living things?

I notice _____

_____

_____

What do you wonder about the effects a volcanic eruption would have on the environment?

I wonder _____

_____

_____

_____

Can You Explain It?

How can a single natural event affect many of Earth's systems? Sketch, write, or model your answer.

Earth Materials Form Systems

At a glance, a coral reef and a coastal forest ecosystem may seem to have very little in common, but you might be surprised by what careful observation of these environments can reveal. Scientists who study environments organize the different parts of these environments into categories to understand how they are related.

Form a question Ask a question about how things found in very different environments are related.

Did you know?

Earth's atmosphere goes up to 100 km, but most of our air is within 15 km of Earth's surface.

_____

_____

_____

POSSIBLE MATERIALS

☐ nature magazines

STEP 1   **Classify** Study two different ecosystems, such as a coral reef and a forest. Sort all the things you see into two categories, and make a table to show your work.

STEP 2   What things are part of both ecosystems? How do they interact?

Draw conclusions Make a **claim** about what different environments have in common. Use **evidence** and **reasoning** to support your claim.

Making Sense

How does knowing the materials found in most environments help to identify Earth's different systems affected by the volcanic eruption?

Interactions of Systems Shape Landforms

It would be very hard to find a place on Earth not affected by water. Look at any environment, and you will find evidence of water's importance. Water determines where most living things on the planet are found. It also changes Earth's surface over time.

Form a question   Ask a question about modeling the effects of water on Earth's surface materials.

Did you know?

Water is called the universal solvent. It dissolves more things than any other substance.

POSSIBLE MATERIALS

- [ ] plastic tray
- [ ] 20 sugar cubes
- [ ] modeling clay
- [ ] water
- [ ] book (about 4 cm thick)
- [ ] effervescent tablet
- [ ] paper towels
- [ ] goggles

STEP 1 As a class, review the questions you recorded and pick the questions that the class thinks are the most important ones to answer.

STEP 2 **Investigate your question** How can you investigate the questions your class chose as most important? Think about the materials your teacher shows you and what else you might need. Write a summary of your plan in the space provided. Show it to your teacher for approval and to see if you can get the things you need. If you use other things than those shown by your teacher, be sure to include them in your list.

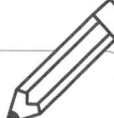

STEP 3 **Organize** Carry out your plan, and record your results. Present your data in a way that everyone can see what you did and what happened. You might choose a table or a graph as a presentation tool. Or you might choose a poster with photos.

Draw conclusions What do each of the materials that you used in your model represent? What kinds of changes did you observe in your model? How do these changes relate to the interactions between water and Earth's surface materials?

_____

_____

_____

Make a **claim** based on your model. Describe an effect you would expect to see in the real world involving water and Earth's surface materials. Use **evidence** to support your answer, and explain your **reasoning**.

_____

_____

_____

_____

Making Sense

How does understanding more about how water and Earth's surface materials interact support your explanation of how one event such as a volcanic eruption can affect many Earth systems?

_____

_____

_____

How did your team make sure everyone's ideas were heard while deciding what to model?

_____

_____

_____

_____

Earth's Major Systems

Systems on Earth

Look at the satellite image of Earth from space. Which of the four basic materials that make up all of Earth's systems can you identify? Long before we could see Earth from space, scientists had identified four major Earth systems.

Explain Study the images on these pages, and read their descriptions. Why is it possible to model Earth as both a single system and a system made up of other systems?

_____

_____

_____

Atmosphere

The **atmosphere** is a system made up of air, and it surrounds Earth. Our planet's atmosphere is responsible for the weather.

. . . .

Hydrosphere

The **hydrosphere** is the system that includes all of Earth's water in all three states. Most of Earth's water is found in the ocean. But water can also be found underground, in streams and lakes, as ice at the poles, and as a gas in the atmosphere.

. . . .

Scientists develop and use models of Earth systems. These models help scientists understand phenomena such as weather in the atmosphere, earthquakes in the geosphere, population growth in the biosphere, and ocean currents in the hydrosphere. By modeling these systems, scientists can identify and explain patterns of interactions between different systems.

Geosphere

The **geosphere** is the solid part of Earth. This system includes features such as rocks, soil, mountains, and volcanoes, as well as things found deep within Earth.

Biosphere

The **biosphere** is the Earth system that includes all living things, or life. Plants, animals, and all other organisms make up the biosphere.

Making Sense

How do these categories or systems help to describe the many interactions in a single volcanic eruption?

_____

_____

_____

Natural Events Connect Systems

One Event, Many Systems

When you studied food webs earlier, you tracked the flow of matter and energy through different ecosystems. Think about the roles that matter and energy play in other systems, such as volcanoes in the geosphere.

Mount Pinatubo's eruption was the second largest of the 20th century (1900–1999).
. . . .

In 1991, the eruption of Mount Pinatubo in the Philippines produced high-speed avalanches of hot ash and gases, giant mudflows, and a cloud of volcanic ash hundreds of kilometers across and 35 km (22 mi) high. Roofs collapsed under the weight of rain-soaked ash.

Make a model to show how the Pinatubo eruption interacted with living things, water, and the atmosphere.

Similar to volcanic eruptions, earthquakes are natural events that occur within the geosphere. Both of these events can release lots of energy. The energy released by an earthquake is capable of moving large sections of rock. A single earthquake can reshape existing landforms or make new ones.

This is Earthquake Lake near Cameron, Montana. The treetops sticking out of the lake show that the area was once dry land.

What change do you think caused Earthquake Lake to form? Which Earth systems interacted during that change?

When an earthquake or a volcanic eruption takes place, matter and energy can flow from the geosphere to other systems.

Which system is most affected by a volcanic eruption? Turn to a partner to share your claim and argue for it with evidence and reasoning.

Adding to the Atmosphere

Earth's atmosphere covers all of the planet. In this view of Earth from space, notice how thin the atmosphere is compared to the geosphere. All of Earth's systems interact with the atmosphere.

Plants give Earth's surface its green look. They and other living things take in air and release waste gases back into the atmosphere.

The atmosphere interacts with Earth's oceans. Water and heat energy move between the oceans and the atmosphere. Powerful storms often result. Winds in the atmosphere move storms onto land. Many land organisms need water from these storms to live and grow.

Winds in the atmosphere can shape landforms, such as sand dunes.

With a partner, describe an event or process that can cause matter and energy to flow into the atmosphere from other Earth systems.

_____

_____

_____

_____

Ash, dust, and other volcanic particles can flow into the atmosphere during volcanic eruptions.

No Stopping the Biosphere

The environment is made up of living and nonliving things. The nonliving part contains materials that organisms need to live and grow. In your group, discuss how a sudden change in an Earth system may affect the biosphere. Then examine the before and after images of the eruption Mount St. Helens in 1980.

Before eruption

Late May 1980

2016

Events such as volcanic eruptions can quickly change environments. Damage is the most obvious change from an eruption. Volcanoes also can enrich the soil. Over time, this can speed up the regrowth of plants.

Ten years after the eruption of Mount St. Helens, some plants had grown back. Gradually, insects and animals returned. More than 40 years after the eruption, even the areas closest to the volcano have recovered a lot.

Which claim about change and stability in the biosphere can be supported using the images of Mount St. Helens as evidence?

a. In time, a damaged environment can recover.
b. Ash and other volcanic matter are harmful to the environment.
c. All changes to ecosystems caused by natural events are permanent.

A Home for the Hydrosphere

During eruptions, snow and glaciers on volcanoes melt and mix with ash and sediment to cause mudflows.

Water vapor is one gas released into the air during volcanic eruptions. The water may have come from rain that seeped into the ground. It may also have come from ocean water.

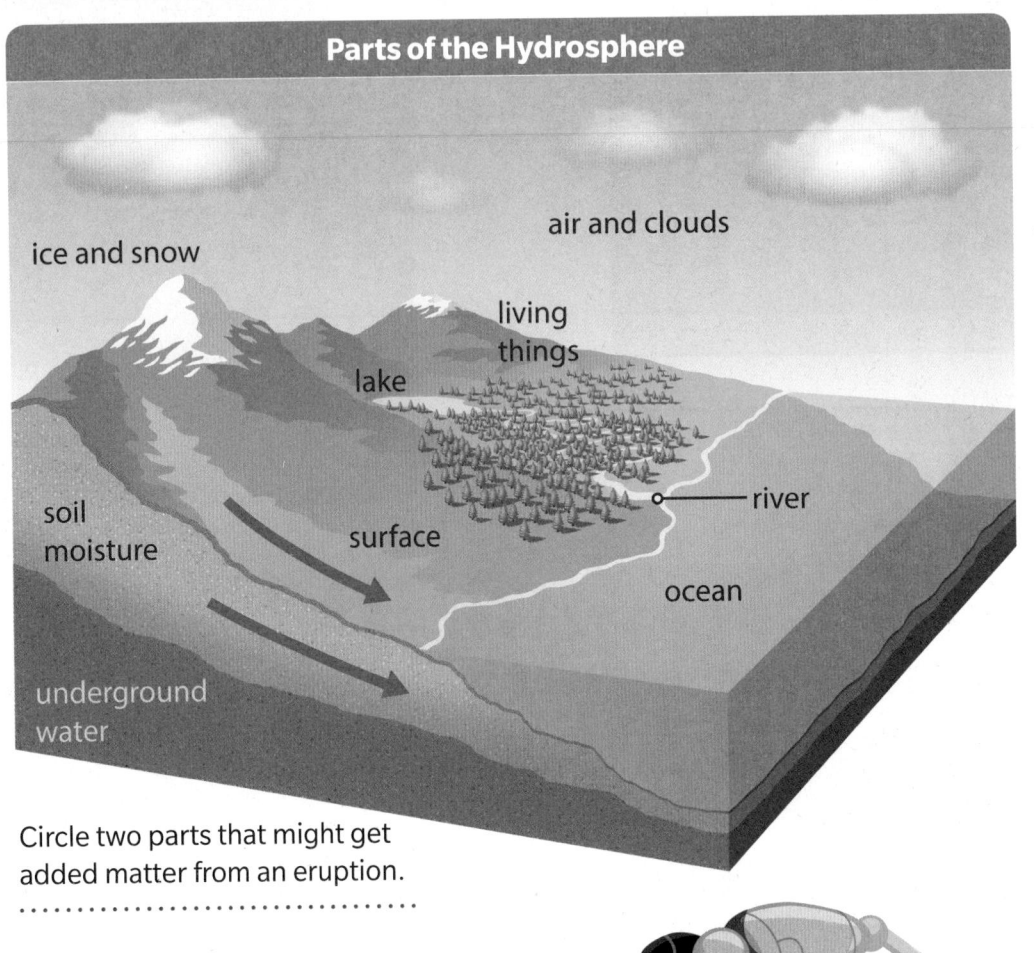

Parts of the Hydrosphere

air and clouds

ice and snow

living things

lake

soil moisture

surface

river

ocean

underground water

Circle two parts that might get added matter from an eruption.

Making Sense

How does knowing what can come out of a volcano add to your explanation of how a single event can affect several systems?

_____

_____

_____

Lesson Check

Can You Explain It?

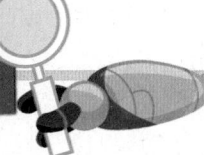

Review your ideas from the beginning of this lesson about how a single natural event can impact many of Earth's systems. How have your ideas changed?

Be sure to do the following:

- Explain Earth's systems, including those you cannot see in the image.
- Describe how energy and matter interact among the systems.

Now I know or think that _____

_____

_____

_____

Making Connections

What Earth systems do you see interacting in the photo of a seaside cliff? How do you know?

_____

_____

_____

_____

Checkpoints

1. When wind blows sand to form large sand dunes, which two systems are interacting?

    a. biosphere and geosphere

    b. hydrosphere and biosphere

    c. atmosphere and hydrosphere

    d. geosphere and atmosphere

2. Choose the correct words to complete the sentences.

> ecosystem
> biosphere
> atmosphere
> geosphere
> hydrosphere
> system

Reef organisms use gases that come from the _____ and

dissolve in seawater, which is part of the _____ .

3. Draw lines to connect the Earth system to an example of something in that system.

biosphere   plants

hydrosphere   air

geosphere   ocean

atmosphere   rock

4. Which of the following is an example of the hydrosphere interacting with the biosphere?

a. A tsunami forms as the result of an earthquake.

b. The weather cools after a volcanic eruption.

c. Rainwater is used by plants and animals on the land.

d. Wind blows small organisms to new places on Earth.

5. Identify the pair of Earth systems interacting in each of the following events.

A hurricane begins as a tropical storm that draws matter and energy from the ocean.   _____

Molten rock, ash, and hot gases are released during a volcanic eruption.   _____

Plant leaves have structures that enable them to take in and release air.   _____

6. Draw and label a model that shows matter and energy exchanging among the biosphere, atmosphere, hydrosphere, and geosphere during a volcanic eruption.

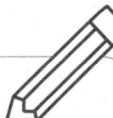

Water in Earth's Systems

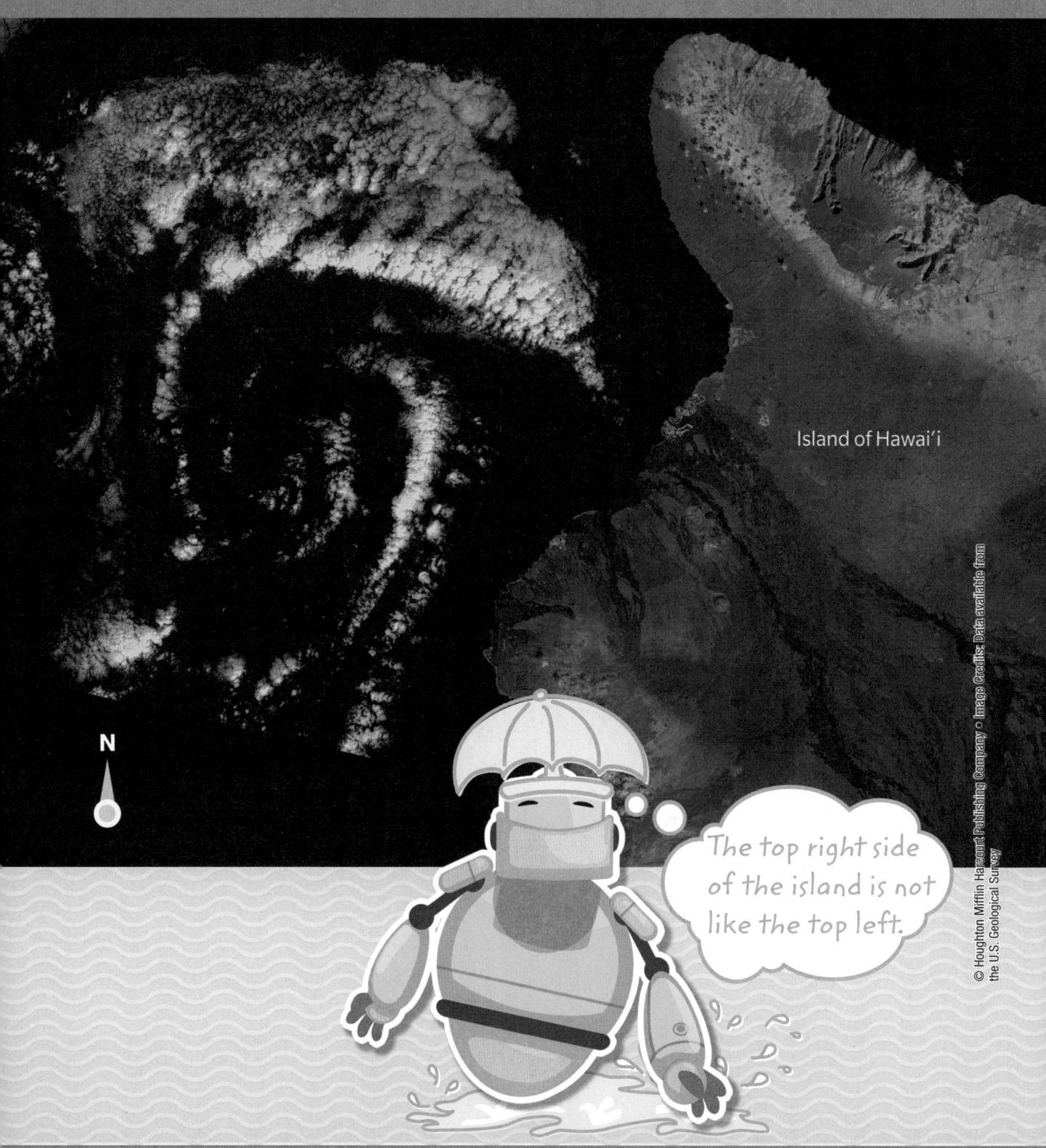

Island of Hawai'i

N

The top right side of the island is not like the top left.

© Houghton Mifflin Harcourt Publishing Company ○ Image Credits: Data available from the U.S. Geological Survey

What do you notice about the colors showing on the sides of the island of Hawai'i?

I notice _____

_____

_____

_____

What do you wonder about the processes that shape what you can see?

How does this relate to Hawai'i being a volcanic island chain?

I wonder _____

_____

_____

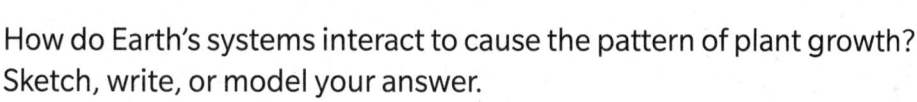

Can You Explain It?

How do Earth's systems interact to cause the pattern of plant growth? Sketch, write, or model your answer.

Water Moves among Earth's Systems

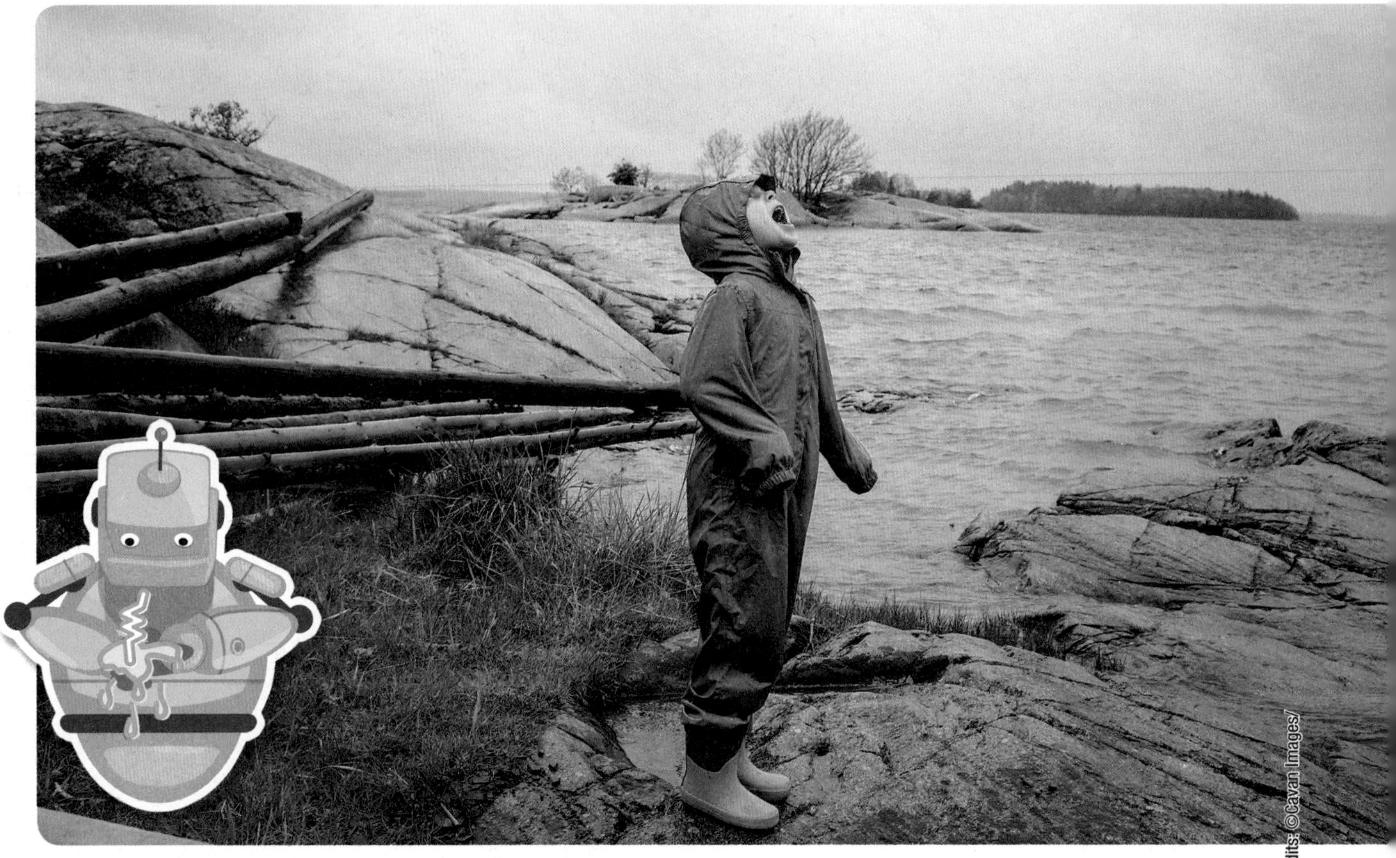

Rain is always fresh water, meaning it has no dissolved salt. Water vapor, the gas phase of water, is what condenses to form clouds and rain. Interactions among the geosphere, hydrosphere, and atmosphere affect where and how much it rains.

Form a question Ask a question about water movement and Earth's systems.

Did you know?

Mt. Waialeale on the island of Kaua'i in Hawai'i gets more than 11 m (36 ft) of rain each year. It's one of the rainiest spots on Earth.

© Houghton Mifflin Harcourt Publishing Company • Image Credits: (cr), (br) ©Houghton Mifflin Harcourt

POSSIBLE MATERIALS

- ☐ 2 plastic containers
- ☐ salt
- ☐ 2 rubber bands
- ☐ modeling clay
- ☐ water
- ☐ 2 small weights
- ☐ measuring spoons
- ☐ dropper
- ☐ marker
- ☐ measuring cup
- ☐ plastic wrap
- ☐ masking tape

STEP 1 Label the plastic containers A and B. Make two identical clay landform models in each, and include a lake in each model.

Why do you think it is important that the landform models be identical?

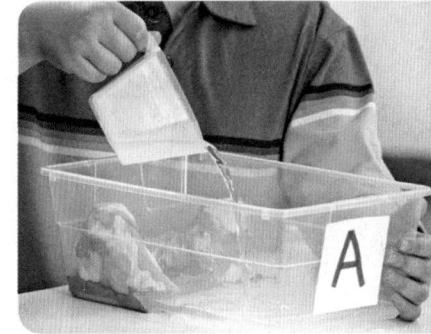

STEP 2 Place the landform models on one end of each container. Each model should take up about ¼ of the space in its container. Stir 2 teaspoons of salt into 2 cups of water until the salt dissolves. Pour the salt water into the empty area in container A. Add 3 drops of fresh water to the lake in A and B.

How is the water in the model lakes different from the water in the model ocean?

STEP 3 **Investigate your question** Cover both containers with plastic wrap, and use a large rubber band to hold the plastic wrap in place. Place a small weight on the plastic wrap directly above the lake in each model. Place both containers indoors in sunlight. Two hours later, observe and record your observations.

Why is the plastic wrap important?

STEP 4   **Analyze your data**   After two hours, how did the amount of moisture on the underside of the plastic wrap compare in the two models?

STEP 5   Did you notice any change in the amount of water in the model lakes? If so, what caused the change?

STEP 6   **Draw conclusions**   Make a **claim** about how water moves and relates to Earth's systems. Cite **evidence** to support your claim, and explain your **reasoning**.

Making Sense

How do the models in this activity add to your explanation of the color difference on the island of Hawai'i?

 How did your group share tasks so that everyone was able to contribute equally?

Water Stores Heat

The movement of heat energy is part of the interaction between the ocean and other Earth systems. For example, the sun evaporates water from the ocean into the atmosphere, which can lead to changes in the weather.

Did you know?

A fluffy cloud one cubic km in size weighs about 500,000 kg.

Form a question Ask a question about heat energy, land, and water.

_____

_____

_____

STEP 1 Fill one plastic cup with water, and fill the other cup with an equal volume of soil.

STEP 2 Place the cups under a heat lamp, and place a thermometer in each cup.

POSSIBLE MATERIALS

- ☐ 2 small plastic cups
- ☐ water
- ☐ soil
- ☐ heat lamp
- ☐ 2 thermometers
- ☐ timer
- ☐ information resources

STEP 3 Set a timer for 20 minutes, and record the temperature for the water and the soil cups. Turn the heat lamp off, and set the timer for another 10 minutes. Record the temperatures again.

	Water	Soil
Heated 20 minutes		
Cooled 10 minutes		

What temperature pattern did you observe?

_____

_____

Temperature changes can cause land breezes and sea breezes. Use information resources to find any patterns of weather that go with them. Summarize here:

_____

_____

Draw conclusions Make a **claim** about heat energy, land, and water. Support your claim with **evidence** from your investigation, and explain your **reasoning**.

_____

_____

_____

●●○○

Making Sense

How does understanding how soil and water store energy add to your explanation of the pattern of extra plant growth on the island of Hawai'i?

_____

_____

Earth's Water Sources

Where on Earth Is the Water?

Most of the water on Earth is found in oceans, or the large bodies of water that separate most continents. Ocean water is different from fresh water because it contains salt.

Some of Earth's fresh water is contained in glaciers, icebergs, and the ice sheets that cover Antarctica and parts of the Arctic.

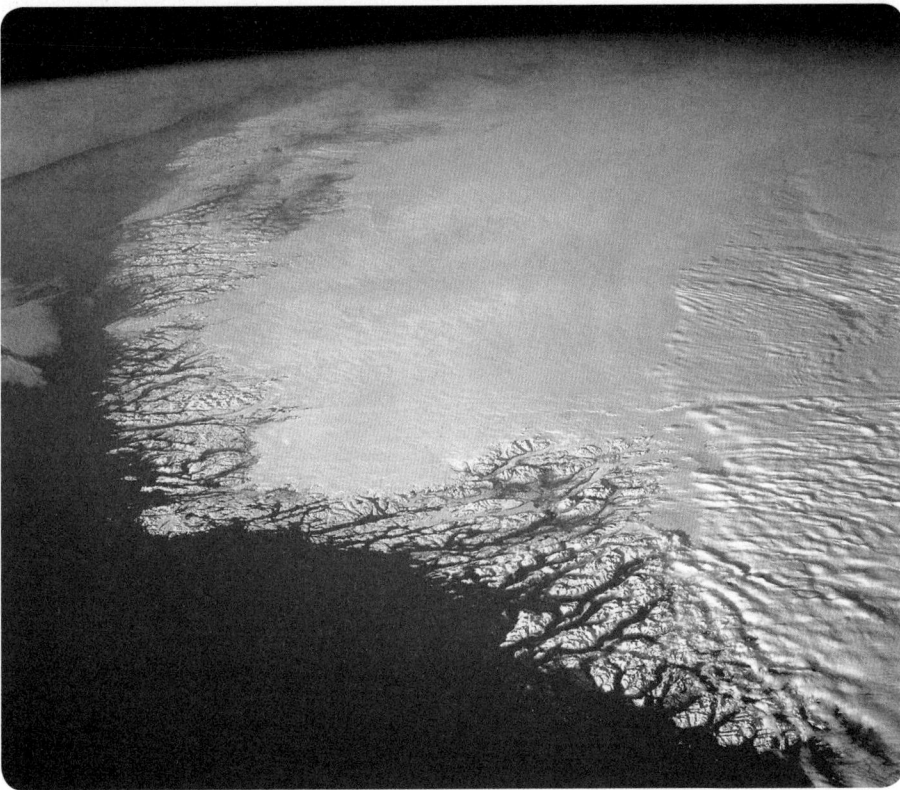

Greenland and the
north polar icecap
. . . .

Lakes, rivers, and streams contain a percentage of Earth's fresh water. Other examples of fresh surface water include snow, ice, and pools of rain or snowmelt.

The remaining fresh water is located underground and is called groundwater. Like fresh surface water, people use groundwater as a source of drinking water.

Iceberg
. . . .

Water Distribution on Earth

Water on Earth can be broken down into many different categories. One category is salt water, which contains salt. Another type is fresh water, which does not contain salt. Surface water is found on Earth's surface, while groundwater is found below. Lakes, rivers, and swamps are sources of fresh surface water.

Use Math Research the percentages of salt water and fresh water found on Earth. Fill in the left key with the terms *salt water* and *fresh water*. Then research the different types of fresh water on Earth. Finally, fill in the fresh water grid and key.

All of Earth's water

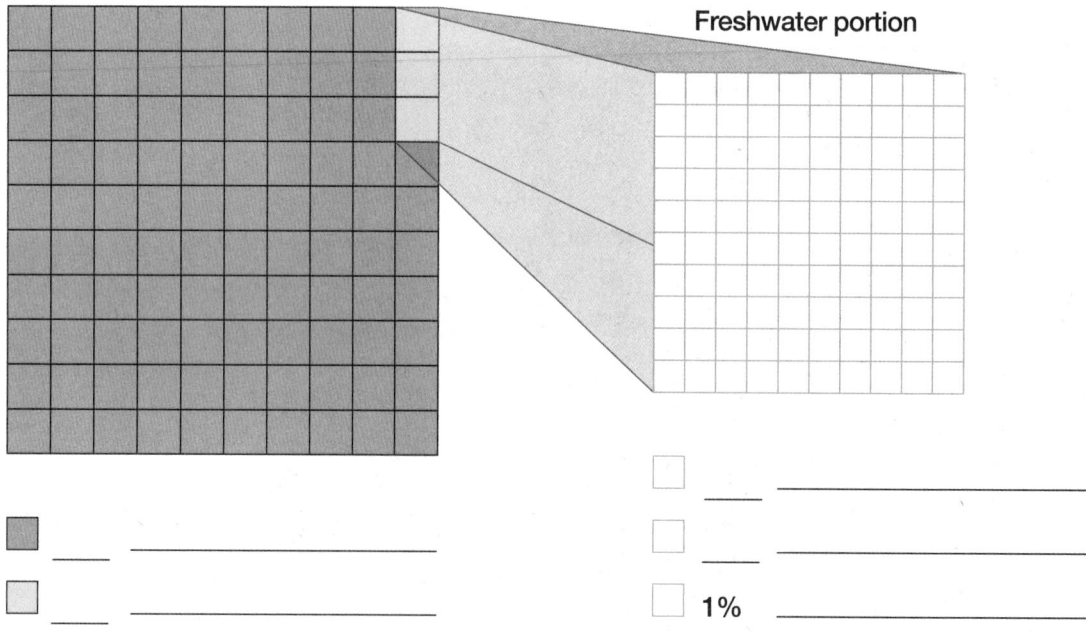

Freshwater portion

____ _____

____ _____

____ _____

____ _____

1% _____

How could you use math to show how living things compete for water as a limited resource?

_____

_____

Making Sense

How can water distribution terms add details to an explanation of the color pattern on the island of Hawai'i?

_____

_____

Water and Earth's Surface

Water Shaping Land

Water affects many processes and materials in Earth's systems. Water is involved in the processes that break down and build up landforms. The oceans and other large water bodies interact with the atmosphere to cause patterns in weather and climate. Organisms in every environment need water to survive.

Rivers provide a habitat for living things. They also drive processes of erosion that carve landforms into the geosphere, such as this canyon.

Currents called longshore currents can reshape coastlines. Coastal communities build structures to manage erosion. The structures are long, narrow and extend tens of meters from the beach into the ocean. They slow down longshore currents, causing them to drop their sand loads.

wave and wind direction

Turn to a partner. Summarize one of the water-caused changes on this page. Then make an argument for a community to control or stop the natural change.

Heat Energy, Water, and Wind

Water is found within every Earth system. The oceans are a major source of water for the atmosphere. Share with a partner what you know about how the ocean affects weather and climate.

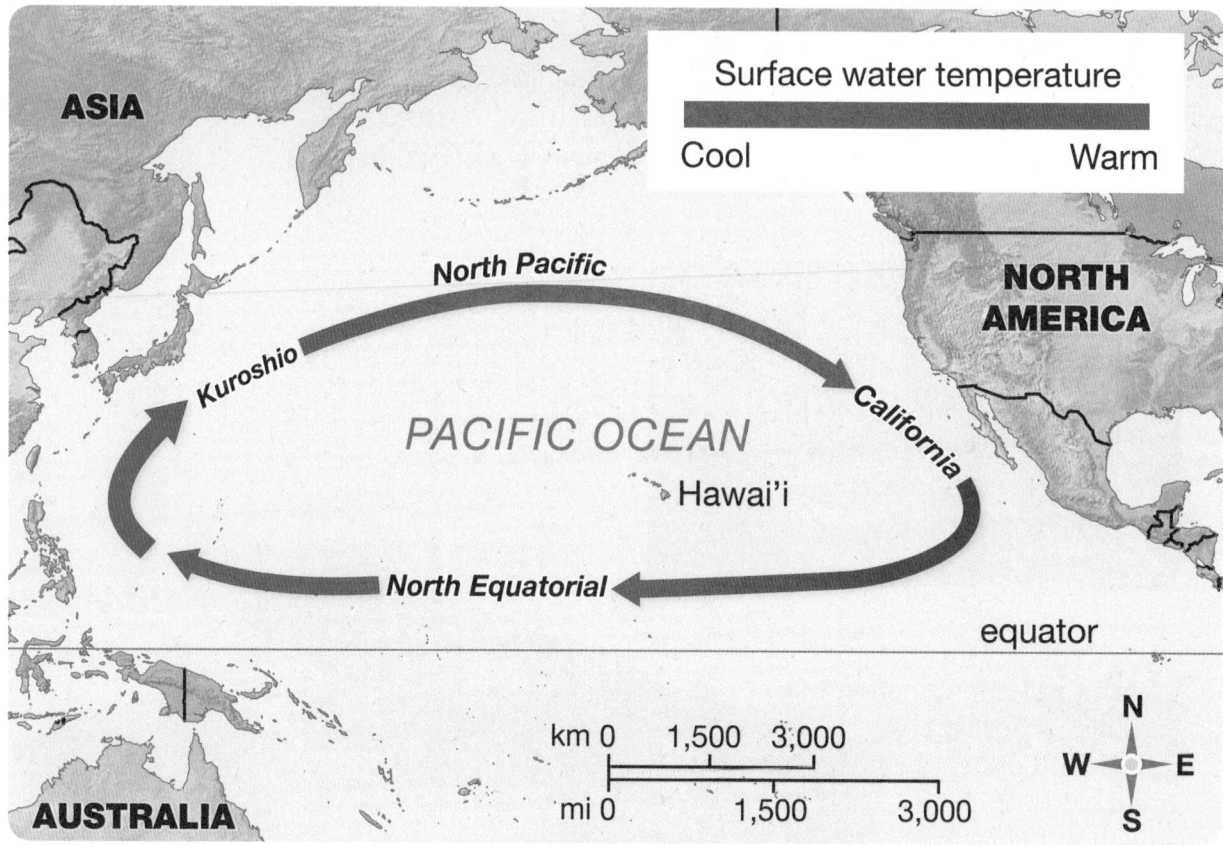

Ocean surface currents move heat energy away from the equator and toward the poles. These currents warm the air and add moisture, causing storms and other types of weather. Global wind patterns are partly responsible for the direction and speed of ocean surface currents. For example, Hawai'i is north of the equator in the Pacific Ocean. Warm, moist *trade winds* blow from the northeast toward the islands.

How do you think air flowing from over the ocean to over land affects the weather on land?

© Houghton Mifflin Harcourt Publishing Company

Rain and groundwater affect what organisms can live and grow in an area.

Picture a storm approaching a coast. In a small group, discuss how far inland the rain-making clouds could travel. How does the geosphere affect the movement of winds and clouds? Look at the diagram below to explore how the atmosphere, hydrosphere, biosphere, and geosphere interact.

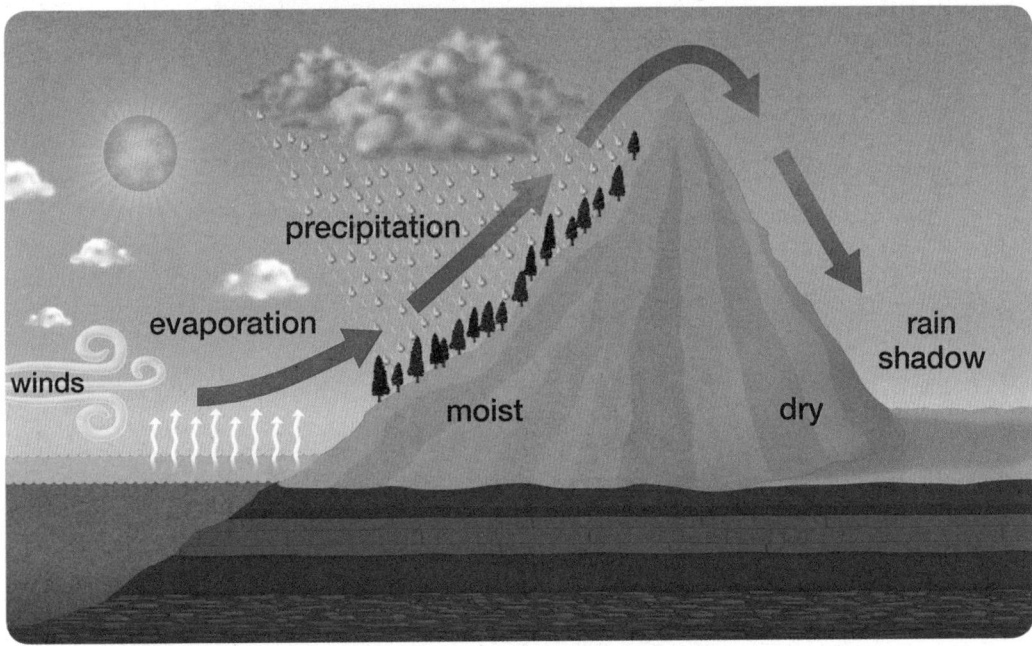

Analyze this image of the rain shadow effect. Explain how the atmosphere, geosphere, and hydrosphere interact. Use evidence and reasoning in your answer.

Water Needed for Life

Plants, plantlike organisms, and animals call the ocean home. The hydrosphere provides habitats for members of the biosphere. The geosphere shapes the depth and contours of the ocean floor. Coastal zone ecosystems are found near the shore in shallow water. Open-sea ecosystems are found where the ocean is deep. In each of these, light level, water depth, water temperature, and available nutrients vary.

Why might light level affect what can live in an ocean zone? (Hint: food chain)

Making Sense

How does knowing about how heat, wind, water, and land interact add to your explanation of the pattern of plant growth on Hawaiʻi?

Name _____

Lesson Check

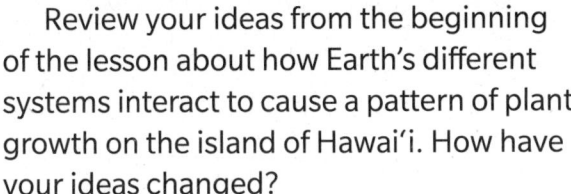

Can You Explain It?

Review your ideas from the beginning of the lesson about how Earth's different systems interact to cause a pattern of plant growth on the island of Hawai'i. How have your ideas changed?

Be sure to do the following:

- Explain how freshwater rain comes from ocean water.
- Tell how land and water temperature differences can cause weather.
- Explain the results of warm, moist air interacting with landmasses.

Now I know or think that _____

_____

_____

_____

Making Connections

How might water interact with other parts of the environment in this image?

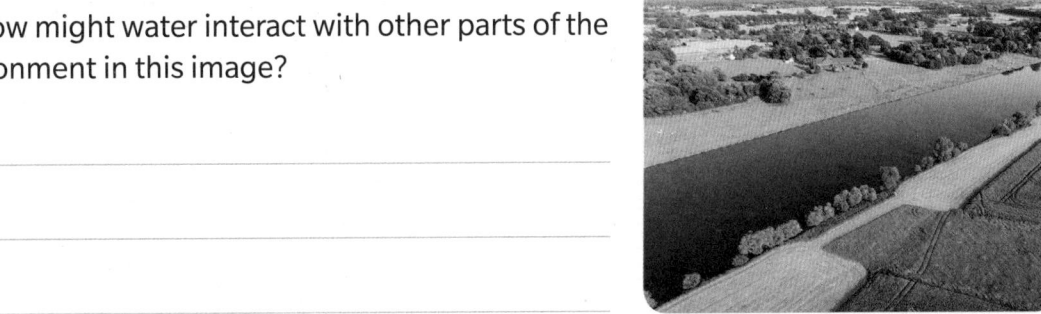

_____

_____

_____

_____

Checkpoints

Use these terms to complete the sentence. Some terms may be used more than once.

cold water   warm water   poles   equator

1. Ocean currents transport _____ from near

the _____ to the _____ and

_____ from the poles to the _____ .

2. Draw and label a model that shows the path of water from the ocean and through its interaction with mountains to produce a rain shadow.

3. You did an activity that modeled rain resulting from salty water. What would happen to the system if you added energy by putting a heating pad under the container with the salt water reservoir? Why?

_____

_____

_____

4. Land (soil) and water warm up and cool down at different rates. Because of this, the interactions of ocean water and nearby land can produce which daily weather pattern?

a. rain shadows

b. land and sea breezes

c. surface currents

d. trade winds

5. Nine tenths of water on Earth is in the ocean. About how much of the water on Earth is salt water, and how much is fresh water? Do the math.

   a. 90% salt water, 10% fresh water

   b. 40% salt water, 60% fresh water

   c. 60% salt water, 40% fresh water

   d. 10% salt water, 90% fresh water

6. Why is the water from this spring (water flowing out of the ground) fresh water?

_____

_____

_____

_____

7. The ocean provides habitats for many types of organisms. The amount of light can limit how much food is available from producers. What is another ocean characteristic that might limit where organisms can survive? Why?

_____

_____

8. How can you use these images to support an explanation of green and brown land patterns on Earth's surface?

_____

_____

I've got to dig
a little deeper.

What do you notice about the land around the aqueduct, or artificial river?

I notice _____

_____

_____

_____

What do you wonder about the needs and cost of getting water and making aqueducts to transport it? How might getting resources be difficult on an island chain like Hawai'i?

I wonder _____

_____

_____

Can You Explain It?

How do people use systems to safely get, transport, and use natural resources? Sketch, write, or model your answer.

Houghton Mifflin Harcourt Publishing Company

LESSON 3 • Resource Use Affects the Environment   209

Engineer It
Squeaky Clean Water

Cities prefer relatively clean drinking water sources like this lake. Notice the building, which holds a pipe that takes in water. In some cases, though, water needs to be cleaned before it can be used. Suppose that you have been hired by a water treatment company to build a water filtration system to clean contaminated water.

Form a question Ask a question about cleaning water.

_____

_____

_____

_____

> **Did you know?**
>
> Pure water is clear, tasteless, colorless, odorless and has no food energy (calories).

POSSIBLE MATERIALS

- ☐ 250 mL of dirty water $0
- ☐ graduated cylinder $0
- ☐ large jar $0
- ☐ 3 rubber bands $1

- ☐ 2 stirring sticks $1
- ☐ gauze squares $3
- ☐ wire screen $3
- ☐ coffee filter $3

- ☐ 5 cotton balls $1
- ☐ 5 paper towels $1
- ☐ pebbles $4

With a budget of $10, your goal is to make the water appear clear while preserving, or keeping, at least 200 mL of water. The water clarity level should be 10 or less on the scale defined in the image in Step 4.
DO NOT DRINK THE WATER AT ANY TIME!

Explore

STEP 1 **Research** Begin by conducting research about how to build a water filtration system, and then write your findings below.

STEP 2 **Define the problem** Review the scenario above, and then jot down your criteria and constraints below.

Criteria	Constraints

STEP 3 **Brainstorm solutions** Look over the materials provided by your teacher, and then brainstorm multiple solutions for your problem. Keep in mind the criteria and constraints. Finally, evaluate your solutions and choose the best one.

Solutions	Evaluation

Make and Test

STEP 4 **Develop a model** Sketch your design on a separate piece of paper, labeling all parts. Also write down your filtration procedure.

_____

_____

Have your teacher review your design, and then build and test it. Use the water clarity scale to judge your water clarity, or how clear the water is, after each step in your filtration process.

| | 25 | 20 | 15 | 10 | 5 |

Steps	Clarity number	Notes

Improve and Test

STEP 5 **Test a new model** Were you able to get the water completely clean? Why or why not?

_____

_____

Did you meet the criteria and constraints? How could you improve this design?

_____

_____

 Turn to a partner and explain something that you learned from a design that didn't work.

Communicate Compare each group's results.

Group	Clarity level	Evaluate their success or failure

Why did some designs fail? How could you improve the designs that failed?

_____

_____

This water is not potable, or safe to drink. What can still be in the water that the filter did not remove?

_____

_____

Draw conclusions Make a **claim** based on your investigation, and support it with **evidence** and **reasoning**.

_____

_____

_____

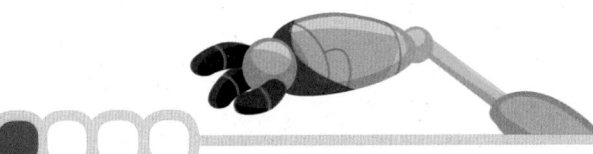

Making Sense

How does what you've discovered in this activity add to your explanation of how people get and use resources like water?

_____

_____

HANDS-ON ACTIVITY

Getting to a Resource

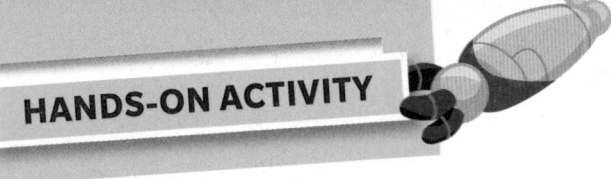

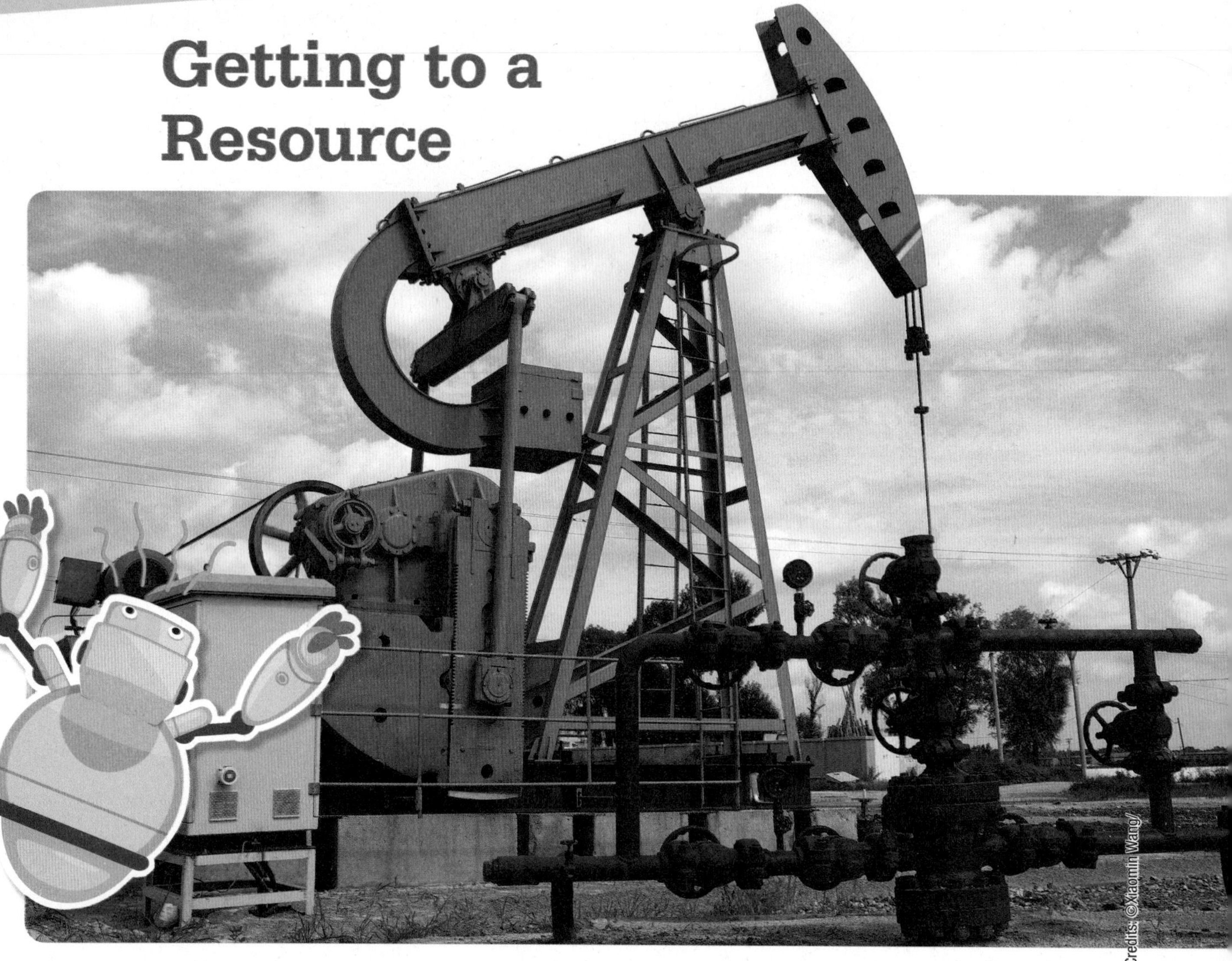

People tend to use the easiest and most readily available methods to find resources. For example, the apples lowest on a tree get picked first. Similarly, a source of oil that is easy to find and gushes from the ground by itself is used up first.

Form a question Ask a question about how harvesting a resource changes over time.

Did you know?

Mponeng gold mine in South Africa is the deepest in the world. The mine's tunnels go almost 4 km (2.5 mi) below Earth's surface.

POSSIBLE MATERIALS

☐ sponge circle
☐ 2 clear plastic cups
☐ water
☐ paper towels
☐ graduated cylinder
☐ funnel
☐ pencil

STEP 1 Place the sponge in the bottom of a cup. Add water to fully soak the sponge, and fill the cup to the level of the sponge.

STEP 2 **Investigate your question** How much water can you get out of the cup? Try each method in the table in order. For each try, catch the water in the second cup, and then use the funnel to add the water to the graduated cylinder. Measure and record.

Method	Total collected (mL)	Water gained (mL) (previous – current)
Just pour		
Push in pencil's eraser		
Squeeze by hand		

Draw conclusions Make a **claim** about the effort and the resulting harvest of resources over time. Support your claim with **evidence** from your investigation, and be sure to explain your **reasoning**.

_____

_____

_____

Making Sense

How does what you've discovered in this activity help you explain how people use systems like the aqueduct to get resources?

_____

_____

Earth's Resources and Human Activities

People have basic needs—water, food, air, shelter, and clothing. Resources are materials from the environment that people obtain and use to meet these needs. What resources are used to meet other needs?

Study the picture. Identify a need and the item that meets the need. Then, identify at least one major resource used to make the item. If you need help, use Internet resources to find out how the item is made.

Need	Item meeting need	Resource(s) to make item
1.		
2.		
3.		

Turn and talk to a partner about your response. Add their answer to your table. Then, work together to add another row of responses.

Results of Use

People turn to the environment to gather the resources they need, for example, water, air, food, wood, rocks, minerals, renewable energy, and fossil fuels. Some resources are plentiful or are renewable. Renewable resources can be replaced naturally in a relatively short time. Other resources are nonrenewable. Earth has a limited supply of them.

Trees are cut down and their branches trimmed off. Then trucks take them to a sawmill. Wood is a renewable resource. However, cutting down large areas of trees can damage ecosystems.

Trees were sawed into boards and the wood was dried. What need are the boards helping to meet now?

What are other uses for wood?

Coal is mined deep underground and on Earth's surface. Surface mining can leave behind scars on the land that take time to recover. Coal and other fossil fuels are nonrenewable resources.

An important use of coal is generating electricity. Electricity is delivered by a system of wires and controls. Burning coal adds pollution the air.

Irrigation systems move water to grow food crops. Agriculture uses a large amount of water to grow certain crops. Heavy use of water can dry up rivers and lakes.

Water and electricity are two resources that are often delivered to people. Identify another resource that is delivered to you through a system. Tell the need it meets.

_____

_____

_____

Complex Resource Situations

Harvesting and using some resources can have negative effects. For example, new roads to reach a mine can destroy wilderness, and mining can produce toxic mine waste. Science can explain the negative effects but not make choices for people. People must evaluate the effects and then make resource choices based on their personal values.

Soil

Plants that grow in soil are renewable. It's easy to grow more in a human lifetime. Soil itself is a nonrenewable resource.

Many farms use chemical fertilizers and pesticides to extend soil life and boost crop production. Health concerns connected to these substances have led some farmers to use methods that help protect the soil, water, and crops, and are safe for people.

This plane is spraying pesticide to kill insects. Pesticides help farms to grow enough food to meet people's needs.

This dam is releasing extra water. The building where machines generate electricity is to the right.

Many dams are a renewable source of electricity. This conserves other energy sources. But, dams also redirect the flow of rivers and streams. That destroys habitats, and disrupts the life cycles of organisms. Some dams are being removed in an effort to restore habitats and other resources.

Making Sense

How does what you've learned about coal, wood, and other resources add to your explanation of why people built the aqueduct and how the aqueduct affects the environment?

_____

_____

Getting and Using Resources

Humans Cause Changes

Apply Work in a small group to list two or more ways humans change the environment.

Animals affect the environment. Humans affect it the most. Humans cause changes when they build cities to live, work, or go to school. Humans also change the environment when they grow food and make products. Pollution occurs when human processes release wastes that harm the land, air, or water.

People changed the natural environment in big ways to build buildings, roads and other structures.

Human pollution affects all the parts of the environment. This person is attempting to clean a bird that was affected by an oil spill.

Some forms of pollution can directly affect living things in an ecosystem. Others may result in population booms of algae and bacteria that make life more difficult for other organisms.

When humans cut down trees to build homes, roads, and farms, the environment changes. Humans can also plant trees to replace trees that were cut down.

Space Junk

Space has become an important Earth resource. Spacecraft in orbit around Earth help us monitor and track the paths of severe weather, talk to each other over great distances, and find our way when we are lost. However, like other forms of technology, satellites become obsolete.

Scientists estimate that 500,000 pieces of space debris are orbiting Earth. These objects include old satellites, parts of satellites, and meteoroids. Some 20,000 of these pieces of debris are larger than a softball. These can be dangerous to space stations, astronauts, and probes. The entire collection of all these objects is referred to as space junk. How can we safely get rid of space junk? How can we satisfy the constraint of limited fuel?

One solution is to use a satellite with a large net to capture the cube satellites. After capture, both satellites would descend into Earth's atmosphere. There, they would burn up.

The most practical solution seems to be using a satellite that acts as a slingshot. It captures the space debris, flings it down to Earth's atmosphere to burn up, and then uses energy from the flinging motion to accelerate toward the next piece. This helps save fuel.

In a group, design a device to clean up the debris. Describe what the device must do and how the parts will work together as a system.

_____

_____

_____

_____

Medium-Rare or None?

Americans love meat! The average American eats 125 kg (275 lb) a year. That's about twice as much meat as the world average. Meat is a great source of nutritional needs such as iron, zinc, protein, and calcium. Producing meat uses a lot of water. Unlike plants that produce their own food, animals that are grown for meat need to be fed. This means that farmland must be used to produce food for the animals. Finally, livestock produce large quantities of waste that can harm Earth's spheres.

Should Americans eat less meat? Do additional research on this issue. Provide an argument with evidence to support your ideas.

_____

_____

_____

● ● ● ●

Making Sense

How does understanding some of the effects of humans' resource choices add to your explanation of how people get and use resources?

_____

_____

_____

_____

Name _____

Lesson Check

Can You Explain It?

Review your ideas from the beginning of this lesson about how people use systems to safely get, transport, and use natural resources. How have your ideas changed? Be sure to do the following:

- Describe safe use of resources such as water.
- Tell some renewable and nonrenewable resources that people use.
- Explain how getting and using resources can affect the environment.

Now I know or think that _____

_____

_____

_____

_____

_____

Making Connections

What type of resource is shown here, and how may it be used?

_____

_____

_____

Checkpoints

1. When water is treated, why might it be filtered multiple times? Choose all that apply.

    a. to get air out

    b. to remove as many particles as possible

    c. to raise the temperature of the water

    d. to return water to streams before it is piped to homes

2. Which of the following are true about fossil fuels such as coal? Select all that apply.

    a. They are renewable resources.

    b. Their supplies are limited.

    c. They are only found in the hydrosphere.

    d. They can pollute air when they are burned.

    e. They can be used to generate electricity.

3. Select the best answer for the question. What is one of the biggest challenges of solving the space debris problem?

    a. finding out where the space debris is

    b. knowing how many pieces of space debris there are

    c. having enough fuel to gather the space debris

    d. figuring out what to do with the debris once it's gathered

4. How can gathering an important natural resource be harmful to an ecosystem?

_____

_____

_____

_____

5. Renewable energy resources usually pollute less than nonrenewable fossil fuels. What is an example of another form of ecosystem damage from obtaining renewable energy?

_____

_____

_____

_____

6. Things that you do every day involve resource use. Describe a daily activity, one natural resource involved, and negative effects, if any, of using it.

_____

_____

_____

_____

7. Which of these is an example of a renewable natural resource? Choose all that apply.

   a. coal

   b. wood

   c. crops

   d. soil

8. Explain why you chose one of your answers to Question 7.

_____

_____

_____

People Can Protect the Environment

What do you notice about the city photograph?

I notice _____

_____

_____

_____

What do you wonder about these rooftops and buildings? Why might people on islands like Hawai'i use roofs like these?

I wonder _____

_____

_____

_____

Can You Explain It?

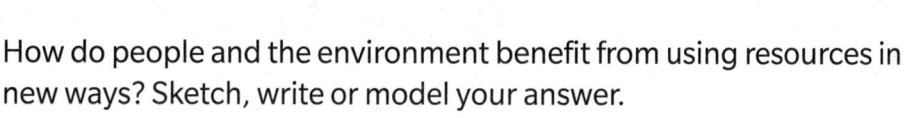

How do people and the environment benefit from using resources in new ways? Sketch, write or model your answer.

Engineer It
Pocket Park

Small "pocket" parks can be a place to play or just enjoy being outdoors. Trees and other plants can help keep the area cool and also provide homes for other living things. Cities use pocket parks to make the best use of small spaces.

Form a question Ask a question about how to design a pocket park.

> **Did you know?**
>
> The world's smallest park is Mill Ends Park in Portland, Oregon. It's about 0.6 m (2 ft) wide.

POSSIBLE MATERIALS

☐ pencil, pen, or markers

☐ copy paper

☐ graph paper, ¼-inch scale

☐ ruler

You are to design a 30 m × 30 m, $10,000 pocket park for Busyville. The park should feature:

- accessibility for children with special needs
- green space
- play area of at least 80 square meters

- dog park
- community garden, 8 × 8 m
- rest areas
- ground cover
- lighting

Explore

STEP 1 **Research** Use books or online resources to find out about parks, accessible playgrounds, and community gardens. Jot down your findings below.

_____

_____

STEP 2 **Define the problem** Review the scenario above, and write down your criteria and constraints.

Criteria	Constraints

Pocket Park Per-Item Prices:

Garden—$20 per sq. meter

Trees—$25 each

Inclusive playground—$55 per sq. meter

Conventional playground— $40 per sq. meter

Trash or recycle bin—$25 each

Recycled picnic table—$125 each

Bench— $50 each

Brick pavers—$15 per sq. meter

Grass—$4 per sq. meter

Electric-powered light—$75 each

Solar-powered light—$150 each

Dog park with fence—$750 for 64 sq. meters

Dog park with green retaining wall—$1,500 for 64 sq. meters

STEP 3 **Brainstorm** Discuss what features to include in order to make the park accessible to all people, and agree on a solution to model. Consider how the parts will work together as a system.

What features will you include to make the park accessible to all people?

_____

_____

_____

_____

Make and Test

STEP 4 **Develop a model** Use the graph paper to make models, with each square representing a square meter. Show the dimensions of the park and the location of each feature. Keep track of the items, their cost, and the requirements they meet in a table similar to the one shown below.

Item	Quantity	Cost ($)	Total ($)	Justification
recycle bin	2	25	50	green feature

STEP 5 **Communicate** Choose your best model and present it to the Busyville Planning Committee—your classmates. Use their feedback to identify possible improvements to your model.

_____

_____

_____

_____

Improve and Test

STEP 6 **Develop a new model** Make your final model using the feedback from the Busyville Planning Committee.

What tradeoffs did you make in your final model in order to best meet the most design requirements?

_____

_____

_____

Make a **claim** supported by **evidence** and **reasoning** to answer the question you formed.

_____

_____

_____

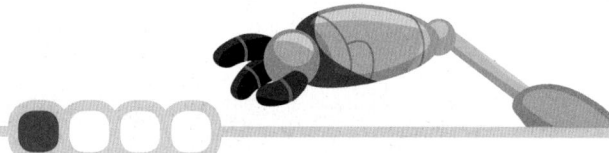

Making Sense

How does the role green spaces play in park design help you explain why people would put plants on top of buildings?

_____

_____

 Which part of this design activity was most challenging to you, and how did you cope with the challenge?

_____

Engineer It
Reusing at Home

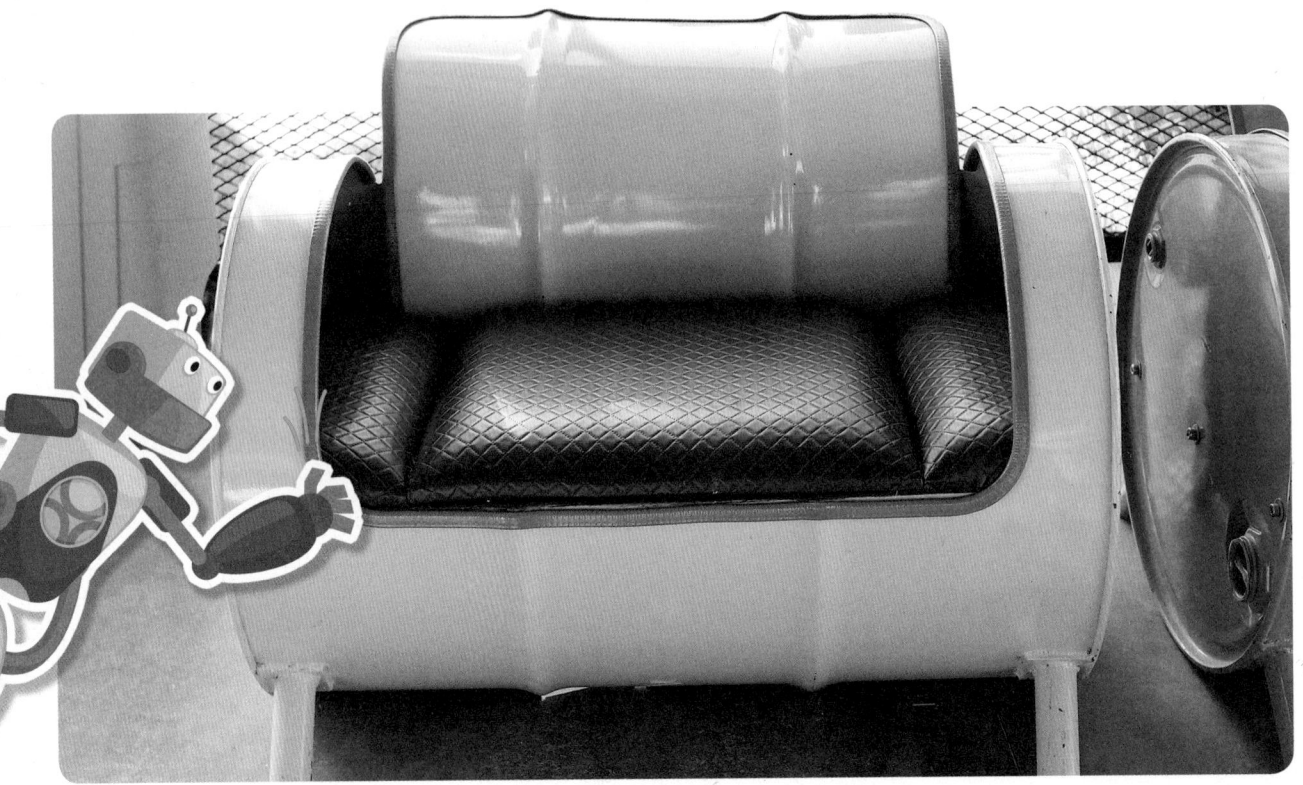

This unusual chair was made from a metal barrel that would otherwise have gone to a landfill. Many items we discard—glass, plastic, wood, metal, rubber, and paper—can be reused.

Form a question Ask a question about how materials can be reused.

_____

_____

_____

_____

Did you know?

Some steel barrels are reused as musical instruments. Parts of the barrels are hammered and shaped so that they play notes.

POSSIBLE MATERIALS

☐ household items   ☐ masking tape

☐ scissors   ☐ glue

STEP 1 **Research** Look around your home or classroom for items that are likely to be discarded. List them in the table.

Item	How can it be reused?

STEP 2 **Brainstorm** Think of ways to reuse these items to solve a problem or to meet a need.

STEP 3 Follow the engineering design steps to design a solution. If possible, get permission, and then build and test a prototype.

Analyze the data in the table and the usefulness of your solution. Make a **claim** about how materials can be reused, explain how the **evidence** supports your claim, and share your **reasoning.**

Making Sense

How does using resources in new ways help people and the environment?

Conservation's Three Rs

The "three Rs"—reduce, reuse, recycle—is a strategy people and communities use to decrease the amount of waste. The U.S. Environmental Protection Agency (EPA) has a priority approach to waste management: first reduce, then reuse, and, lastly, recycle.

Back to Basics

When we **recycle**, we use materials in old things to make new things. This can involve breaking the item down to its raw ingredients. Food scraps can be composted or made into biofuel, but they don't go in recycling bins. Read below to learn about the different items that can be recycled.

- PET (polyethylene terephthalate) plastic is used to make drinking bottles.
- Paper products range from milk cartons to newspapers.
- Soda cans, food cans, and aluminum foil/containers are made of metals.

- Glass containers for food and liquids can be clear, brown, or green.
- Polystyrene foam containers are not usually recyclable unless carefully cleaned.
- Some areas have food waste recycling collection services where you can dispose of your food scraps.

Science can only point out the effects of recycling. People choose to recycle based on their values and needs. What is one reason people might choose to recycle and one they might choose not to?

Now let's take a closer look at some of these recyclable items. Read through each description to learn more.

Paper or cardboard items are used by people every day. In fact, many of the paper items you use are probably made from recycled paper or cardboard. In the United States, almost 63% of all the paper products used are recycled.

Not all glass can be recycled, but brown, green, and clear glass can. Most glass containers made in this country are at least one-fourth recycled glass. Recycling glass conserves sand and the fossil fuels used in glass production.

What are some recyclable items that you use every day? How does recycling help the environment?

_____

_____

_____

Using Less

Categorize Look at each of the products below. Circle the items that are the best for helping to reduce waste.

a.

c.

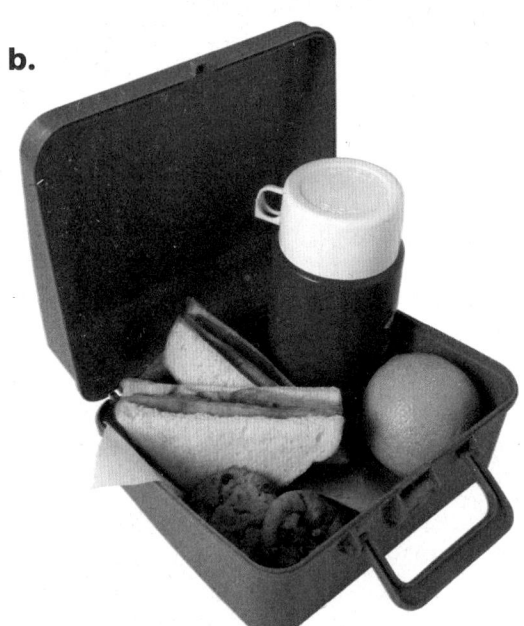

b.

d.

One way to help the environment and its resources is to reduce your use of materials. When you reduce your use of an item, you make the size, number, or amount of that item smaller. Product packaging produces a lot of waste that often ends up in landfills or burned.

Making Sense

What makes a refillable water bottle an example of green technology, like a green roof?

_____

_____

Conserve and Protect the Environment

Green technology is innovative ways of using resources to minimize human impact on the environment. One example is biodegradable food utensils that are designed to decompose in compost.

Green Technology

This is the Supertree Grove at a Singapore theme park. Each "tree" has various plants, solar electric cells, and a rainwater collector. The trees supply electricity and irrigation water for the park.

The open pattern on this building is made of a smog-eating material. The material breaks down air pollution when exposed to sunlight.

Green walls are becoming popular. These building surfaces are covered with plants. Some benefits are shade, lower noise, and cleaner air.

Research to find out about green technology used in your area. Evaluate the technology and report your findings.

Paper or Plastic Bag Debate

Have you ever gone to the grocery store with your parents and heard the checkout clerk ask, "Paper or plastic?" What do you think the difference is between using paper or plastic bags?

Prepare to debate the question, *Which is more environmentally friendly—paper bags or plastic bags*? Research the pros and cons of each. Decide which least impacts the environment

Use the table to record your claim about plastic and paper bags. Enter at least three pieces of evidence to support your claim.

Claim	Supporting evidence

Ocean animals such as sea turtles confuse discarded plastic bags with jellyfish and eat them. Dead turtles and other marine animals have been found with these bags in their stomachs. Communities have passed laws that ban the use of plastic bags. People claim the laws protect wildlife. However, others argue that plastic bags are cheap and convenient to use.

 Collaborate in a small group develop an argument for or against a plastic bag ban. Summarize your argument in the space below. Tell how your group agreed on its position.

Cities Conserving Resources

Many cities around the country are doing what they can to conserve resources. People want to conserve materials, reduce fossil fuel use, and improve energy efficiency, which involves using less energy to get the same amount of work or service from a product.

CITIES GO GREEN

Cities around the world have found creative ways to help the environment. Look at each image, and read each caption to learn more about what cities are doing to improve energy efficiency.

This Texas park has trees, a lake, and wildlife. The park uses renewable energy and was built of ecologically friendly materials.

Portugal plans to double its output of renewable energy by 2030. Now, they sometimes generate more than needed.

Separate protected lanes make bicycling a safer choice. Benefits are more physical activity and less pollution from cars.

Green rooftops help cool cities. They also lower heating and cooling costs for buildings and improve air quality.

Conservation at Home

At home, you can also conserve natural resources and help protect the environment. Look at the picture below. Consider the larger scale "green" choices you've just seen. Then tell how you could apply what you know about conservation to this room.

Making Sense

Why is green technology, such as green roofs, an example of people and the environment benefiting from using resources in new ways?

Name _____

Lesson Check

Can You Explain It?

Review your ideas from the beginning of this lesson about how people and the environment benefit from using resources in new ways. How have your ideas changed? Be sure to do the following:

- Identify an example that shows green technology protecting the environment.
- Explain how the example protects the environment.
- List some other ways in which people can protect the environment.

Now I know or think that _____

_____

_____

_____

Making Connections

Composting turns food and yard waste into fertile soil. Explain how composting is an example of green technology.

_____

_____

_____

_____

Checkpoints

1. A family wants to move to a city with lots of green technology. Which features of a city would they find more appealing? Circle the correct answer.

   a. a city that replaced one of its parks with apartments

   b. a city that is building two new landfills outside of town

   c. a city with a large community garden and a recycling program

   d. a city with a natural gas power plant and a coal power plant

2. A friend doesn't think that the Three Rs protect the planet. What would you tell them to change their mind? Where could you obtain more information to support your argument?

   _____

   _____

   _____

   _____

   _____

3. Which of the following are examples of someone practicing at least two of the "three Rs"? Circle all that apply.

   a. After using a zip-top plastic bag to store a loaf of bread, James realizes he can also use the bag to hold a bottle of sunblock and a small tube of toothpaste in his luggage for his trip.

   b. Grant decides to install a water filter on the faucet of his kitchen sink instead of spending money on 5-gallon bottles of spring water.

   c. Maria finishes using a bottle of water. She then cuts it into two halves to make small pots for growing tomato seeds. After transplanting the seedlings to a garden, she recycles the bottle halves.

   d. Hyun decides to "green" his restaurant by using washable stainless steel chopsticks instead of disposable wooden ones.

4. How is green technology helping to protect the environment? Circle all that apply.

    a. by using more renewable energy sources

    b. by using more nonrenewable energy sources

    c. by establishing extensive recycling programs

    d. by offering transit systems that run on clean energy

5. Circle all the ways to reduce the number of new small plastic water bottles being produced.

    a. Use them as planters.

    b. Put them in a recycling bin.

    c. Use a filter to purify tap water.

    d. Buy a smaller number of larger bottles of water.

6. Choose the words that correctly complete the sentences below.

> renewable   nonrenewable   environment   energy efficiency

The purpose of green technology is to keep _____

resource use at a minimum and _____

resource use at a maximum. The main reason many cities are

switching to green technology is to find ways to protect our

_____. Cities are doing what they can to improve

_____.

Unit Review

1. For each Earth system, give an example of how it can interact with the geosphere during a volcanic eruption.

Sphere	Interaction
Hydrosphere	
Atmosphere	
Biosphere	

2. If Earth is mostly water, why are people concerned with saving water in Earth's systems? Choose all that apply.

  a. Most of it is salt water.

  b. Most of the fresh water is frozen.

  c. People are adding pollutants to the water.

  d. Earth is producing less water.

3. *Runoff* is rain that flows across Earth's surface and into streams and lakes. In cities, it often carries pollution with it. Community leaders want to decrease the stream pollution from runoff by half. Currently, all of the area in the city is paved. Based on the research data in the table, how do you recommend they replace the paved areas? Be sure to support your argument with numerical evidence.

Effect of Paving on Runoff

	Natural ground	One-fourth paved	Half paved	All paved
Rain Runoff	10%	20%	30%	55%

_____

_____

_____

4. Building dams affects Earth's systems. Identify the two systems most affected and describe one interaction between them. What is a question about this you could investigate?

_____

_____

_____

5. In Ms. Hauser's class, students are learning about how Earth systems interact and affect Earth's surface materials and processes. Jaquan and his group drew the model shown here to show their understanding.

Analyze the student model. Select all the changes they can make to improve the model.

   a. Add clouds in the sky and arrows leading to them from the ocean to show how the biosphere and hydrosphere interact.

   b. Draw a beach and waves crashing on it to show a way the hydrosphere and geosphere interact.

   c. Draw an erupting volcano to show how the geosphere and the atmosphere interact.

   d. Add a river cutting through the land to show how the hydrosphere shapes the geosphere.

6. Give an example of a negative effect from gathering a natural resource and an example of a negative effect from using a natural resource. Why do people still choose to use these resources, given the negative effects? What information could you collect to support an argument for your answer?

_____

_____

_____

_____

7. Savannah's class surveys students at her school and finds that 75% of them walk to school, recycling bins are in every classroom, and the school participates in a water conservation program.

Based on the findings, which does Savannah's school need to focus on **most** to be more "green"?

   a. putting two or more recycle bins in each classroom

   b. limiting the amount of water used by each student

   c. trying to get more students to take the bus

   d. rewarding use of refillable water bottles

8. Write the human activities in the table columns based on their effect on the environment. Some items may appear in both columns. Add an example of data you could gather to support one of your choices.

- farming
- green roofs
- dams
- recycle bins

Positive	Negative

9. Draw and label a model to show how the ocean can interact with a landform to form a system of rainy and dry areas.

10. Engineers are making a system to gather and clean water for an island city. One prototype uses ocean water, and the other uses stream water. How can they determine which prototype best solves the problem? What might cause them to choose one over the other?

In Unit 5, you used models and computational thinking to describe and explain patterns in Earth systems. In this unit, you will analyze data to describe patterns on Earth and in the sky over the course of a day, a month, and a year, and explain how the sun compares with other stars.

UNIT 6 Patterns in the Sky

LESSON 1
Gravity Affects Matter on Earth

Things look different from up here!

© Houghton Mifflin Harcourt Publishing Company • Image Credits: ©freefly/Adobe Stock

What do you notice about Earth's shape and the skydivers?

I notice _____

_____

_____

_____

What do you wonder about the cause of the skydivers' motion?

I wonder _____

_____

_____

_____

Can You Explain It?

Why do the skydivers fall to Earth and not fall away from Earth's curved surface? Sketch, write, or model your answer.

An Ant's View of the World

Even though Earth is round, it looks flat to people standing on its surface. For example, the horizon in a vast open area appears to be a straight line. It is difficult to tell that Earth is round.

Form a question Ask a question about the fact that Earth's surface appears flat to people who are standing on the ground.

> **Did you know?**
>
> The diameter of Earth at the equator is about 12,800 km (7,900 mi).

_____

_____

_____

STEP 1   **Model** Hold the small ball 15 cm (about 6 in.) from your face, and observe its shape. Keeping your head still, notice what you can see above, below, and to the sides of the ball.

Repeat Step 1 with the other two balls. Sketch what you see in the boxes below.

POSSIBLE MATERIALS

☐ balls, small, medium, and large

Apply Now imagine an ant on a large ball. As it looks across the ball, what does it see? Would it know that it is on a huge ball?

_____

_____

Explain Write in the missing cause or effect.

Cause	Effect
	I could see the whole round shape.
The ball was large.	

Make a **claim** about why Earth's surface appears flat from the ground. Support your claim with **evidence**, and explain your **reasoning**.

_____

_____

Making Sense

As the skydivers fall, how does Earth's shape appear to change?

_____

_____

HANDS-ON ACTIVITY

A Trip around the World

Auckland, New Zealand, and Seville, Spain, are antipodes, or opposite points on Earth's surface that can be connected by a straight line through Earth's center. People living in both places experience the ground as being down and the sky as being up because gravity pulls objects on Earth's surface toward its center.

Form a question Ask a question about how people on different sides of Earth experience the direction of the ground and the sky.

> **Did you know?**
>
> There is no place in North America where a path through the center of Earth would end in China.

© Houghton Mifflin Harcourt Publishing Company • Image Credits: (l) ©Rafael Ben-Ari/Adobe Stock; (r) ©lleandralacuerva/Adobe Stock

POSSIBLE MATERIALS

- [ ] clear inflatable globe with labeled continents and compass rose
- [ ] small plastic figures
- [ ] transparent tape

STEP 1   Inflate the globe.

STEP 2   Tape at least one standing figure to each of the seven continents on the globe: North America, South America, Europe, Asia, Africa, Australia, and Antarctica.

STEP 3   Hold the globe in front of your face. The North Pole should be at the top, and the South Pole should be at the bottom. Turn the globe so you are looking at the figure you placed on North America. Then, look through the center of the globe and toward the figure you placed on Africa.

How would you describe the figure's position?

_____

_____

_____

_____

_____

_____

STEP 4   Place your eyes near the feet of one of the figures. Look across the surface of the globe, as though you are that figure.

Can you see the other figures? What parts of their bodies are closest to you?

_____

_____

STEP 5   Hold the globe away from you with the North Pole on top and the South Pole on the bottom. Look at the figure that is taped to Australia.

How would you describe the position of the figure on Australia?

_____

_____

STEP 6   Hold the globe away from you with the North Pole on top and the South Pole on the bottom. Describe the figures that are standing on the continents in the Southern Hemisphere—that is, those on the southern half of the globe.

_____

_____

What is causing different figures to appear upside down?

_____

_____

Do you think Earth really has a top or bottom? Why?

_____

STEP 7 Flip the globe so that the figure in Australia is upright. Look through the globe from the view of the Australian person. How does the figure in North America look?

_____

Draw conclusions Which way does the force of gravity pull, and how was the tape used in this activity to mimic the force of gravity?

_____

_____

Some of the figures in your model appeared sideways or upside down to you, but people always feel upright no matter where they are standing on Earth's surface. Make a **claim** explaining why this is true. Use **evidence** from this activity to support your argument and explain your **reasoning.**

_____

_____

_____

 What other questions do you have about the similar and different experiences of people living all over the world?

_____

_____

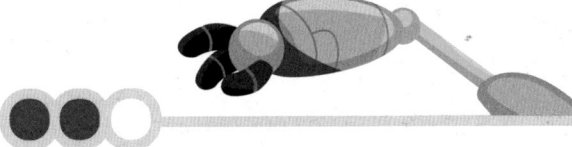

Making Sense

Based on your investigation, would you say that skydiving is a similar experience at different locations on Earth? Explain.

_____

_____

An Attractive Sphere

We have all seen images of a round Earth from space. Are there ways to tell that the surface of Earth is curved while standing on it? The images below show some evidence that can be used to prove Earth's shape.

The View from Above

Study the pictures, then answer the questions.

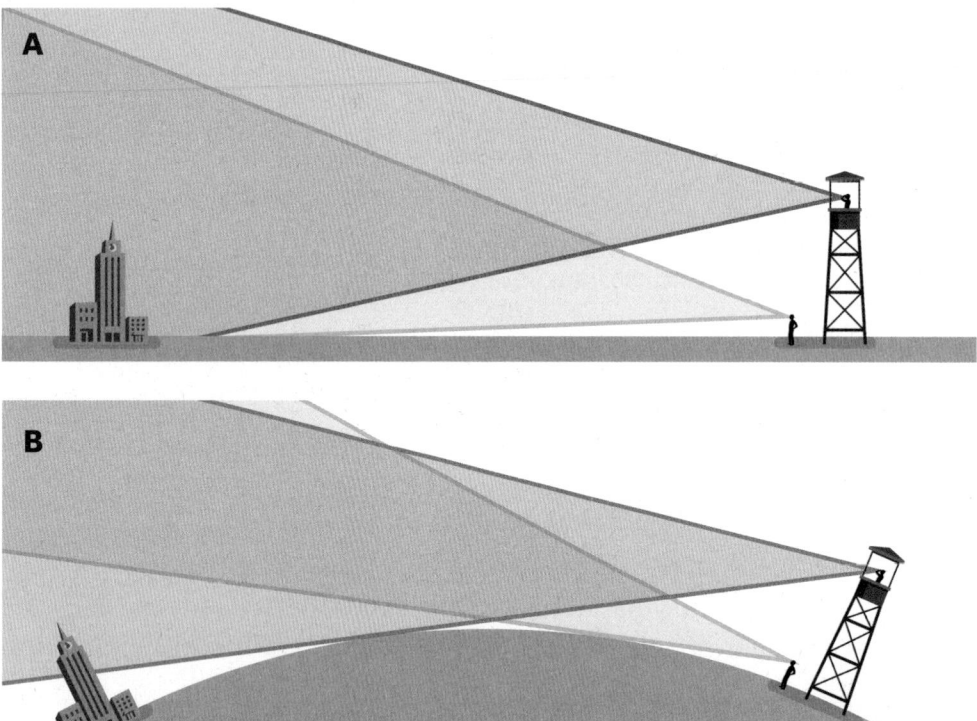

a. Look at the top image, labeled A. Compare what the person on the tower and the person on the ground can see.

_____

_____

b. Look at the bottom image, labeled B. Compare what the person on the tower and the person on the ground can see.

_____

_____

One piece of evidence that Earth is round is that you can see more of Earth's surface when you climb up high. Is there more evidence?

The images below show what you would see if you saw a ship approach land from the horizon, the area where the sea and sky appear to meet. Why does the entire ship appear as though it's rising from under the water?

The model above shows what you would see at the beach if a real ship was sailing toward you. Compare the two images below. Which one supports the model above? Use these images to support the argument that Earth is a sphere.

_____

_____

_____

_____

© Houghton Mifflin Harcourt Publishing Company

Earth's Shape and Gravity

You probably already have some ideas about gravity. **Gravity** is a force that attracts all objects in the universe toward one another. How exactly does gravity affect objects on Earth?

Study the illustration below to explore what happens to objects on different places on Earth. Draw arrows to show which direction the pizza dough will drop when the man throws the dough into the air.

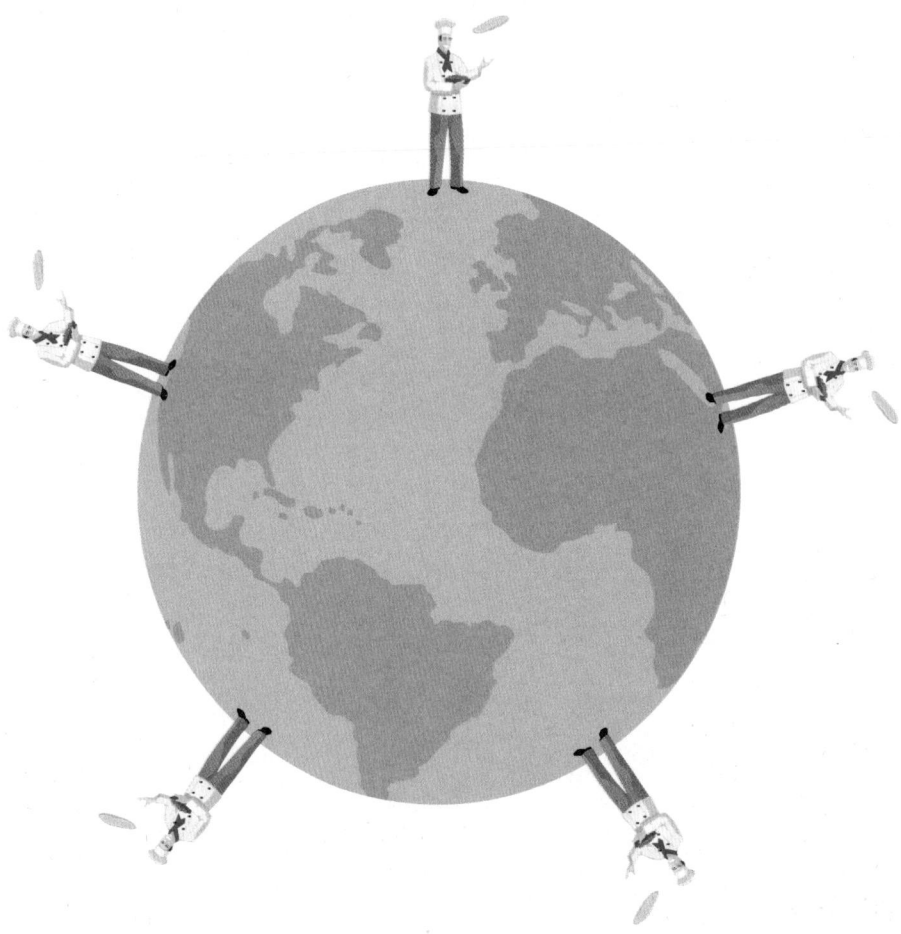

Explain why you drew the arrows the way you did. What do you already know about gravity that made you draw the arrows this way?

_____

_____

_____

_____

Does location affect the direction of gravity? No matter what hemisphere, or half, of Earth you live on, gravity is pulling down on you. Use the photos to discuss the questions below with your classmates.

These penguins are located in Antarctica. Why don't they fall off Earth's surface? Explain your answer.

These people are located in Australia. If one of them dropped his or her phone, which way would it fall? Explain your answer.

These falls are located in New York and Ontario, Canada. Why doesn't water flow uphill? Explain your answer.

How does gravity affect you?

_____

_____

What is meant when someone says that an object "falls down"?

_____

_____

Playing Ball

We know that no matter where you are on Earth, all things fall down toward Earth's surface. But is that where gravity stops? Have you ever dug a hole and dropped something into it? If you have, you know that the object would continue to fall down until it reaches the bottom. That is because gravity pulls all matter toward the center of our planet.

Analyze Look at the photo of the boy about to catch the soccer ball that his friend has just thrown. How will the soccer ball move? Does your answer depend on any assumptions about where on Earth the boy is playing?

 Reflect on the evidence you have collected for Earth's shape and the pull of gravity. Assess whether you have enough evidence to make and support a claim about why the skydivers won't fall away from Earth's curved surface. Work with your teacher to make a plan to gather any additional evidence you feel you need.

Making Sense

What does your evidence for Earth's shape and the pull of gravity tell you about the path of the skydivers?

Lesson Check

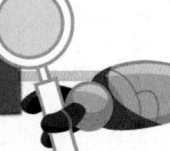

Can You Explain It?

Review your ideas from the beginning of this lesson explaining why skydivers do not fall away from Earth's surface as they fall through the air. How have your ideas changed?

Be sure to do the following:

- Identify the force that keeps everything on Earth's surface.
- Explain why people on opposite sides of the globe do not feel upside down or sideways.
- Describe what it means for an object to fall down.

Now I know or think that _____

_____

_____

_____

_____

_____

Making Connections

Scientific satellites and communications satellites move in curved paths around Earth, called *orbits*. Based on what you have learned about the skydivers, why don't satellites fly away from Earth?

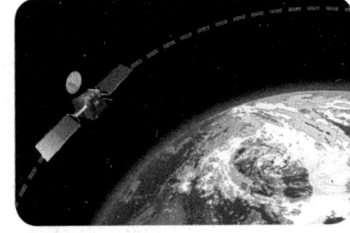

_____

_____

_____

Checkpoints

1. Which of the following observable patterns could be used as evidence to argue that Earth is a sphere? Choose all that apply.

   a. Higher elevations allow you to see around the curve of Earth's horizon.

   b. You see only the top part of a ship as it sails over the horizon.

   c. The sun and stars travel across the sky from east to west.

2. Objects on Earth fall toward its center. What causes this? Choose the correct answer.

   a. Earth's shape   **c.** Earth's size

   b. gravity   **d.** pressure

3. Choose the correct phrase to complete the sentences.

to the right	away from Earth's center
to the left	toward Earth's center

   The most accurate way to explain what a downward direction

   means is to say that "down" is the direction _____.

   The most accurate way to explain what an upward direction means

   is to say that "up" is the direction _____.

4. You and a student in Australia each have a tennis ball, which you both drop from a height of 1 m. Make a claim about what each of you will observe, and support your claim with patterns from the lesson.

   _____

   _____

© Houghton Mifflin Harcourt Publishing Company

5. Explain what causes the round Earth to appear flat to people standing on its surface. Support your claim with evidence.

_____

_____

_____

6. Which image correctly shows a model of Earth and the direction of the force of gravity in the Earth system?

1.

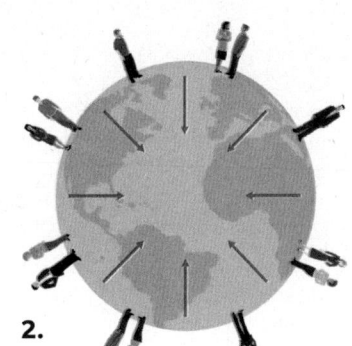
2.

3.

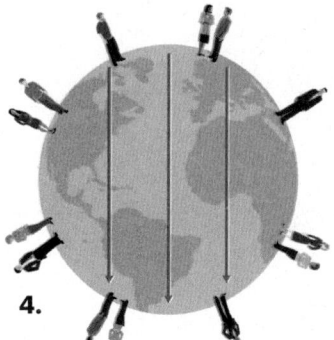
4.

7. Explain how gravity affects people in different parts of the world, using the model you selected to support your explanation.

_____

_____

8. Which of the following are true statements you could use to construct an explanation about gravity? Select all that apply.

a. Gravity is a force.

b. Gravity affects all matter on Earth.

c. There is no gravity in the Southern Hemisphere.

d. Gravity is caused by air pushing down on things.

Sky Patterns over Time

What do you notice about the sunset?

I notice _____

_____

_____

_____

What do you wonder about the time that the sun sets? How might Earth's
shape relate to the sun set?

I wonder _____

_____

_____

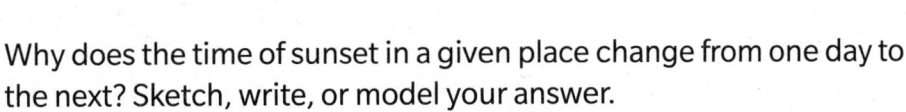

Can You Explain It?

Why does the time of sunset in a given place change from one day to
the next? Sketch, write, or model your answer.

Shadows

A shadow forms when an object blocks light from hitting a surface. Shadows can vary in length, shape, darkness, and other ways. A single object can cast shadows with different characteristics. With the right lighting, these students can cast shadows much longer than they are tall.

Form a question   Ask a question about how shadows from sunlight change throughout the day.

Did you know?

Solar eclipses involve huge shadows. The moon blocks the sun's light from hitting Earth!

© Houghton Mifflin Harcourt Publishing Company • Image Credits:
©Zurijeta/Shutterstock

POSSIBLE MATERIALS

☐ new pencil or dowel   ☐ metric ruler   ☐ other objects you need to complete your plan

☐ modeling clay   ☐ marker

☐ posterboard

Look!

STEP 1

With your class, select the most important questions about shadows. Write down the questions here.

_____

_____

_____

STEP 2

How can you investigate the questions your class chose as most important?

Think about the materials your teacher provides and what else you might need. Write your plan and show it to your teacher to see if you can get the other things you need. If you use objects other than those provided by your teacher, be sure to include them in the list above.

_____

_____

_____

_____

_____

Carry out your plan, and record your results. Present your data in a way that helps everyone see what you did and what happened. You might use a table, a graph, or a sketch as a presentation tool, or you might choose to make a poster with photographs.

What patterns did you notice in your data?

_____

_____

_____

Compare and contrast your results with the results of other groups.

_____

_____

_____

Draw conclusions Make a **claim** that answers the question or questions your class decided to explore. You may need to have a claim for each question. Support your claim with **evidence** from your investigation, and use **reasoning** to explain how the evidence supports your claim.

_____

_____

_____

 Reflect on how your team worked together to carry out your investigation. Discuss one positive way each member of the group contributed their skills and strengths to help the team.

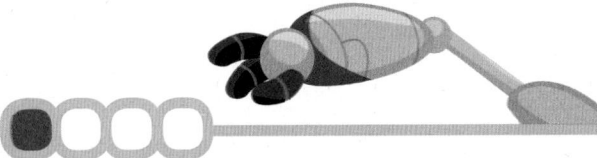

Making Sense

What caused shadows to change throughout the day? How could this be related to the sunset?

_____

_____

_____

HANDS-ON ACTIVITY

The Night Moves

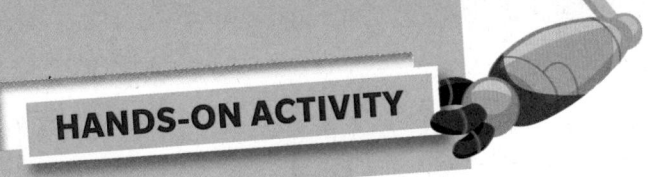

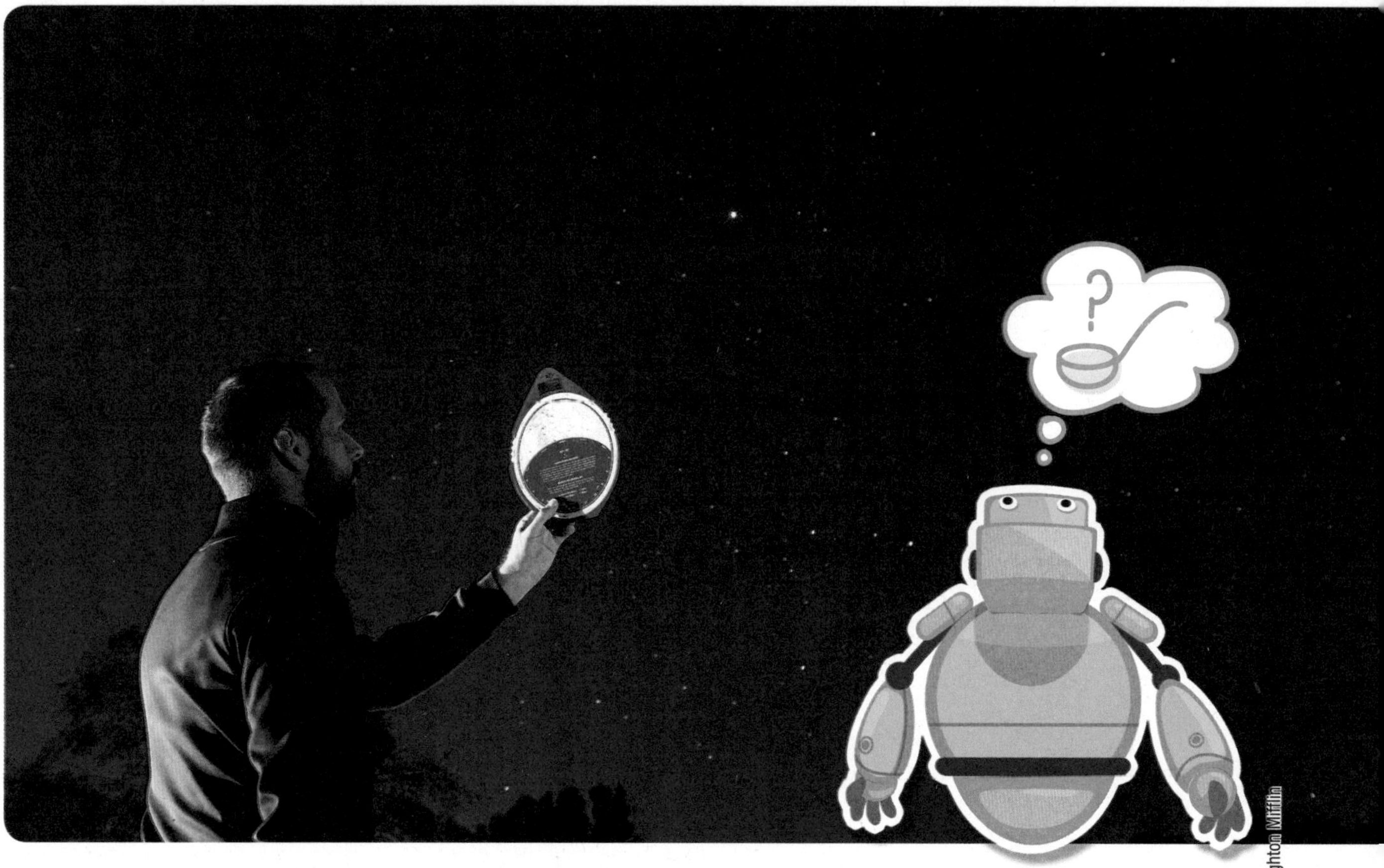

Some groups of stars, called **constellations,** appear to make patterns in the night sky. Your teacher will have placed a model of the sun in the middle of the room and posted names or images of constellations around the room. Imagine that your head is Earth and that it is nighttime when your back is to the sun and you can see the constellations. Explore a pattern in the sky caused by Earth's motion.

Did you know?

Astronomers officially recognize 88 constellations.

Form a question Ask a question about how Earth's motion relates to which constellations are visible.

STEP 1 Stand in front of the sun model with your back to it. You are modeling Earth at night during a given time of year. Record your observations of the constellations you see in front of you.

STEP 2 Revolve one-quarter of the way around the sun in a counterclockwise direction, keeping the sun at your back. This position represents Earth at a different time of year. Record your observations of the constellations. Repeat Step 2 two more times until you are back to your starting position, making sure to always keep the sun at your back and to record your observations.

STEP 3 At your starting position, rotate counterclockwise to model Earth's rotation. Record your observations, and be ready to explain how this motion changes your view of the sky.

Make a **claim** about why different stars are visible during different times of the year. Cite **evidence** to support your claim, and explain your **reasoning**.

Making Sense

What patterns can be explained by Earth's revolution around the sun?

Objects in the Sky

The Moving Sun

Each day, the sun appears to rise in the east and set in the west. What other daily patterns in the sun's motion can be observed?

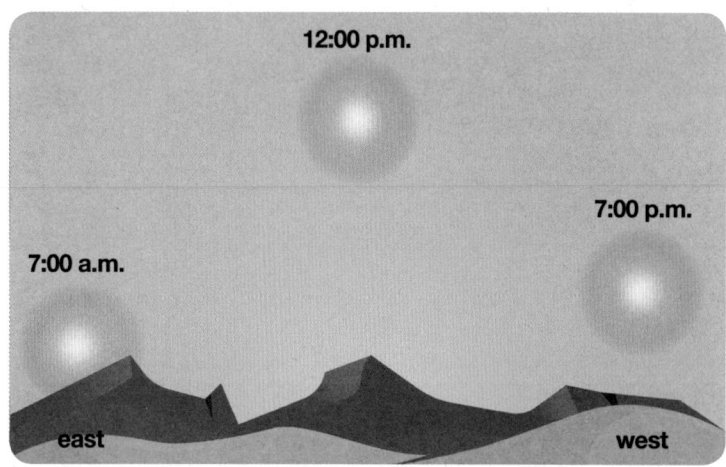

The sun's position in the sky above Earth's surface, or its altitude, can be measured in degrees.

Study the graph below. It shows the sun's altitude for two days in late May, as seen from a city in the United States. Then, answer the question.

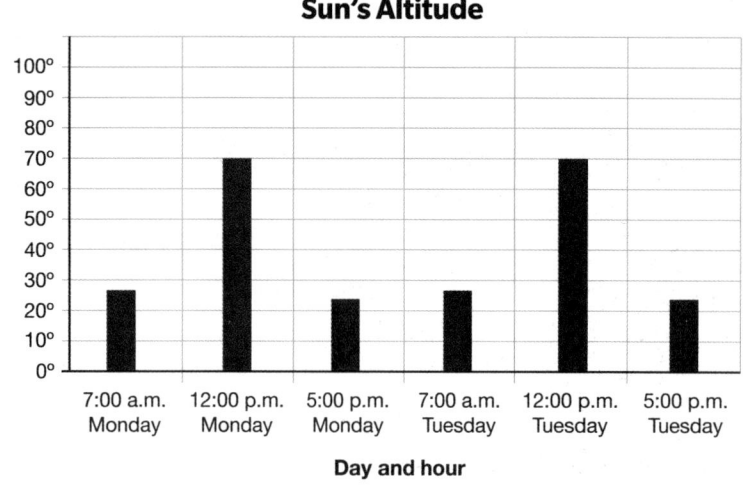

Analyze What patterns do you see in the graph?

The Night Sky

On a clear night, you can see many constellations in the night sky. Like the sun, many stars appear to move across the sky from east to west. Let's camp out overnight to see if the positions of constellations change within one night.

These images show how the night sky changed overnight from Friday to Saturday. Answer the questions under the images.

Friday 10:00 p.m.

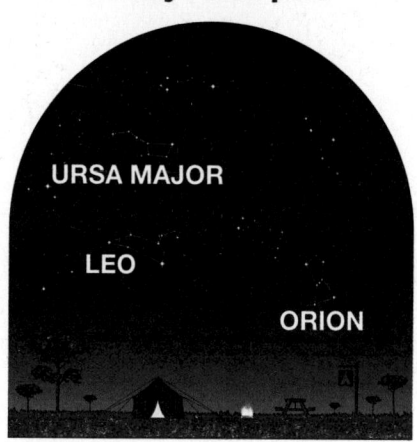

a. What do you notice about the position of the stars?

Saturday 12:00 a.m.

b. How did the stars change?

Saturday 2:00 a.m.

c. What patterns do you see?

Saturday 4:00 a.m.

d. How has Orion changed this night?

Your Turn

Draw a diagram to model and explain your understanding of why the sun and stars appear to change position over the course of 24 hours. Include Earth, the sun, and stars in your diagram.

As the World Turns

Gabriella lives in the United States and has just finished school. She decides to call some of her friends who live all over the world.

Read the following comments that describe Gabriella's phone calls to her friends to discover an effect of Earth's rotation.

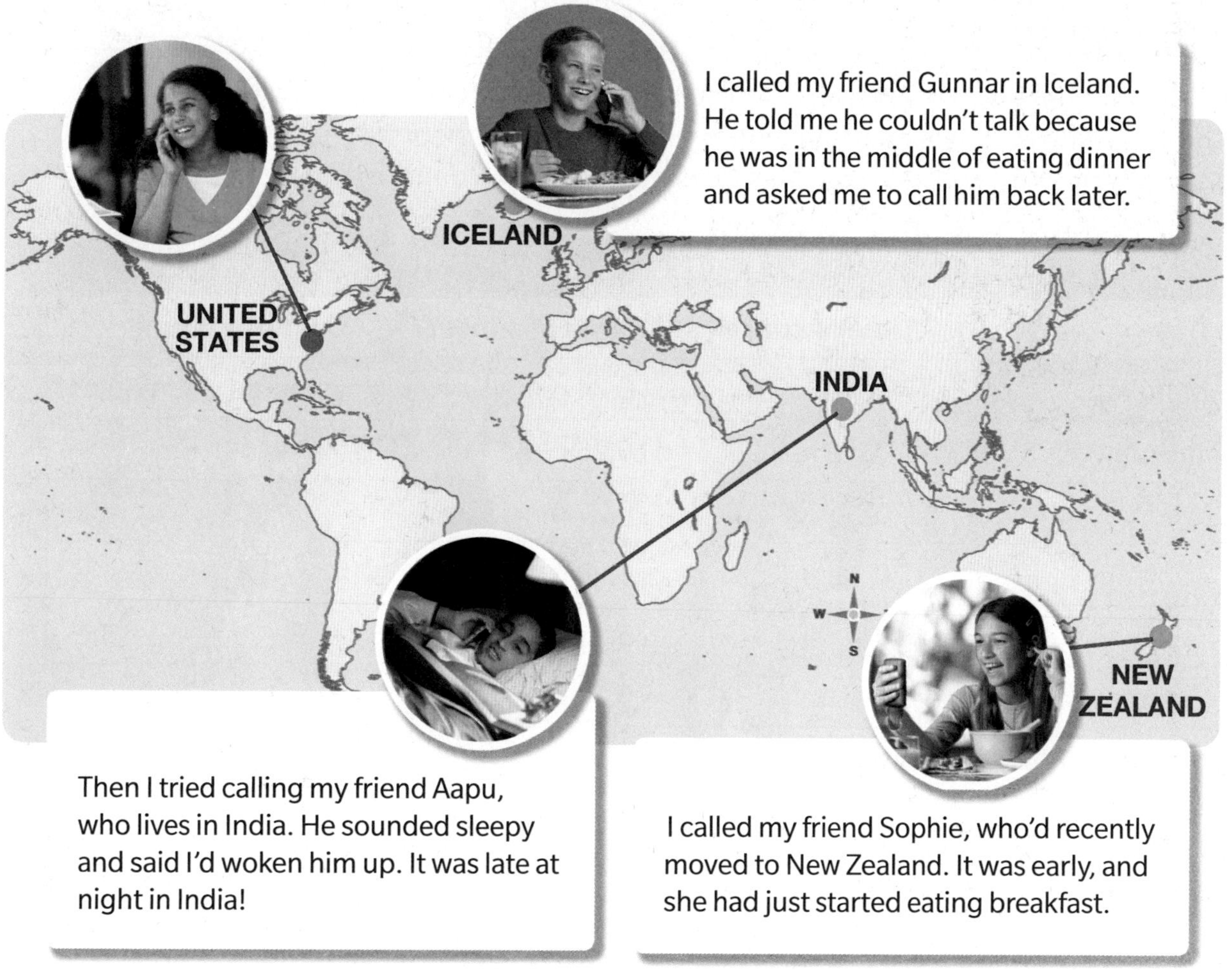

I called my friend Gunnar in Iceland. He told me he couldn't talk because he was in the middle of eating dinner and asked me to call him back later.

ICELAND

UNITED STATES

INDIA

NEW ZEALAND

Then I tried calling my friend Aapu, who lives in India. He sounded sleepy and said I'd woken him up. It was late at night in India!

I called my friend Sophie, who'd recently moved to New Zealand. It was early, and she had just started eating breakfast.

Compare Identify the time of day in each place that Gabriella calls.

_____

_____

_____

Infer Why do you think the time of day is different in each place?

_____

_____

_____

 **Turn and Talk** How would a friendship with someone far away in another country be similar to and different from a friendship with someone who goes to your school?

Daylight

Look at the table. It shows times of sunrise and sunset for a location over the course of one week. Calculate the number of daylight hours for each day. Then look for patterns. The first calculation has been done for you.

Hours of Daylight			
Day	**Time of sunrise**	**Time of sunset**	**Daylight hours**
Monday	7:05 a.m.	6:24 p.m.	11 hours, 19 minutes
Tuesday	7:03 a.m.	6:25 p.m.	
Wednesday	7:02 a.m.	6:27 p.m.	
Thursday	7:00 a.m.	6:28 p.m.	
Friday	6:58 a.m.	6:29 p.m.	
Saturday	6.57 a.m.	6:31 p.m.	
Sunday	6:55 a.m.	6:32 p.m.	

Use your data to make a bar graph to reveal patterns of daily changes at this location for one week. Label the graph's axes and give it a title.

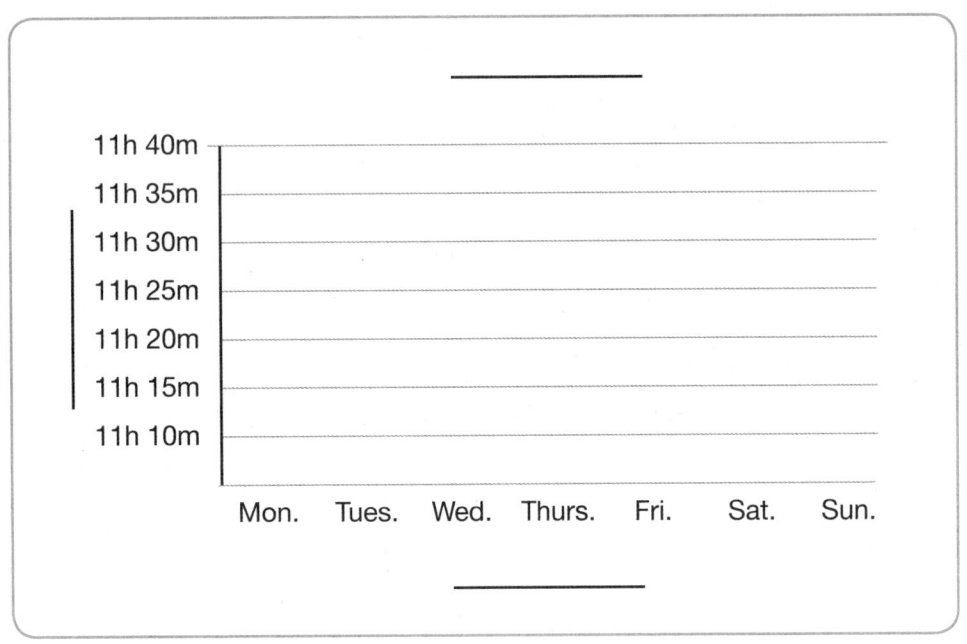

If this pattern continues, I predict that there will be _____ nighttime hours in the coming days.

History of Telling Time

Did you know that ancient people kept track of time using shadows cast by the sun? Study the images to see how technology engineered to tell time has improved throughout history.

A **sundial** may be the oldest means of telling time. The stick's shadow is long in the morning, shortest at noon, and lengthens towards sunset. Most sundials have hours marked on the disk.

An **hourglass** has two bulbs connected by a narrow neck. Grains of sand trickle through the neck at a known rate. When all the sand has moved to the bottom, an hour has passed.

Mechanical clocks were invented in the late 1300s. They used weights to mark each hour with a bell ring. Later clocks had hour and minute hands, making it easier to tell time.

The first **atomic clock** was invented in 1949. These clocks are so accurate that it would take 300 million years before the time would be incorrect by one second.

Around We Go

Look at the two images. The person represents your position in space at the given time. As Earth rotates, your view changes.

6:45 p.m.

3:00 a.m.

Identify Choose the correct words to complete each sentence.

Earth's _____ causes the _____ to appear to rise in the east in the morning, move across the sky, and set in the west in the late afternoon. Earth's movement also causes the stars to appear to _____ from the east to the west each night. The same Earth movement also causes _____ and night .

| rotation |
| be still |
| move |
| day |
| moon |
| shape |
| sun |

Making Sense

How do observable patterns in the sky relate to how Earth moves in space?

_____

_____

_____

_____

© Houghton Mifflin Harcourt Publishing Company

What Patterns Do the Sun and Moon Cause During the Year?

Round and Round

Each year, Earth makes one complete orbit around the sun. Earth is not the only object orbiting the sun in space. All of the objects in the solar system orbit the sun. Some planets also have moons orbiting them.

The moon is a natural satellite of Earth. It takes the moon about a month to make one **orbit** around Earth. An orbit is the path of one object in space around another.

Earth orbits the sun in an almost perfect circle. This movement of Earth one time around the sun is called a **revolution**. It takes about 365 days for Earth to make one revolution around the sun. Our year is based on this movement of Earth.

Explain What patterns do you think are caused by the revolutions of Earth and the moon?

_____

_____

_____

_____

_____

Moon Shapes

Have you ever seen a full moon? How about a crescent moon early in the morning? Each month, the moon goes through phases, or changes in its appearance as seen from Earth. Look at the sequence of moon phases observed in August. Look for a pattern as you study these phases.

Model Fill in the missing moon phases in the September calendar by drawing moons of the correct shape.

Describe What patterns in phases did you observe using the calendars?

Revolution and Patterns

The moon's phases are patterns of light and darkness caused by the moon's revolution around Earth. What patterns are caused by Earth's revolution around the sun? View the images below to see one effect of Earth's revolution on the day sky in the Northern Hemisphere.

Look at the sun's position in the sky during different seasons, as seen from the same spot. Note the time and month.

This also shows the sun's position in the midday sky during the same months. Note that this shows a different year.

Chart the Sun

Interpret the information from the images. Then, construct a graph of the sun's noon position above the horizon during the observed time periods.

Sun's Position at 12:00 p.m.

Position

High ———————————————————————

Medium ———————————————————————

Low ———————————————————————

| January year 1 | April year 1 | July year 1 | October year 1 | January year 2 | April year 2 | July year 2 | October year 2 |

Dates

Shifting Stars

Earth's revolution affects how we view the sun's position in the sky. How does it affect our view of the stars at night? Study the images below to explore a pattern in the position of stars as Earth revolves around the sun. Discuss the questions below with a classmate.

10:00 p.m.

On a **summer** night, you see these constellations in the night sky from a given spot on Earth. Which constellations can you see?

....

10:00 p.m.

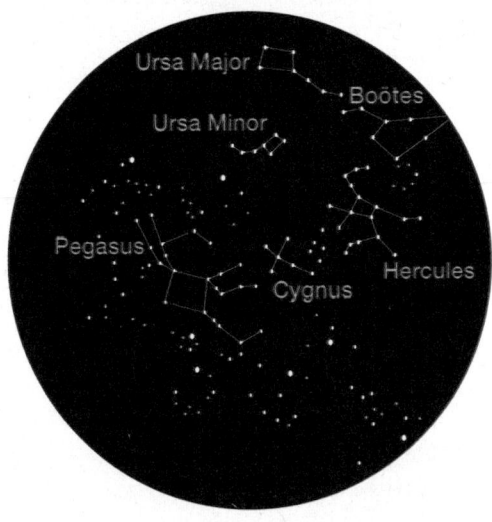

On a **fall** night, you see these constellations in the night sky from the same spot on Earth. How has Hercules changed from the summer view?

....

10:00 p.m.

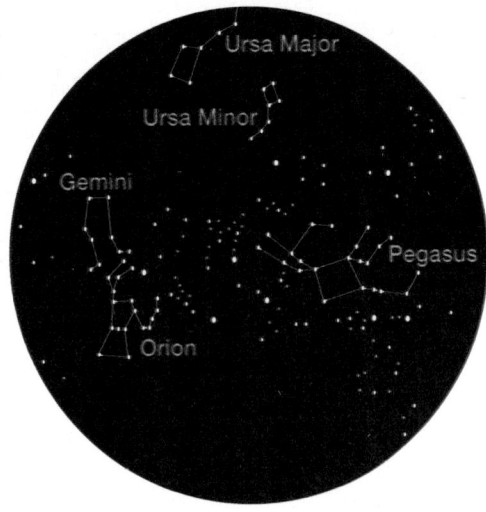

On a **winter** night, you see these constellations in the night sky from the same spot on Earth. Again, the night sky features some different constellations. How has Ursa Minor changed?

....

10:00 p.m.

On a **spring** night, you see these constellations in the night sky from the same spot on Earth. Once again, the night sky looks different. Can you see Pegasus? What do you think happened?

....

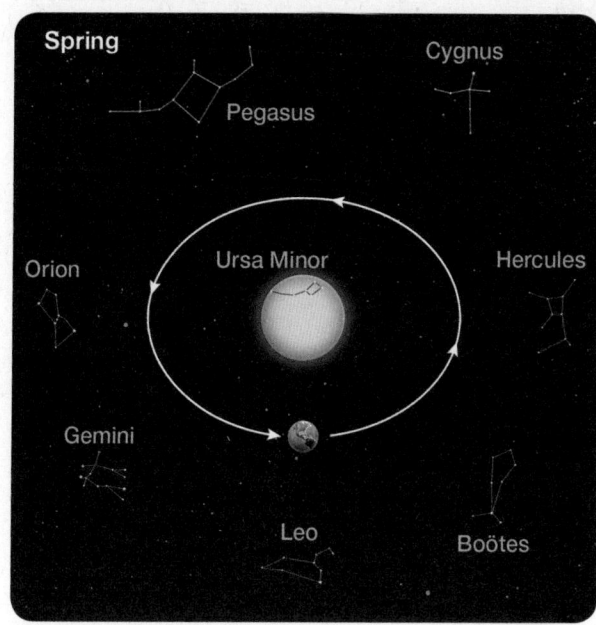

Spring

Cygnus

Pegasus

Orion

Ursa Minor

Hercules

Gemini

Leo

Boötes

Analyze Look back at the spring image on the previous page and take note of the constellations in the sky. Then, look at this star map that shows Earth's location in the spring. (The model is not to scale.) Circle the following: Earth and Pegasus. Explain why you can't see Pegasus in the spring.

_____

_____

_____

Changing Constellations

How do your observations of the constellations change with the seasons? Using the night images on the previous page, complete the data chart to record your observations. Write a large X if you see the constellations during the season. Leave a space blank if you do not see the constellation in that season.

	Summer	Fall	Winter	Spring
Orion				
Gemini				
Leo				
Ursa Minor				
Pegasus				
Hercules				
Boötes				
Cygnus				

Explain Which pair of constellations is visible in winter?

a. Orion and Leo   **b.** Gemini and Hercules

c. Ursa Minor and Boötes   **d.** Cygnus and Pegasus

Campus Constellations

Suppose you attend a school similar to one in this image. How is your ability to see different parts of your campus affected by your position? You are not able to see certain things depending on your location and orientation—the direction you are facing. This model can help you understand why we see different stars in different seasons.

Model Make a model to explain how the motions of Earth and the moon around the sun in space cause specific patterns in the sky. Select a daily, monthly, or yearly pattern to be the focus of your model.

Making Sense

How does evidence for yearly patterns in the sky help you explain why the sun sets at different times from one day to the next?

_____

_____

_____

_____

Name _____

Can You Explain It?

Review your response from the beginning of this lesson explaining why the sun sets at different times each day. How have your ideas changed? Write your answer below. Be sure to do the following:

- Relate Earth's rotation to the apparent movement of the sun.
- Describe how the angle of the sun changes throughout the day.
- Explain how the changing angle of the sun affects shadows.

Now I know or think that _____

_____

_____

_____

_____

Making Connections

At some times of year, the sun is already up when this family walks to the school bus. At others, the sun is just rising. Based on what you learned about the varying time of sunset, why does the time the sun rises change from one day to the next?

_____

_____

_____

Checkpoints

1. The drawings show the sun at different times of day. Write the time shown below each picture: 1:00 p.m., 7:00 p.m., or 6:00 a.m.

_____ _____ _____

2. Make a bar graph to show the pattern in the sun's altitude in the sky. You can use "low" and "high" to represent the sun's altitude on the y-axis, based on the data in the model above. Your graph should show the position of the sun at 6:00 a.m., 1:00 p.m., and 7:00 p.m. each day for three days.

3. The model shows the position of an observer on Earth at 3:00 a.m. What is likely to happen to that position in five hours?

   a. It will remain stationary.

   b. It will rotate and face the sun.

   c. It will rotate and face away from the sun.

3:00 a.m.

4. The images show the night sky at a given location in summer (top) and winter (bottom). Which of the following statements is the most accurate explanation of why the night sky changes?

a. Because Earth revolves around the sun, Earth is in different positions each season. In summer, Earth is on one side of the sun, and then in winter, it is on the opposite side. This affects what can be seen in the night sky.

b. Because Earth revolves around the sun, on some nights the sky is visible in one direction, and the next night it's in the other direction. It's just random that the two images are different.

c. The rotation, or spin, of Earth means that the sky always looks different from month to month. It is hard to predict which constellations can be seen each season.

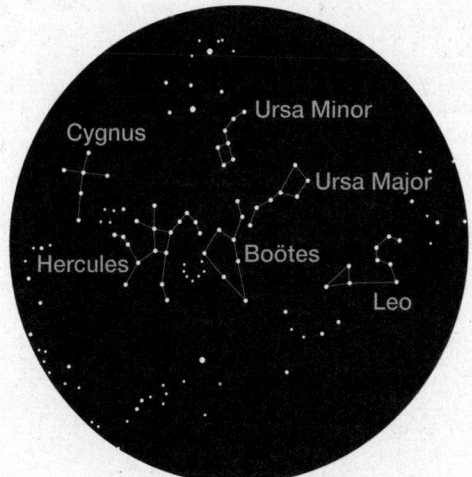

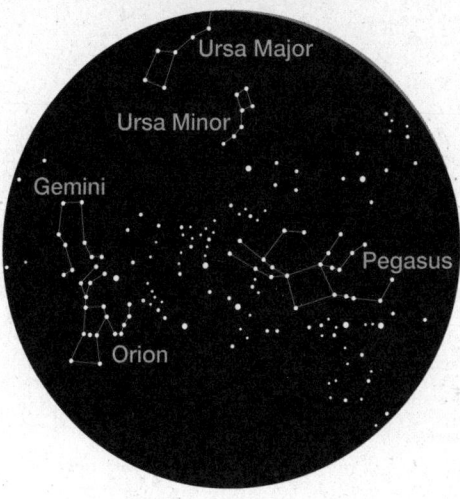

5. Choose the correct words to complete the sentences.

| sun   moon   day   month   180   365 |

Earth revolves around the _____

in a circular path. It takes about _____

days for Earth to make one revolution around the sun. The

_____ revolves around Earth. It takes about one

_____ to complete one revolution around Earth.

6. A student measures the length of a shadow at three different times during the day. She forgets to record her measurements in her data chart. Think back to the data you collected about shadow patterns to help her fill in the correct measurements.

| 2.1 meters   0.2 meters   4.0 meters |

Hour	8:00 a.m.	10:00 a.m.	12:00 p.m.
Shadow length			

LESSON 3

The Sun

Need some more light?

What do you notice about how this student is reading outdoors?

I notice _____

_____

_____

What do you wonder about why this student is using a light to read? How might Earth's shape relate to when we have light and when we don't?

I wonder _____

_____

_____

_____

Can You Explain It?

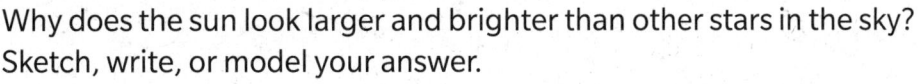

Why does the sun look larger and brighter than other stars in the sky? Sketch, write, or model your answer.

Glowing Light

We see stars because they produce light. The sun is a star, and we can see the sun because of the light it produces. The light from the sun helps us see many other objects that reflect the sun's light. What factors do you think affect a star's brightness?

Did you know?

Light from the sun takes about 8 minutes to reach Earth.

Form a question Ask a question about why the sun looks brighter than other stars in the sky.

As you work through the activity, use a table like the one below to record your observations.

Step	Observations	Why did this happen?	How is this similar to stars?
Step 1: Size			
Step 2: Distance			
Step 3: Temperature			

STEP 1   Activate one large and one small glow stick. When your teacher turns off the lights, record your observations.

STEP 2   Activate two small glow sticks. Place one close to you and one far away from you. Again, record your observations.

STEP 3   Fill the three cups with water: one cold, one room temperature, and one warm. Place a small glow stick in each cup of water. When your teacher turns off the lights, record your observations.

POSSIBLE MATERIALS

☐ 4 glow sticks (one large and three small)

☐ water

☐ cups

☐ thermometers

Draw conclusions   Write a **claim** about your investigation using **evidence** to support it. Then, explain your **reasoning**.

_____

_____

_____

Apply   To compare the brightness of stars, scientists determine what stars would look like if they were all at the same distance from Earth. What properties of a star would not change if all were the same distance away?

_____

_____

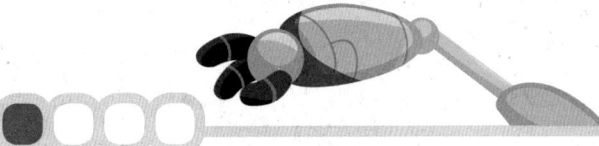

Making Sense

Based on your investigation, what might be true about the sun that would make it appear much brighter than other stars?

_____

_____

HANDS-ON ACTIVITY

Color Provides the Final Clue

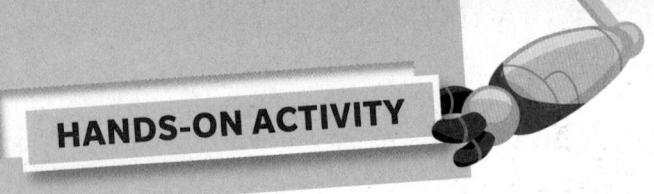

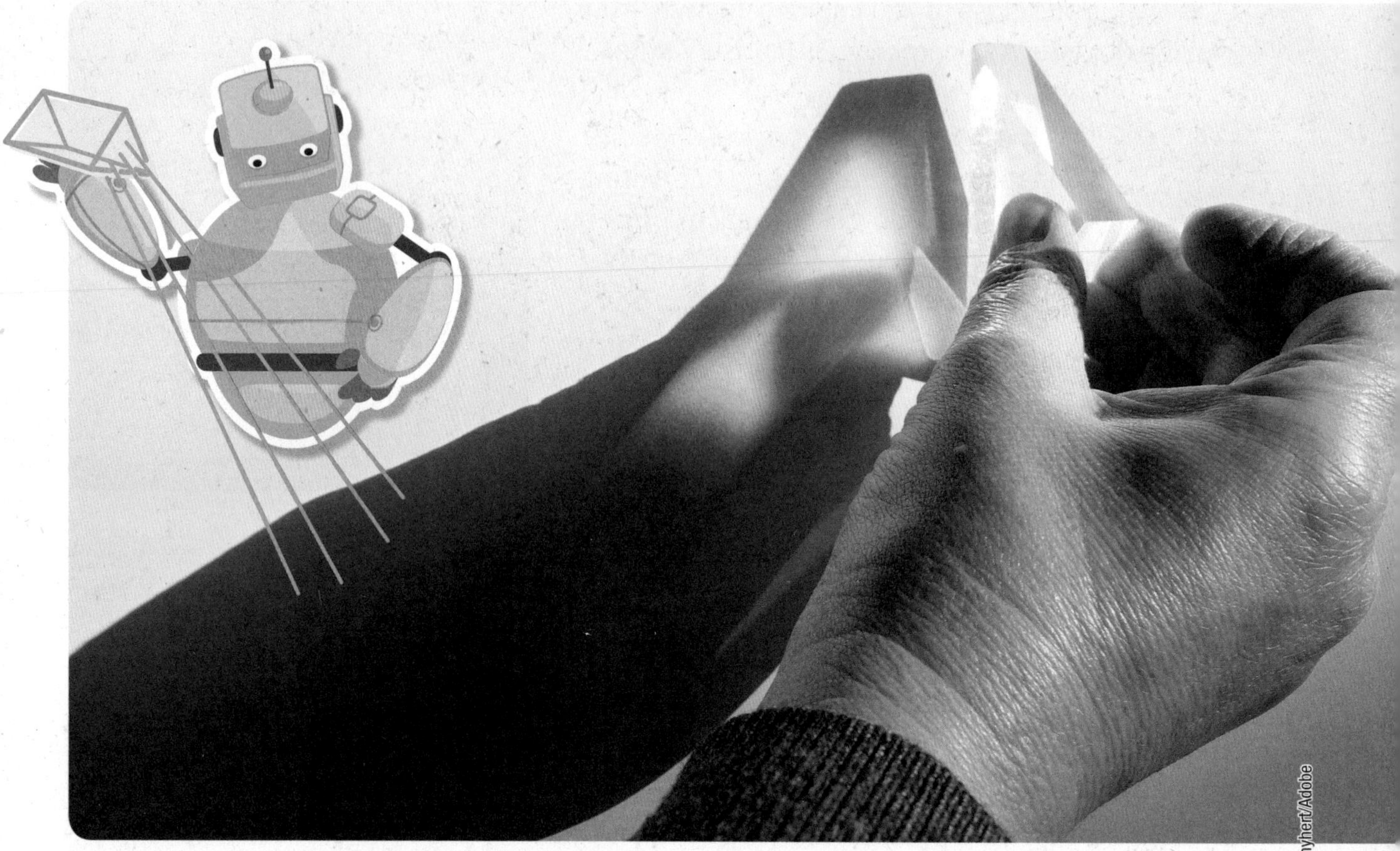

Stars are celestial bodies that emit light. A long time ago, some scientists claimed that the sun was a star. However, their claims could not be supported until two scientific advancements in the 1800s allowed scientists to collect important evidence. The first was the ability to measure the distances to the closest stars, and the second came from the instrument that you will make in this activity.

Did you know?

The sun is roughly 4.5 billion years old.

Form a question Ask a question about how scientists know that the sun is a star.

STEP 1 Pick up the diffraction grating slide with two fingers so you do not touch the middle of the slide. A diffraction grating is a piece of clear plastic with thousands of tiny lines in it. Examine it carefully.

CAUTION: Do NOT look directly at the sun or other very bright lights through the diffraction grating.

POSSIBLE MATERIALS

☐ cardboard tube

☐ diffraction grating slide

☐ electrical tape, black

☐ masking tape

☐ various lights, including fluorescent and incandescent lights

STEP 2 Hold up the diffraction grating and look at a light through the center. Turn the grating so you see colorful images to the left and right (not up and down).

What colors do you see?

_____

_____

_____

_____

STEP 3 Look at other types of lights with your diffraction grating, and describe any differences that you see.

_____

_____

_____

Where do you think these colors came from?

_____

_____

STEP 4   **Build**   A spectroscope is an instrument that allows you to see more clearly the different colors coming from a light. Here's how to make one.

Cover one end of the cardboard tube with black tape, except for an open slit about ¼" wide. Hold the diffraction grating over the other end of the tube as you look through it at a bright light. Turn the slide until you see the colors to the left and right, and then tape it in place.

When you look through the spectroscope at a bright light, how is it different from using just the diffraction grating?

The range of colors that comes from a light is called its *spectrum* (plural *spectra*). Choose two lights that have very different spectra and describe them, or use colored pencils or crayons to show what their spectra look like.

Light A: What kind of light is this?   Light B: What kind of light is this?

The spectrum of Light A   The spectrum of Light B

STEP 5   Improve your spectroscope. A better spectroscope spreads out the colors farther so you can see if there are additional faint colored lines that were not visible before.

How could you change your spectroscope to spread out the colors even farther? Make sure each member of your group gets a chance to share an idea before you decide which improvement to try.

Neat!

Check your plan with your teacher. If you have permission, try your plan to see if it works.

Use your spectroscope to look at as many different kinds of lights as you can find. If possible, find lights that have different shapes but the same colors. If two lights have the same colored lines, they probably have the same glowing gases. Describe your observations below.

Make a **claim** about how scientists study the sun and the stars. Support your claim with **evidence** from your investigation, and explain your **reasoning**.

Making Sense

Different glowing gases in stars produce spectra with different bright lines. How could scientists use this information and data from spectroscope investigations to provide evidence that the sun is a star?

How Does Distance Affect the Apparent Size of Objects?

Light-Years

Distances between stars are enormous. If we used units such as kilometers, we would end up with very big numbers. To measure the huge distances in space, scientists use a unit of measurement called a light-year. A light-year is how far light travels in one Earth year. The distance traveled is about 9,500,000,000,000 kilometers (9.5 trillion km).

All of the stars in a constellation may appear to be the same distance from Earth, but they are not. Below you will find some of the stars that make up the constellation Leo and how far they are from Earth. Use this information to correctly name and color the stars on the diagram on the next page. One has been done for you.

Algieba 126 light-years

Adhafera 260 light-years

Zosma 58 light-years

Algenubi 250 light-years

Denebola 36 light-years

Rasalas 133 light-years

Regulus 77 light-years

Explain Why are distances to stars measured in light-years instead of other units of distance such as kilometers or miles? Choose the correct answer.

a. Stars are very far from Earth, so very large units are used to measure their distances.

b. Stars give off light, so light units are used to measure their distances.

c. It takes a long time to travel to stars, so time units are needed to measure distances to stars.

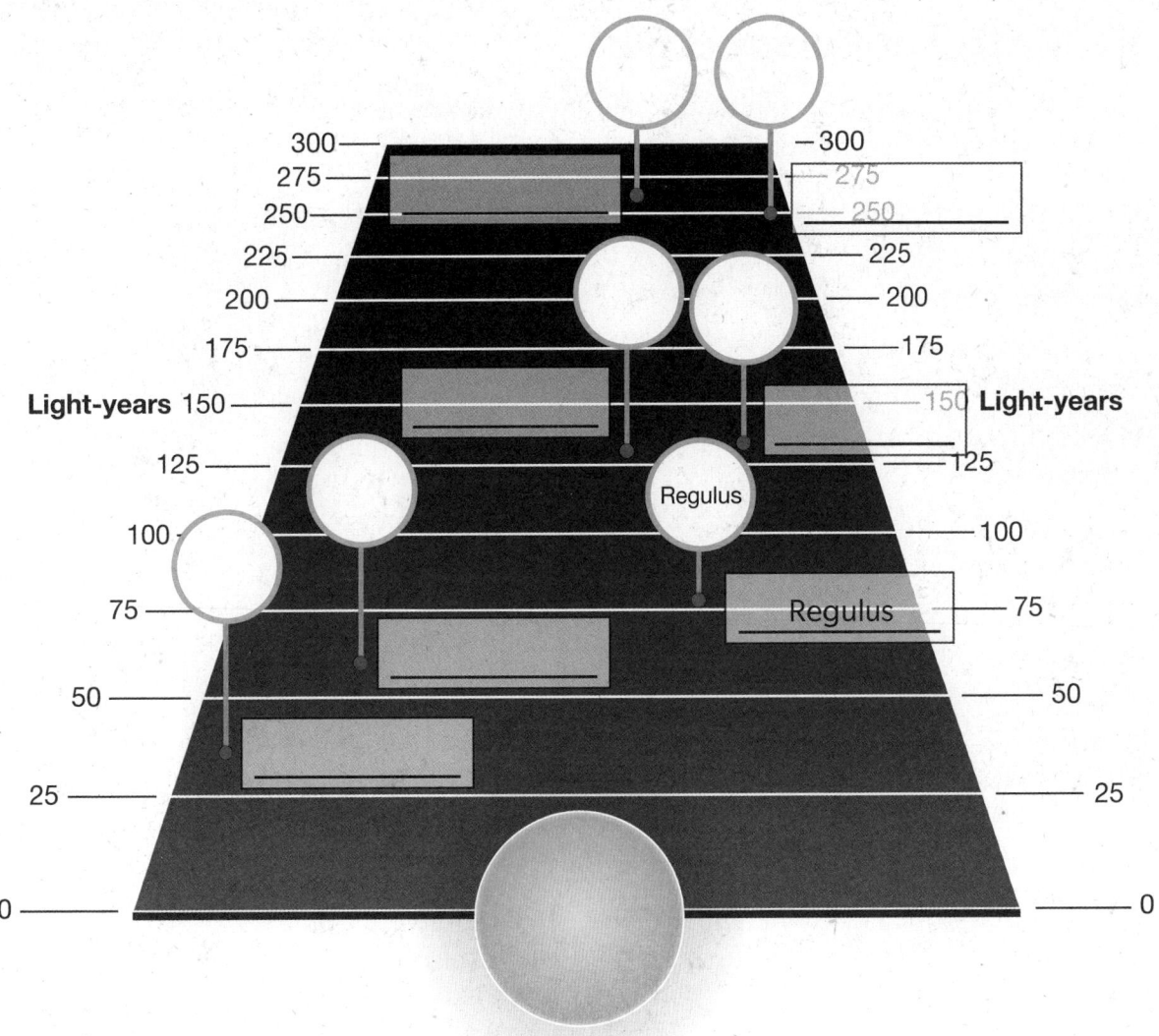

The diagram shows that stars vary greatly in their distance from the sun and Earth. Using the most advanced, current technology, it would take over a million years to travel to Denebola, which is the closest star shown here!

Which statement about stars is true? Choose the correct answer.

a. They are all the same distance from Earth.
b. They are closer to Earth than the sun is.
c. They vary greatly in their distance from Earth.

Why does the sun appear larger than other stars such as Zosma? Support your argument with evidence and reasoning.

It's a Matter of Perspective

Have you ever seen a large building or skyscraper in the distance? It looks very small, doesn't it? Discuss and answer the questions below with a partner.

Explain Why does the airplane in the image appear smaller than the car?

a. The airplane is a smaller size than the car.
b. The airplane is farther away from the viewer than the car is.
c. The airplane is not as shiny as the car, so it is harder to see.

Infer Which statement best explains why the streetlights in the distance in the picture don't look as bright as the streetlights closer to the car?

a. They are a different shape.
b. They are a different size.
c. They are in the distance.

Compare the scale of two other objects in the image.

_____

_____

_____

_____

_____

Observed Sizes

Your ideas about the size of an object are affected by the actual size of the object and its distance from you. When you compare the sizes of objects, you are comparing their scale. The skyscraper looked small to you because of its position far in the distance.

Discuss Look at the chairs around your classroom. Discuss how the size of the chairs near you compares to the size of the chairs farther from you. Make a **claim** about how distance affects the size objects appear to be. Support your claim with **evidence** from your chair observations and explain your **reasoning**.

Turn and Talk With just your eyes, the moon looks like a small white and gray circle. Photographs and first-hand accounts from astronauts who explored the moon show that the moon is very large from up close. In a small group, take turns listening and speaking to explain how distance can affect our view of objects.

Making Sense

How does the scale of distances in space relate to the brightness of the sun in relation to other stars in the sky?

What Are the Sun's Characteristics?

A Close-Up View

On a sunny day, you can feel the sun warming you and your surroundings. You can see its light shining all around you. Without the sun, life would not be possible on Earth.

Identify What else do you know about the sun?

This image shows the sun's disk from Earth's surface. We are used to seeing the sun from this distance.

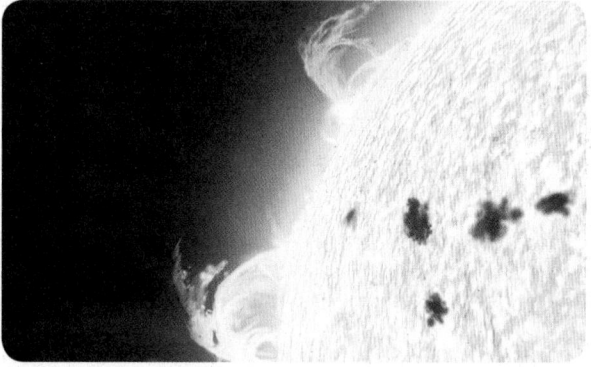

This image shows a close-up view of the sun. Compare the scale, or size, to the view from Earth.

Analyze Study the images of the sun. Notice the color, size, and how bright the sun appears in each. Fill in the top and bottom rows of the chart below. In a small group, take turns listening and speaking to compare and contrast the images and to explain any differences.

View	Color	Scale and brightness	Characteristics
From Earth			
Close-up			

Stellar Details

Scientists studied the sun and stars by measuring the light that reaches Earth. They compared characteristics of the light from their measurements, and they determined that the sun is a star. What else have scientists figured out about the sun? For instance, the sun is big, but exactly how big is it? Why is it bright?

Solar System Giant

The sun is the largest object in our solar system. It makes up nearly 99.9% of the mass of our solar system. The sun has a diameter of about 1.4 million km (about 869,920 mi). You could line up about 110 Earths across the sun's diameter and fit more than one million Earths inside its volume! The sun makes its own energy and light which provides most of the energy for Earth.

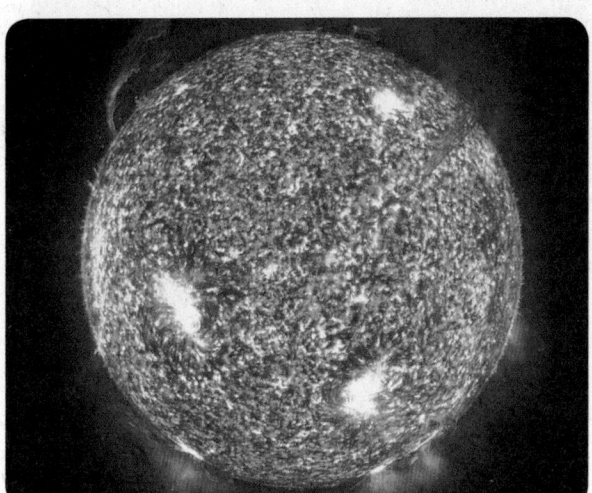

Traveling by Light Speed

The sun is at the center of our solar system. All the planets in our solar system revolve around the sun. The sun is about 150 million km from Earth, but it only takes about eight minutes for light from the sun to reach Earth. Other planets of the solar system are much closer or much farther away. Mercury is the closest planet to the sun, and it takes sunlight about three minutes to reach its surface. Saturn is farther from the sun than Earth. Sunlight takes over one hour to reach Saturn.

Infer After reading the passages, what can you infer about the sun's light?

Choose the correct answer.

a. Sunlight takes the same amount of time to reach all the planets.

b. Sunlight takes longer than one hour to reach Neptune, the farthest planet.

c. Sunlight does not reach some of the farthest planets.

d. Sunlight provides the same amount of energy to each planet.

Objects in the Night Sky

There are many different types of objects in the night sky. Billions of them are stars, but stars are not the only objects in the night sky.

Look at each picture. As you read about the objects, think about whether they are stars or not. Underline characteristics that can help you decide and then label each picture as a star or not a star.

Halley's Comet is made of ice, dust, and gases. It can't make its own light. It can be seen about every 75 years when its orbit around the sun brings it close to Earth.

Betelgeuse is around 1,000 times bigger than the sun, but it is not quite as hot with a temperature of 3,226 °C. It is very bright. It is made of gases and produces its own light.

The **sun** is made mainly of the gases hydrogen and helium. It provides light and heat for Earth. Its temperature is about 5,504 °C.

Mars is found in our solar system. It is made of rock and does not produce its own light. It orbits around the sun. It is cooler than Earth.

Vega is made of gases. It produces light and is much brighter than the sun. Its temperature is about 9,500 °C.

Let It Shine!

Look at the dusk scene shown here. The sun certainly looks brighter than all other stars. How else do these stars differ? Work with others in a group to describe the stars and to identify factors that can affect their brightness.

You may have noticed that the stars in this picture have different colors. A star's color is an important property that provides clues about its temperature.

Star	Distance in light-years (ly)
sun	0.00001
Sirius	9
Capella	45
Betelgeuse	520

The stars in the picture appear to have different sizes, colors, and brightness. Of these factors, brightness and size are the most affected by the star's distance from Earth.

Compare Use the image and the table above to fill in the boxes and to answer the question below.

a. Write the names of the stars in order from dimmest to brightest as viewed from Earth.

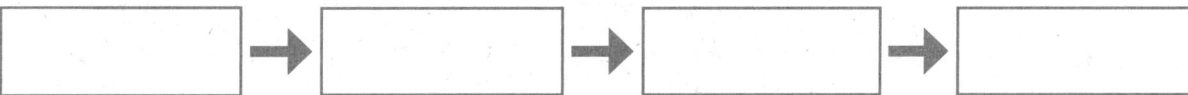

b. What pattern can you recognize based on your observations?

© Houghton Mifflin Harcourt Publishing Company

The Modest Sun

Think about the glow sticks at the beginning of this lesson. How did size affect the brightness of the glow sticks? Discuss with a partner.

This is what these stars would look like if they were next to one another.

Can you find the sun in the model above? Look back at the night view of the sky on the previous page. Do you see how Betelgeuse seems much smaller and dimmer than the sun? In reality, Betelgeuse is around 1,000 times bigger and about 100,000 times brighter than the sun. Remember that natural objects exist from the very small to the immensely large.

Explain Why did the star Betelgeuse appear to be the dimmest when you looked at the picture of it from Earth? Choose the correct answer.

a. Betelgeuse looks like a bright star because it is farthest from Earth.

b. Betelgeuse looks like a bright star because it is closest to Earth.

c. Betelgeuse looks like a dim star because it is farthest from Earth.

d. Betelgeuse looks like a dim star because it is closest to Earth.

Making Sense

How does the sun's distance from Earth cause it to look larger and brighter than other stars, allowing people to read by sunlight but not by starlight? Support your argument with evidence.

_____

_____

_____

Lesson Check

Can You Explain It?

Review your response from the beginning of this lesson explaining why the sun looks much larger and brighter than other stars. How have your ideas changed? Be sure to do the following:

- Compare the distances between Earth and both the sun and other stars.
- Describe how greater distance affects the appearance of an object's size and brightness.

_____

_____

_____

Making Connections

When spending time in the sun, people use sunscreen, hats, sunglasses, and other methods to protect themselves against certain light energy from the sun. Consider what you learned about why the student needs a light in addition to the stars in order to read at night. Why don't people need to protect themselves against light energy from other stars?

_____

_____

_____

_____

Checkpoints

1. Ms. Barazi is testing two incandescent light bulbs. She places a high energy light bulb in a lamp at the end of a hallway and a low energy bulb in a lamp at the opposite end near her students. The bulbs are the same size. This demonstration could be used to support which claim below? Choose all that apply.

   a. The sun only appears brighter than other stars because it is closer to us.

   b. The sun only appears larger than other stars because it is closer to us.

   c. The sun only appears larger than other stars because it is made of gas, not rock.

   d. The sun only appears brighter than other stars because it makes its own light.

2. Study the model. Then choose the correct answer. From which planet would the sun look smallest?

   a. Mars

   b. Neptune

   c. Earth

   d. Saturn

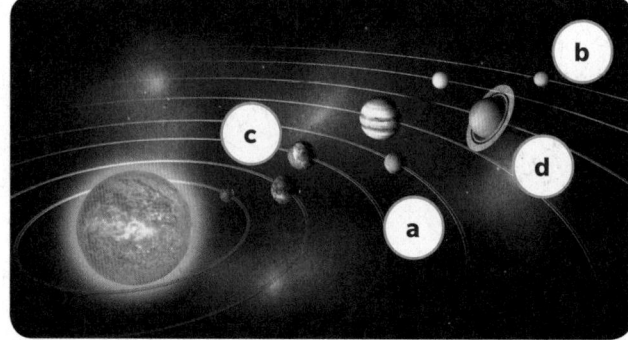

3. Make a model to explain why the sun appears larger and brighter than other stars.

4. Identify which of the objects in these images are stars, and use evidence and patterns from the lesson to support your argument that they are stars.

 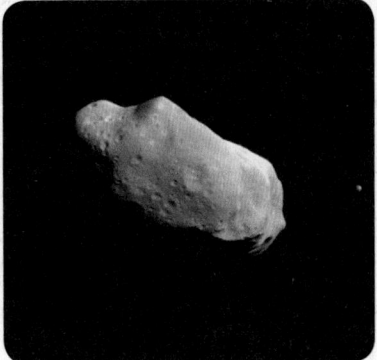 

_____

_____

_____

_____

5. Which of the following statements describe the sun and all other stars? Think about patterns in the information you have learned about stars. Choose all that apply.

a. It orbits around another star.

b. Temperatures on its surface are very high.

c. It makes its own light.

d. It is made of gases.

6. Choose the correct words to complete each sentence.

| light-year | gravity | megameter |
| the sun | light | Betelgeuse |

To measure the vast distances in space, scientists use a unit called a

_____, which is how far _____ travels

in one year. The closest star to Earth is _____ .

Unit Review

1. You want to prove to someone that Earth is not flat. Which of these pieces of evidence support your claim? Choose all that apply.

   a. climbing down into a valley to see more of Earth's surface

   b. climbing to the top of a mountain to see more of Earth's surface

   c. standing on a beach and watching a ship disappear over the horizon

2. Circle the area in the photo where gravity is causing something to fall down.

3. Which of these describes how gravity affects objects near Earth's surface?

   a. It pulls everything to the center of Earth.

   b. It pulls everything toward the Southern Hemisphere.

   c. It pulls everything toward the North Pole.

   d. It pulls everything south.

4. Explain the pattern the moon goes through about once a month and what causes that pattern. Cite evidence from the photo to support your explanation.

   _____

   _____

   _____

   _____

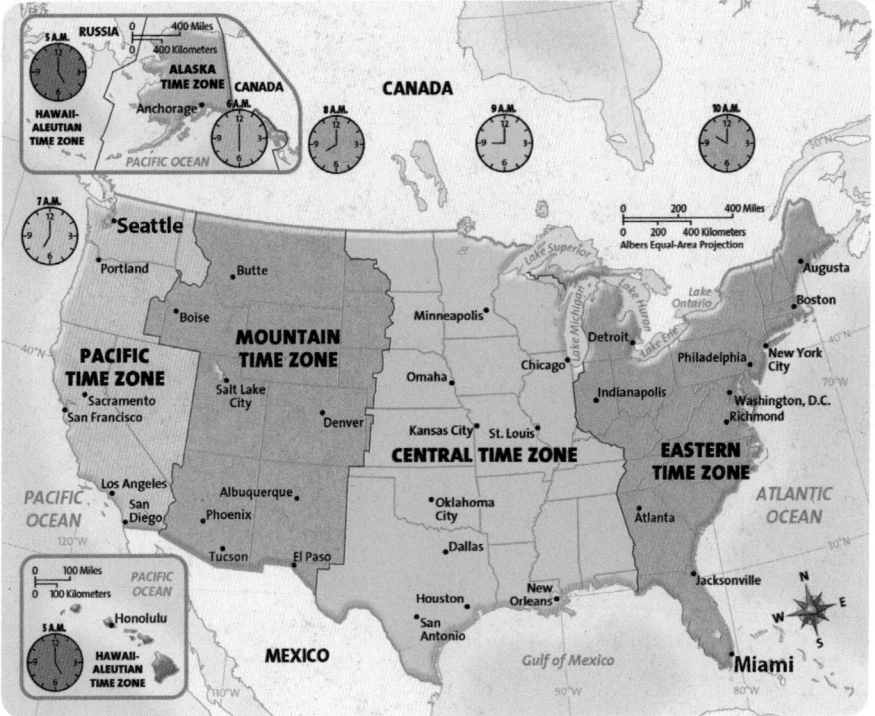

5. Ruby is in Miami and texts her cousin, Xavier, in Seattle. Ruby's clock says 10:00 a.m. When Xavier texts back, he tells her she woke him up. Which of the following is the best explanation as to why Xavier is still in bed? Use the map above to help you answer.

    a. It is 10:00 a.m. in Seattle. Xavier likes to sleep in late.

    b. It is 7:00 a.m. in Seattle. The time difference is caused by Earth's daily rotation.

    c. It is 7:00 a.m. in Seattle. The time difference is caused by Earth's revolution around the sun.

    d. It is 4:00 a.m. in Seattle. The time difference is caused by the moon orbiting Earth.

6. At what time of day is the sun at its highest point in the sky?

    a. around sunrise   **b.** around noon   **c.** around sunset

7. From Earth, the sun appears larger and brighter than other stars. Explain why by providing two pieces of evidence to support that distance affects how things are seen.

_____

_____

8.

Betelgeuse	the sun	easy	difficult	small	great

The scale, or the comparative size, of stars is _____

to judge due to the _____ distances between

them. The closer an object is, such as _____ , the

larger it appears.

9. The data in the graph below show the pattern of daylight hours throughout the year. Use the graph to select the best answer.

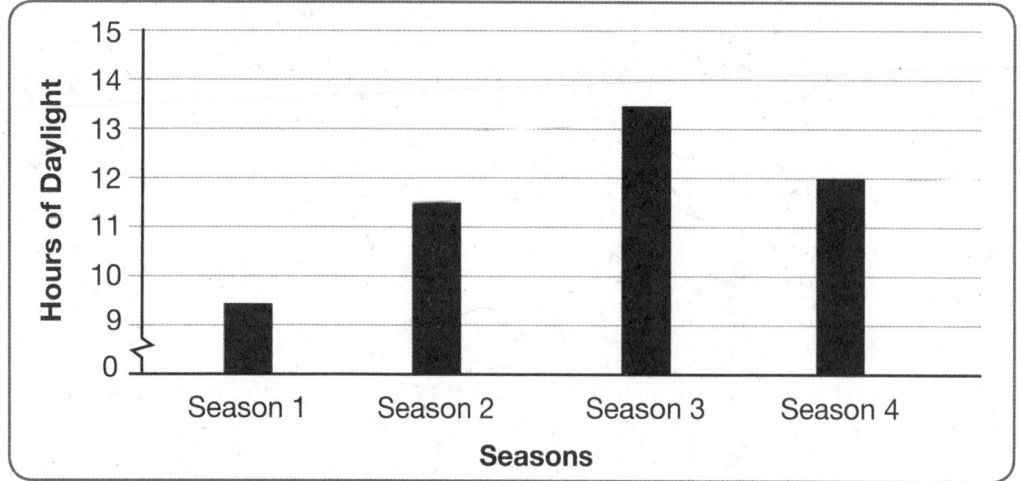

Which season represents the hours of daylight in the summer months of the United States?

a. Season 1   c. Season 3

b. Season 2   d. Season 4

10. Look at the image of the constellation Orion shown in winter.

If you look at the sky at the same time a few months later, in spring, where will Orion be located? Choose the image that shows the correct pattern of movement for Orion.

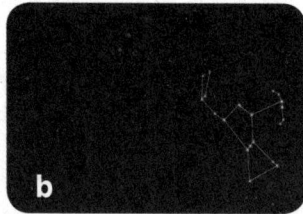
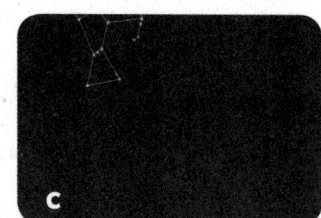

Interactive Glossary

As you learn about each item, add notes, drawings, or sentences in the extra space. This will help you remember what the terms mean. Here's an example:

fungi (FUHN•jy) A group of organisms that get nutrients by decomposing other organisms

hongos Un grupo de organismos que obtienen sus nutrientes al descomponer otros organismos.

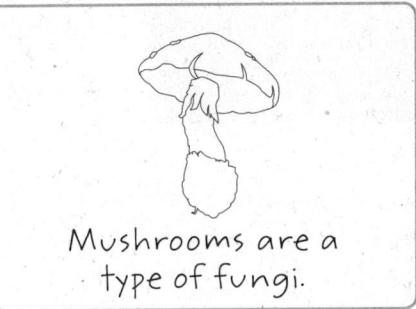

Mushrooms are a type of fungi.

Glossary Pronunciation Key

With every Glossary term, there is also a phonetic respelling. A phonetic respelling writes the word the way it sounds, which can help you pronounce new or unfamiliar words. Use this key to help you understand the respellings.

Sound	As in	Phonetic Respelling
a	bat	(BAT)
ah	lock	(LAHK)
air	rare	(RAIR)
ar	argue	(AR•gyoo)
aw	law	(LAW)
ay	face	(FAYS)
ch	chapel	(CHAP•uhl)
e	test	(TEST)
	metric	(MEH•trik)
ee	eat	(EET)
	feet	(FEET)
	ski	(SKEE)
er	paper	(PAY•per)
	fern	(FERN)
eye	idea	(eye•DEE•uh)
i	bit	(BIT)
ing	going	(GOH•ing)
k	card	(KARD)
	kite	(KYT)
ngk	bank	(BANGK)

Sound	As in	Phonetic Respelling
oh	over	(OH•ver)
oo	pool	(POOL)
ow	out	(OWT)
oy	foil	(FOYL)
s	cell	(SEL)
	sit	(SIT)
sh	sheep	(SHEEP)
th	that	(THAT)
	thin	(THIN)
u	pull	(PUL)
uh	medal	(MED•uhl)
	talent	(TAL•uhnt)
	pencil	(PEN•suhl)
	onion	(UHN•yuhn)
	playful	(PLAY•fuhl)
	dull	(DUHL)
y	yes	(YES)
	ripe	(RYP)
z	bags	(BAGZ)
zh	treasure	(TREZH•er)

A

atmosphere (AT•muh•sfir) The mixture of gases that surround a planet. (p. 182)

atmósfera Mezcla de gases que rodean a un planeta.

B

biosphere (BY•oh•sfir) The system that includes all the living things on Earth. (p. 183)

biósfera Conjunto de todos los seres vivos de la Tierra.

C

chemical change (KEM•ih•kuhl CHAYNJ) Change in one or more substances, caused by a reaction, that forms new and different substances. (p. 70)

cambio químico Cambio en una o más sustancias, causado por una reacción que genera sustancias nuevas y distintas.

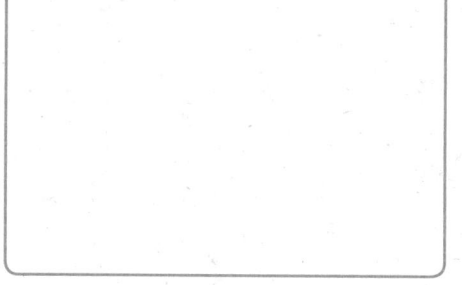

conservation of matter (kahn•ser•VAY•shuhn UHV MAT•er) A law that states that matter cannot be made or destroyed; however, matter can change into a new form. (p. 72)

conservación de la materia Una ley que enuncia que la materia no puede ser creada ni destruida; sin embargo, la materia puede cambiar de una forma a otra.

constellation (kahn•stuh•LAY•shuhn) A group of stars that appears to make a pattern in the night sky. (p. 270)

constelación Patrón de estrellas que forman un diseño o dibujo imaginario en el cielo.

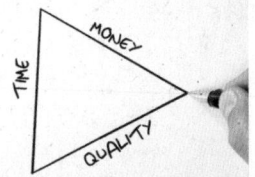

constraint (kuhn•STRAYNT) An absolute limit on acceptable solutions. (p. 15)

restricción Un límite absoluto para las soluciones aceptables.

consumer (kuhn•SOOM•er) A living thing that cannot make its own food and must eat other living things. (p. 105)

consumidor Ser vivo que no puede producir su propio alimento y por eso debe alimentarse de otros seres vivos.

criteria (kry•TIR•ee•uh) The desirable features of a solution. (p. 15)

criterios Características deseables para una solución.

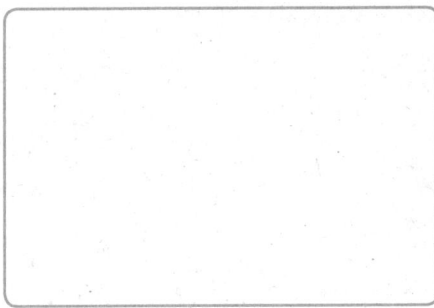

decomposer
(dee•kuhm•POH•zer) An organism that breaks down dead organisms and animal wastes into simpler substances, which are then returned to the environment. (p.125)

descomponedor Ser vivo que se encarga del aprovechamiento de organismos muertos y residuos de animales y los convierte en sustancias más simples, las cuales regresan al medio ambiente.

ecosystem (EE•koh•sis•tuhm)
A system in which organisms interact and exchange matter and energy. (p. 138)

ecosistema Un sistema en el cual los organismos interactúan e intercambian materia y energía.

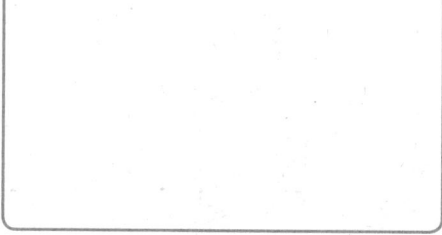

environment
(en•VY•ruhn•muhnt) All of the living and nonliving things that surround and affect an organism. (p. 144)

medio ambiente Todo los seres vivos y no vivos que rodean y afectan a un organismo.

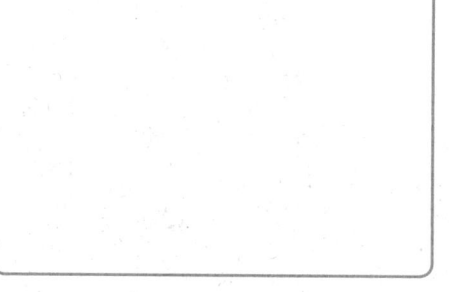

food chain (FOOD CHAYN) The
transfer of food energy between organisms in an ecosystem. (p. 124)

cadena alimentaria Transferencia de energía alimentaria entre organismos en un ecosistema.

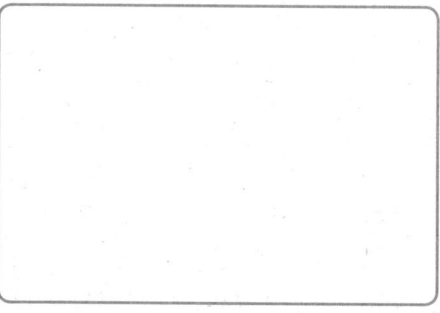

© Houghton Mifflin Harcourt Publishing Company • Image Credits: (t) ©Ed Reschke/Getty Images; (tc) ©Aleksander Bolbot/Shutterstock; (bc) ©Georgette Douwma/Photodisc/Getty Images

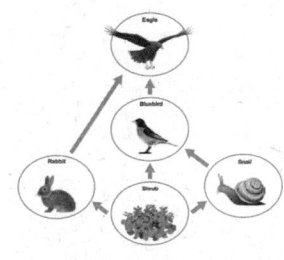

food web (FOOD WEB) A group of food chains that overlap. (p. 127)

red alimentaria Grupo de cadenas alimentarias que se superponen.

gas (GAS) The state of matter that does not have a definite shape or volume. (p. 41)

gas El estado de la materia que no tiene una forma o volumen definido.

geosphere (JEE•oh•sfir) The solid portion of Earth including rocks, soil, mountains, and materials deep within Earth. (p. 183)

geósfera La parte sólida de la Tierra que incluye rocas, barro, montañas y los materiales en las partes profundas de la Tierra.

gravity (GRAV•ih•tee) A force that attracts all objects in the universe toward one another; near Earth's surface, a force that pulls things toward the center of Earth. (p. 258)

gravedad Una fuerza que atrae a todos los objetos uno hacia el otro en el universo; cerca de la superficie de la Tierra, una fuerza que jala objetos hacia el centro de la Tierra.

green technology (GREEN tek•NAHL•uh•jee) Innovative ways of using resources that minimize human impact on the environment. (p. 237)

tecnología verde Maneras innovadoras del uso de recursos que minimizan el impacto de los humanos en el medio ambiente.

hydrosphere (HY•droh•sfir) All of Earth's water, taken together in all states of matter. (p. 182)

hidrósfera Toda el agua de la Tierra, considerada en conjunto en todos los estados de la materia.

invasive species (in•VAY•siv SPEE•sheez) A nonnative species that is better able to compete for resources than the existing species in the ecosystem. (p. 156)

especie invasiva Una especie que no es nativa en un ecosistema y que tiene mayor capacidad de competir por recursos que las especies existentes en ese ecosistema.

liquid (LIK•wid) A form of matter that has a volume that stays the same but has a shape that can change. (p. 41)

líquido Una forma de materia que tiene un volumen que permanece igual pero tiene una forma que puede cambiar.

© Houghton Mifflin Harcourt Publishing Company • Image Credits: (t) ©vuk8691/E+/Getty Images; (tc) ©Corbis; (bc) ©Steve Nudson/Alamy; (b) ©Picsfive/Adobe Stock

matter (MAT•er) Anything that takes up space. (p. 32)

materia Cualquier cosa que ocupa espacio.

mixture (MIKS•cher) A combination of two or more different substances in which the substances keep their identities. (p. 57)

mezcla Combinación de dos o más sustancias diferentes en la que estas mantienen sus identidades.

orbit (AWR•bit) The path of one object in space around another object. (p. 279)

órbita La trayectoria de un objeto alrededor de otro en el espacio.

physical change (FIZ•ih•kuhl CHAYNJ) A change in which the shape or form of the substance changes but the substance still has the same physical makeup. (p. 69)

cambio físico Transformación en la que cambia la figura o forma de una sustancia pero esta mantiene su composición física.

predator (PRED•uh•ter) An animal that hunts, catches, and eats other animals. (p. 123)

depredador Animal que caza, atrapa y come otros animales.

prey (PRAY) Animals that are caught and eaten by predators. (p. 123)

presa Animales que son atrapados y comidos por los depredadores.

producer (pru•DOO•ser) A living thing, such as a plant, that can make its own food. (p. 105)

productor Ser vivo, como las plantas, que es capaz de producir su propio alimento.

prototype (PROH•tuh•typ) A model for testing. (p. 18)

prototipo Un modelo para poner a prueba.

recycle (ree•SY•kuhl) To use the materials in old things to make new things. (p. 234)

reciclar Utilizar los materiales de cosas viejas para crear cosas nuevas.

revolution
(rev•uh•Loo•shuhn) The movement of Earth one time around the sun. (p. 279)

revolución Movimiento de la Tierra a lo largo de una órbita completa alrededor del Sol.

 S

scavenger (SKAV•in•jer) An animal that feeds on dead plants and animals. (p. 125)

carroñero Animal que se alimenta de plantas y animales muertos.

solid (SAHL•ID) The state of matter that has a definite shape and a definite volume. (p. 41)

sólido El estado de la materia que tiene una forma definida y un volumen definido.

solubility
(suhl•YUH•bil•uh•tee) How much of a substance will dissolve in a given amount of a different substance. (p. 58)

solubilidad Qué tanto de una sustancia se puede disolver en una cantidad dada de una sustancia diferente.

solution (suh•LOO•shuhn)
A mixture that has the same composition throughout because all its parts are mixed evenly. (p. 57)

solución Mezcla que mantiene la misma composición a través de ella porque todas sus partes se han mezclado uniformemente.

 T

tradeoff (TRAYD•awf) A decision to give up one quality or feature of a solution to gain a different quality or feature. (p. 22)

intercambio Una decisión de abandonar una cualidad o característica de un diseño para obtener una cualidad o característica diferente.

© Houghton Mifflin Harcourt Publishing Company • Image Credits: (t) ©Devon Stephens/ iStockphoto.com/Getty Images; (b) ©Nancy R. Cohen/Photodisc/Getty Images

Index

Index

Index

Index

Index

COLOR Me! Engineering robot

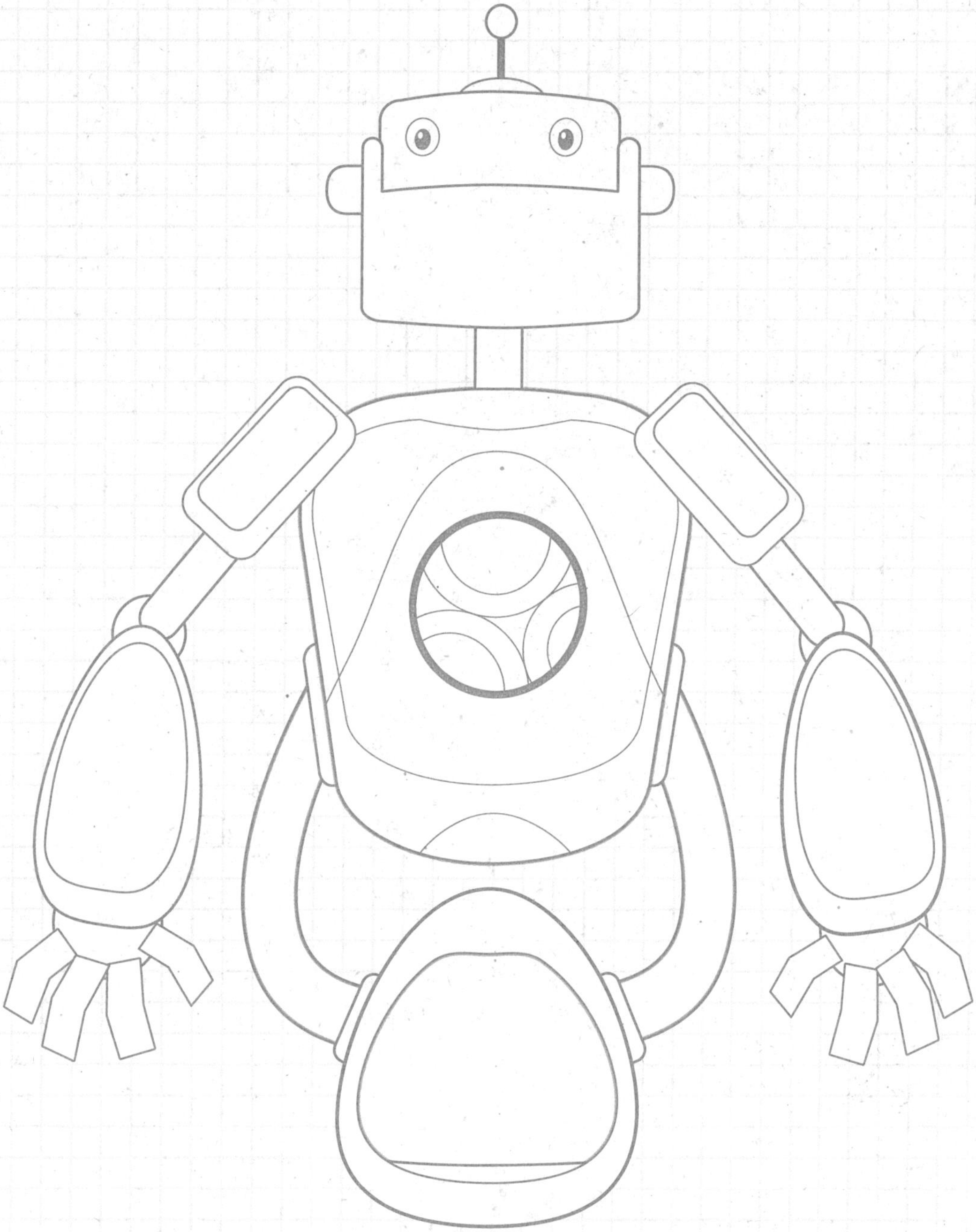

I am a scientist.

COLOR Me! Life Science robot

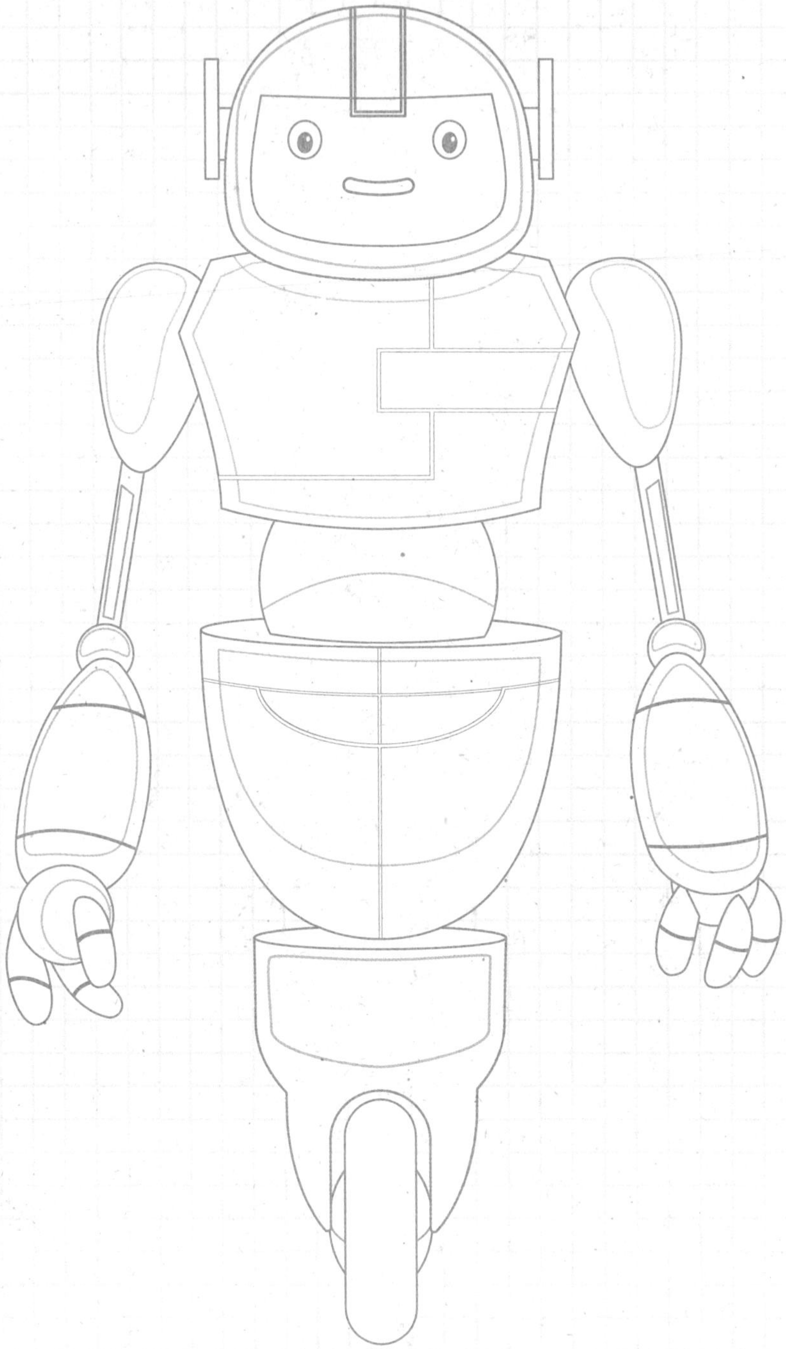

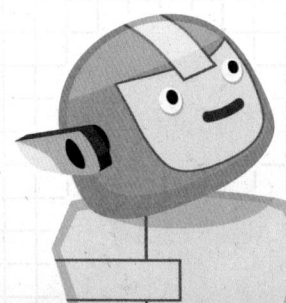

Science is COOL!

COLOR Me! Physical Science robot

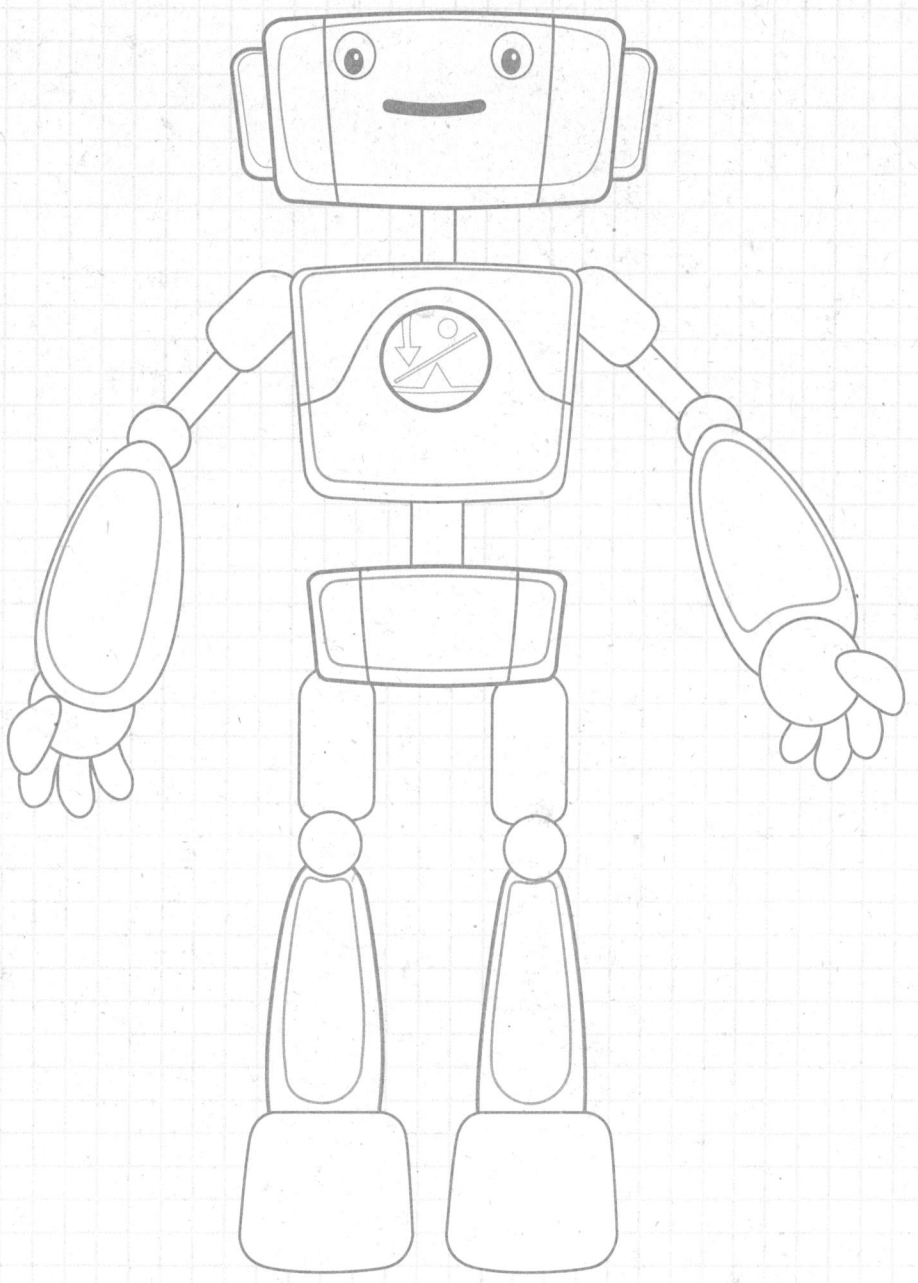

Science is FUN!

COLOR Me! Earth Science robot

SCIENCE is fun!